Tourism Research: A 20-20 Vision

Tourism Research: A 20-20 Vision

**Edited by Douglas G. Pearce
and Richard W. Butler**

(G) Goodfellow Publishers Ltd

(G) Published by Goodfellow Publishers Limited,
Woodeaton, Oxford, OX3 9TJ
http://www.goodfellowpublishers.com

British Library Cataloguing in Publication Data: a catalogue record
for this title is available from the British Library.

Library of Congress Catalog Card Number: on file.

ISBN: 978-1-906884-10-9

 Design and typesetting by P.K. McBride, www.macbride.org.uk

Printed by Baker & Taylor, www.baker-taylor.com

Cover design by Cylinder, www.cylindermedia.com

Contents

List of figures

List of tables

Contributors

Julio Aramberri*
Hospitality Management, Culinary Arts & Food Science, Drexel University, Philadelphia, USA. jraramberri@gmail.com

Tom Baum*
Department of Human Resource Management, University of Strathclyde, Glasgow, Scotland. t.g.baum@strath.ac.uk

Rodolfo Bertoncello
Universidad de Buenos Aires/ CONICET, Argentina. rberton@fibertel.com.ar

Richard Butler*
Strathclyde Business School, University of Strathclyde, Glasgow, Scotland. richard.butler@strath.ac.uk

Chris Cooper *
Business School, Oxford Brookes University, Oxford, UK. ccooper@brookes.ac.uk

Douglas C. Frechtling*
Dept. of Tourism and Hospitality Management School of Business, The George Washington University , Washington D.C., USA. frechtli@gwu.edu

David Harrison*
Tourism and Hospitality Department, University of South Pacific, Suva, Fiji. harrison_d@usp.ac.fj

Cathy H.C. Hsu*
School of Hotel and Tourism Management, The Hong Kong Polytechnic University, Hung Hom, Kowloon, Hong Kong, P. R. China. hmhsu@polyu.edu.hk

Jue Huang
Beijing Hospitality Institute, Beijing, China. huang.jue@bhi.edu.cn

Songshan Huang
School of Management, University of South Australia, Australia. Sam.Huang@unisa.edu.ac.

Myriam Jansen-Verbeke*
Catholic University, Leuven, Belgium, jansen.verbeke@skynet.be

Hoffer Lee
Department of Recreation and Leisure Studies, University of Waterloo Ontario, Canada. Hm5lee@uwaterloo.ca

Bob McKercher*
School of Hotel and Tourism Management, The Hong Kong Polytechnic University, Hong Kong, P. R. China. hmbob@inet.polyu.edu.hk

Gianna Moscardo*
School of Business, James Cook University, Townsville, Australia. Gianna.Moscardo@jcu.edu.au

Douglas Pearce*
Victoria Management School, Victoria University of Wellington, Wellington, New Zealand. douglas.pearce@vuw.ac.nz

Richard R. Perdue*
Pamplin College of Business , Department of Hospitality and Tourism Management,
Virginia Tech, Blacksburg VA, USA. Rick.Perdue@vt.edu

Regina Schlüter*
Universidad Nacional de Quilmes, Argentina. regina_schluter@yahoo.com

Gareth Shaw*
Department of Management, University of Exeter Management School, Exeter, UK.
G.Shaw@exeter.ac.uk

Pauline J. Sheldon*
School of Travel Industry Management, University of Hawaii, Honolulu, Hawaii,
USA. psheldon@hawaii.edu

Egon Smeral*
Austrian Institute of Economic Research, Modul University,Vienna, University of
Innsbruck, Austria. Egon.Smeral@wifo.ac.at

Stephen Smith*
Department of Recreation and Leisure Studies , University of Waterloo, Waterloo,
Ontario, Canada. slsmith@healthy.uwaterloo.ca

Geri Smyth
Faculty of Education, University of Strathclyde, Glasgow, Scotland.
g.smyth@strath.ac.uk

Haiyan Song*
School of Hotel and Tourism Management, The Hong Kong Polytechnic University,
Hong Kong, P. R. China. hmsong@polyu.edu.hk

Timothy J. Tyrrell
School of Community Resources and Development, Arizona State University, Phoenix,
AZ, USA. Timt@asu.edu

Muzaffer Uysal*
Pamplin College of Business , Department of Hospitality and Tourism Management,
Virginia Tech Blacksburg VA, USA. samil@vt.edu

Allan Williams*
Institute for the Study of European Transformations, and Working Lives Institute,
London Metropolitan University, London, UK. Allan.Williams@londonmet.ac.uk

Stephen F. Witt*
School of Hotel and Tourism Management, The Hong Kong Polytechnic University,
Hong Kong, P. R. China. stephen_f_witt@hotmail.com

Shinji Yamashita*
Department of Cultural Anthropology, University of Tokyo, Tokyo, Japan.
cyamas@mail.ecc.u-tokyo.ac.jp

Xinyan Zhang
School of Hotel and Tourism Management, The Hong Kong Polytechnic University,
Hung Hom, Kowloon, Hong Kong, P. R. China

* Fellow of the International Academy for the Study of Tourism

About the editors

Douglas Pearce is Professor of Tourism Management at Victoria University of Wellington in New Zealand. He has published widely on various aspects of tourism including development and planning, tourism organizations, the geography of tourism and urban tourism. Most recently his work has had a New Zealand focus, notably as leader of a major project on tourism distribution channels. Other research interests and consultancy work have taken him to Europe, the South Pacific and Southeast Asia. He is a charter fellow and former vice-president of the International Academy for the Study of Tourism and serves on the editorial boards of a number of journals. With Richard Butler he has co-edited three earlier volumes of the Academy's work: *Tourism Research: Critiques and Challenges* (1993); *Change in Tourism: People, Places, Processes* (1995); and *Contemporary Issues in Tourism Development* (1999).

Richard Butler is Emeritus Professor at Strathclyde University in Glasgow, Scotland, having also taught at the University of Surrey and the University of Western Ontario. His research interests have been primarily in destination development processes and impacts, sustainability of tourism, particularly in islands and remote areas, and the relationship between tourism and indigenous peoples. His most recent publications include books on the role of key individuals in the development of tourism, political change and tourism, and sustainability of tourism in small islands. His primary research areas have been Canada and Scotland, but he has taught and conducted research in Australia, South East Asia, and Europe also. He is a charter fellow of the International Academy for the Study of Tourism, and served as its first Secretary and then two terms as President.

1 Introduction: looking back, moving forward

Douglas G. Pearce

Tourism research continues to expand at a rapid rate as testified by the ever-growing number of journals, books and conferences in this field. Whether there has been a commensurate increase in our understanding of tourism, however, is another matter, for this explosion in output has meant it is increasingly difficult to keep pace with what is being produced. Tourism research remains of mixed quality, studies are often fragmented, lack a clear sense of direction and are often not underpinned by a sound theoretical basis. As a result, progress has been variable, opportunities have been missed and the platform for future research on tourism is perhaps not as solid as it might be.

These issues were addressed by fellows of the International Academy for the Study of Tourism at their biennial meeting held in Mallorca in June 2009. The Academy was established in Santander, Spain in 1988 and held its first biennial meeting the following year in Warsaw and Zakopane, Poland (Dann, 2009). Founded at the initiative of Jafar Jafari, the Academy is an international, limited membership, multidisciplinary body whose goals are 'to further the scholarly research and professional investigation of tourism, to encourage the application of the findings, and to advance the international diffusion and exchange of tourism knowledge'. In celebrating the 20th anniversary of the meeting in Poland it was deemed appropriate to focus on what progress had been made in tourism research over the previous two decades and to consider where research in this field might go in the future, hence the theme of the meeting and the title of this volume which contains a selection of the revised papers presented in Mallorca. The evolution of tourism research over this period, including that presented at meetings of the Academy, can be contextualized in terms of developments in tourism and broader changes in society at large.

Development

Over the last two decades the volume of international tourist arrivals worldwide has more than doubled (Table 1.1). While the current global economic recession has clearly dented projections in the near term – UNWTO (2009) figures show international arrivals were down 7 per cent in the first eight months of 2009 – tourism in the past has proved resilient and continued growth seems assured once economies recover. Table 1.1 also illustrates some significant redistribution in the global pattern of arrivals over the last 20 years, notably the emergence of the Asia Pacific region, a trend which seems set to continue. Moreover, in many places domestic demand is greater than international and the Asia Pacific region in particular, especially China, has also experienced a significant increase in domestic tourism.

Table 1.1: Evolution of international arrivals (millions) by world region: 1989-2030. Sources: 1989-2020 UNWTO (2006a, b), 2030 Yeoman (2008)

	Europe	Americas	Asia/Pacific	Africa	Middle East	World
1989	250.7	86.9	49.4	13.9	9.2	410.1
	61%	21%	12%	3%	2%	100%
1999	370.5	121.9	98.7	27	21.5	639.6
	58%	19%	15%	4%	3%	100%
2008	487.9	147.2	184.1	47	55.6	922
	53%	16%	20%	5%	6%	100%
2020	717	282	416	77	69	1561
	46%	18%	27%	5%	4%	100%
2030	799.9	309.8	546.5	101.8	158.9	1897
	42%	16%	29%	5%	8%	100%

Much of the growth in tourism research might therefore be attributed quite simply to the fact that there has been more tourism to study in new and different places. It is, therefore, perhaps not surprising that research on the development of tourism has been a recurrent theme in meetings of the Academy. Increasing interest and concern with the way tourism was developing in the 1980s resulted in a focus on 'alternative tourism' at the Academy's 1989 meeting (Smith and Eadington, 1992). That concept was subject to much scrutiny and debate, with the resultant book's title, *Tourism Alternatives*, reflecting the view that those present saw little merit in a single way forward. Environmental and community issues associated with tourism development were addressed at the Cairo meeting in 1995 (Cooper and Wanhill, 1997), with a range of associated issues and approaches also being explored at the following meeting in Melaka, Malaysia (Pearce and Butler, 1999). A characteristic of several of the papers at the latter meeting was that they dealt with parts of the world where tourism was just developing (Ghana, Samoa, Vietnam and India's Bhyundar Valley) and with other regions such as Patagonia that have a longer tradition of tourism but where there had previously been little material available in English. Other papers considered the factors underlying growth, both in terms of supply and demand, and showed how tourism development was being linked to other processes such as heritage conservation or the spread of casino gambling. Many of the papers presented in Beijing in 2005 considered implications for destination management, planning for tourism development and human capital issues (Gartner and Hsu, in press). Wang and Wall (in press), for example, compared planning models used in the host country, China, and in the West, highlighting the need to recognize different approaches throughout the world.

This growth in tourism has also been accompanied by a considerable amount of change, not only in the scale and form of tourism which has occurred, but also in the world in which this development has taken place. This introduction is being written as events are being held to commemorate the fall of the Berlin Wall and the end of the Cold War, events which occurred only a few months after the Academy's first meeting in Poland in August 1989 and which were subsequently to have a major impact on tourism flows and developments in Europe and elsewhere. Likewise, the events in Tiananmen Square earlier that year did little to herald the emergence of China as a leading tourism destination 20 years later (Aramberri and Xie, in press; Hsu *et al.*: Chapter 12). The Mallorca meeting took place in the shadow of the global economic recession, growing concern about global warming and the uncertain threat of the outbreak of the influenza A (H1N1) virus. Many participants had travelled to Mallorca on low-cost airlines, booking their tickets online from home, a stark contrast to the complicated and costly arrangements made to travel to Warsaw 20 years earlier and a clear illustration of how far-reaching some changes in international travel and distribution have been.

Change in tourism was the theme of the Academy's Seoul meeting in 1993 (Butler and Pearce, 1995). In his introduction to that volume, Butler (1995) reviewed not only political changes but also others that have a pronounced impact on the growth and nature of tourism: economic conditions, societal values, technological advances… The different impacts of these changes on tourism were illustrated in chapters dealing with such topics as nostalgia in Japanese domestic tourism, tourism between quasi-states, and the constraints of water supply. Gartner (2005) set the papers presented at the Macao meeting (2001) against five trends: consolidation, consumption centre development, devolution, public involvement and the coming of age of tourism research. Gosar's (2005) account of the impact of the creation of new nation states (Slovenia and Croatia) on tourism in Istria is a good example of how broader political changes have impacted on tourism and created new topics to pursue. Various emerging forms of tourism were also discussed in Beijing such as entertainment tourism, extreme tourism and space tourism (Gartner and Hsu, in press). Further change can be anticipated as the 21st century advances. Drawing on a range of mega drivers, Yeoman (2008) paints an intriguing picture of what world tourism might look like in the year 2030. It is one in which tourists seek new benefits and experiences, some unlikely destinations emerge, novel forms of tourism appear and new considerations come in to play. Such changes greatly increase the scope of tourism research in coming years.

Critiques and reviews of tourism research

A continuing concern with papers presented at Academy meetings has been a critical assessment of the research being done on tourism, whether in terms of the broader themes outlined above or tourism research more generally. Foreshadowing sentiments presented at subsequent meetings, the editors of the first Academy volume noted in their introduction that '...the body of data to test and verify theory in many of these areas [relating to alternative forms of tourism] is not yet at hand or is in need of refinement. Meanwhile, development goes forward...and the need for direction and greater understanding by and for policy makers remains a most significant challenge', (Eadington and Smith, 1992:12). The volume resulting from the papers presented at the Calgary meeting in 1991, entitled *Tourism Research: Critiques and Challenges* (Pearce and Butler, 1993), focused more directly on how tourism research at that time was being conducted. In the introduction (Pearce, 1993: 1), I commented that much tourism research was being undertaken in an uncritical manner:

> *The emphasis has been on the results with very little attention being paid to the way in which the research has been carried out. Review papers, both disciplinary and thematic, frequently outline what we know rather than how we came to know it. Concepts and techniques are often adopted by researchers from their parent disciplines and applied with little or no modification or explicit rationale to tourism problems. The tourism literature has never been rent by widespread debates about theoretical or methodological issues.*

Papers in that volume attempted to overcome some of these shortcomings and offer ways forward. Cohen (1993), for example, provided a detailed critique of touristic images, Dann (1993) drew attention to limitations in the use of two common variables used in tourism research, while Philip Pearce (1993) evaluated theories of tourist motivation.

In the introductory chapter to the Melaka volume, a tension was noted between 'calls for more generalized, theoretical approaches to research on tourism development and those which have adopted a more case-oriented approach stressing contextual factors' (Pearce, 1999: 9). Dann (1999: 14) offered a provocative critique of the state of tourism research: 'instead of there being a desirable cumulative body of knowledge that is emic, comparative, contextual and processual (Cohen, 1979), what we frequently encounter is a ragged collection of half-baked ideas that constitutes largely descriptive, case-confined wishful thinking'. Jenkins (1999) drew attention to the need for 'bridging the great divide' between tourism academics and practitioners. Later, Gartner (2005) presented a more optimistic assessment, arguing tourism research was coming of age. At the same time he also recognized (p.19) that:

> *significant gaps in knowledge remain and old knowledge should be closely scrutinized and not simply accepted as truth because a number of writings contain this 'knowledge'...there is much we do not yet know or think we know but in reality we do not.*

It is in this context that the Academy took a more concerted approach at its 2009 meeting in Mallorca to reviewing the state of tourism research.

The Academy of course is not alone in reflecting on the ways in which tourism research has evolved and in the directions it has taken. Indeed, reviews of aspects of tourism research appeared early on as bodies of work took shape; the special issues the *Annals of Tourism Research* in the late 1970s early 1980s provide a good overview of the state of the art at that time in various disciplines. Research reviews commonly focus on a particular theme (Ashworth, 2003; Yoo and Weber, 2005; Li, 2008; Getz, 2008); discipline (Ritchie, 1996; Gibson, 2008; Nepal, 2009) or national perspective (P. Pearce, 2005). Others address broader methodological, ontological, epistemological and paradigmatic issues (Riley and Love, 2000; Phillimore and Goodson, 2004; Jennings, 2007; Tribe and Airey, 2007). Reviewers often take a content analysis approach to identify what has been studied and how (Yoo and Weber, 2005; Gibson, 2008; Li, 2008). Such reviews have been facilitated by electronic database search technologies but care must be taken with coverage and conclusions in terms of what is being searched – publications other than journals are frequently excluded – and what key words and classifications are being used. Other reviews are more interpretative and qualitative. In his assessment of tourism marketing research, for example, Ritchie (1996) sought to detect 'pinpoints of light', discussed 'shadows on the field' and identified emerging challenges. Tribe and Airey (2007) offered an analytical framework for understanding change in tourism research and put forward the notion of a knowledge force field whereby the researcher's gaze is influenced by five significant forces: person, position, rules, ends, and ideology.

What constitutes progress in tourism research and how advances might be identified has not been clearly and comprehensively established. In one of the more explicit statements on this topic, Dann *et al.* (1988) used a matrix to model the interplay of what they consider to be the two key dimensions of research: theory and method. Theory was defined (p. 4) as 'that body of logically interconnected propositions which provides an interpretative basis for understanding phenomena' while methodology was said to signify 'the acceptance of standardized procedures; according to which research is carried out and evaluated'. They recognized that both dimensions were essential to any mature research and spoke of 'the desired optimum in which there is a correct balance of theory and method' (Quadrant 4). They followed this up by quantifying the style of research and types of analysis reported in the *Annals of Tourism Research* in the pre- and post-1980 period and concluded (p. 10) that at the time of writing (1988) 'it would be premature to argue that tourism research has reached the happy state of Quadrant 4'.

While improvements in methodological robustness and theoretical sophistication are undoubtedly key elements by which to judge research progress, such criteria alone are not without their limitations and other factors also need to be considered. Focusing solely on theory and method does not address the issue of what is being researched and whether it is important or not. Speaking of the expectations and challenges of using increasingly sophisticated means of analysis in order to be published in journals, Ryan (2005: 8) observes:

researchers seeking publication of their work must be able to display high levels of research skill, be able to demonstrate the rigor of their research methodology, but not to become so wrapped up in the technicalities of the research that the major objectives of demonstrating the significance of the research for theoretical conceptualisation, policy or management is lost.

Crompton (2005: 39) suggests that 'one acid test of importance comes when findings from a research program are disseminated to tourism professionals. Do they care?' This is the 'so what' question but as Philip Pearce (2005: 27) argues, the question of relevance is not just limited to industry interest: '...the question of the relevance of academic work (predominantly research) lies in specifying relevant to whom, in what tourism or development sector, at what scale, over what time period and with what themes'. In an earlier paper he had also addressed the related issue of tourism researchers asking the right questions (Pearce and Moscardo, 1999).

More generally, progress in tourism research might be considered in terms of how our understanding of a particular problem has increased or improved over time. What do we know now that we did not know before the research was undertaken? How does this new understanding of a particular problem contribute to our cumulative knowledge in the broader field of studies or discipline? Likewise in looking ahead, in developing our research agendas and framing our research questions, we need to look more explicitly at what we need to know to increase our understanding of a particular issue or problem and what this new knowledge will contribute both theoretically and practically. In what ways and to what extent is new knowledge being transferred to and applied by the industry, policy-makers and the community? Here it is important to recall that basic research and applied studies are not mutually exclusive (Van Scotter and Culligan, 2003).

The papers presented at the Academy's Mallorca meeting reflect the international and multidisciplinary makeup of its membership, the development of tourism and broader changes discussed above, and the diversity of approaches to reviewing tourism research, identifying advances and establishing future directions. Contributors were asked to adopt both a retrospective and prospective approach, to reflect on how research on a particular theme or topic had developed over the past two decades and to outline agendas that might provide a clearer sense of direction and take research in their selected areas forward. Recognizing the limitations of space, the literature reviewed was to be representative rather than exhaustive.

Structure

The remainder of this book is structured in four parts. The four chapters in Part 1 provide original and stimulating perspectives on progress in tourism research. Aramberri (Chapter 2) presents a provocative overview of the development of tourism research which he argues is characterized by a scissors crisis, by a growing split between the *hows* and the *whys*, between one camp dominated by managerial approaches concerned with applied issues and the other consumed by cultural critiques aimed at exposing modernity. The two camps, he suggests, co-exist in a condition of Mutually Accepted Disinterest (MAD), a condition that may persist and one which has created a chasm in which key issues go unaddressed. Arramberri does not see any middle way out of this predicament as attempts to address this situation are dismissed as blind alleys. Not everyone will agree with his analysis but it does provide a focal point to debate the broader issues he raises. In Chapter 3, Smith and Lee make a very useful contribution to earlier critiques of the adequacy of the theoretical foundations of tourism research. They address this issue directly and systematically by a content analysis of leading tourism journals to examine in some detail how 'theory' has been used by tourism researchers over the last two decades and to devise a sevenfold typology of tourism theory. On this basis Smith and Lee conclude that while there has been relative growth over this period in the theoretical basis of articles published in the journals examined, the term is increasingly being used in ways in which it has no substantive meaning. Although the approach they use to undertake their analysis has its limitations, their results should give us much cause to ponder, not least because of the low frequencies of the term theory reported in the most recent lustrum. In tracing the evolution of research on tourism and development, Harrison (Chapter 4) illustrates links between several of the general points discussed above, notably the growing interest from researchers as tourism has expanded globally and changes in the focus of their research following the decline of broader competing theoretical perspectives (modernization and underdevelopment) as ideological shifts occurred and globalization theory emerged. Theoretical issues remain important but these need to be tested and underpinned by much more empirical research. Harrison also calls for much closer links between academics and other stakeholders who frequently operate in distinct spheres and publish in different outlets. Butler (Chapter 5) then asks why the concept of carrying capacity has largely been ignored in the past two decades when the notion of sustainable tourism has gained increased attention and poses the question of whether tourism researchers regard the problem as irrelevant or insurmountable due to its conceptual complexity and challenges in application. In examining these issues with regard to a particular concept, Butler provides a very interesting illustration of how research on some topics advances or not.

The five chapters in Part II focus more specifically on advances in research on the business of tourism. In many respects these chapters might be seen as being representative of Aramberri's *how to* camp. Methodological aspects and applications are stressed in several of the chapters but conceptual and other issues are also considered. In Chapter 6, Frechtling and Smeral review the way in which approaches to measuring and interpreting the economic impact of tourism have evolved as the emphasis has shifted from multipliers and input–output models to computable general equilibrium (CGE) models and the development of tourism satellite accounts (TSAs). They then identify the importance of measuring the impact of mega-events, both planned and unplanned, and outline methodological considerations and challenges in doing this. Shaw and Williams (Chapter 7) trace changing research agendas in work on tourism SMEs (small and medium enterprises), drawing attention to recurrent themes and highlighting emerging topics. They note that research in this area has often been uneven and that while much progress has been made opportunities have also been missed. In particular there has been a lack of engagement with the wider literature on SMEs and a marginalization of tourism in SME policy. Similar issues are raised by Pearce (Chapter 8) with regard to research on tourism distribution, a phenomenon, he argues, that constitutes a potentially powerful unifying concept as it bridges supply and demand. While there has been significant progress in terms of different approaches, coverage of topics has been rather variable, limited linkages have been made between tourism studies and with the wider distribution literature, and research in the field has often lacked a clear sense of direction. To overcome such problems a systematic research agenda is outlined based on strategy design process which enables key research questions to be identified that might be pursued in coming years. Song, Witt and Zhang deal with a related issue in Chapter 9 where they put forward a collaborative approach to tourism forecasting, one that is structured around the tourism supply chain (TSC). While popular in supply chain management in other areas, such an approach is only now being applied in tourism. After reviewing current approaches to tourism forecasting, Song and his colleagues outline the benefits and challenges of TSC forecasting and discuss design and practical matters in implementing this approach. The way in which key concepts can evolve over time and the implications of these changes are graphically illustrated in Perdue, Tyrell and Uysal's account (Chapter 10) of how the conceptual foundations of the value of tourism have diverged in the past two decades in response to a more future-oriented time perspective and growing awareness of the need to take account of different stakeholder groups. They outline two key conceptual dimensions of the value of tourism and then review the changes that have occurred in its measurement with regard to three groups of stakeholders: tourism businesses, destination marketing/management organizations and community development authorities. These shifts imply a need to give greater weight to balance not growth alone.

The three chapters in Part III have a geographical focus. The first two bring together much new material previously inaccessible in the English language literature and explore the ways in which research is developing in parts of the world where tourism has more recently emerged as a significant economic and social activity: Latin America and China. The third focuses on Bali, one of the more established destinations in Asia. The synthesis and analysis provided by these three reviews offer valuable insights into how contextual factors influence the development of tourism research and show how and why certain broader themes are privileged over others as objects of study. These chapters also provide a counterpoint to material in the rest of the volume which is derived essentially from Anglo-American and European approaches to research. In Chapter 11 Schlüter and Bertoncello provide an insightful account of the way in which tourism research in Latin America has emerged and the challenges that researchers there have faced in terms of publishing in their own languages (Spanish and Portuguese) and of establishing a regional identity while also endeavouring to develop an international profile. With reference to the region's leading tourism journal, established twenty years ago, Schlüter and Bertoncello track a shift in perspective from tourism as a purely economic activity to a social practice, show a broadening of the methodological base of the research being undertaken and conclude with an optimistic outlook. Similar trends emerge from Hsu, Huang and Huang's content analysis of recent trends in tourism and hospitality research in China (Chapter 12). This also reveals a dominant economic/business orientation although studies from a more social science perspective are becoming more common. Methodologically, Chinese scholars are now adopting more quantitative techniques but research in the country still lacks the rigour of academic research elsewhere. However, the authors are optimistic about the future of tourism research as a new generation of scholars comes to the fore. In examining the development of tourism in Bali over the last two decades, Yamashita, a cultural anthropologist, discusses changing concepts of cultural tourism and also demonstrates, through such examples as the reaction to the Kuta bombing, the impact of external events on tourism and the research implications of these (Chapter 13). The paradox he observes in Bali is that 'cultural tourism started so that the Balinese could control their own culture, but as a result of its practice their culture has started moving beyond their control'. He concludes by calling for more 'reflexive tourism' studies in the future.

In Part IV the emphasis moves to more recent and emerging themes in tourism research where the four examples provide insights into how research on new topics arises and might proceed. Baum and Smyth consider the neglected role that refugees and other migrants have played as employees within the labour markets of developed countries (Chapter 14). As is typical when reviewing an emerging theme, Baum and Smyth devote much of their chapter to establishing the nature of the problem, outlining the characteristics of the demand for labour in the tourism sector and the opportunities these create for refugees. In so doing, they also demonstrate the links with research in related areas, in this case refugee studies in general. In Chapter 15 Jansen-Verbeke and McKercher reflect on why and how the issue of tourism development at World Heritage Sites is becoming the subject of a lively interdisciplinary discourse. As is characteristic of work on other emerging themes, much research on World Heritage Sites is fragmented, consisting of individual case studies which have yet to be effectively integrated. What is needed now is 'a more holistic understanding in multiple contextual settings'. The authors call for more effective communication of what is already known and a focus on processes rather than on ad hoc perceptions and descriptions. They conclude by offering a research-based management agenda. Moscardo then addresses a broader issue which has widespread implications for the future direction of tourism research (Chapter 16). She asserts it is important to reflect on the ethics of tourism research practice and to ask if a code of tourism research ethics is necessary, and if so, what such a code might look like. While more established tourism researchers may have been brought up with the codes of ethics of their parent disciplines, such as anthropology or geography, this is not necessarily the case with many younger researchers whose training has come through more recent tourism programmes. In reviewing the ethics debate in the social science literature, Moscardo not only demonstrates the range of ethical issues which we need to consider but again shows the value of broader engagement, especially in the early phases of the development of any new theme. Cooper and Sheldon bring this fourth section to a close by considering another critical and far-reaching theme, knowledge management in tourism, that is, how the knowledge acquired through research can be more effectively applied to deliver a more competitive tourism sector, assist in collaborative research initiatives and create 'learning destinations' (Chapter 17). In tracing the development of this emerging field they argue that tourism is still in the early stages of understanding effective mechanisms for knowledge transfer and that considerable benefit might be derived through a greater crossover with generic knowledge management research. The ideas that Cooper and Sheldon put forward for advancing research in this area will be of interest to all those who not only want to improve the understanding of particular aspects of tourism through research but who also seek to enhance the dissemination of that knowledge through more effective transfer of it.

In the concluding chapter the editors draw out and discuss general trends that emerge from these four sections and offer their thoughts on ways to advance tourism research.

References

Aramberri, J. and Xie, Y. (forthcoming) 'Modern mass tourism in China: some theoretical issues', in W.G. Gartner and C.H.C. Hsu (eds), *A Handbook of Tourism Research*, London: Taylor and Francis.

Ashworth, G. (2003) 'Urban tourism: still an imbalance in attention?', in C. Cooper (ed.), *Classic Reviews in Tourism*, Clevedon: Channel View Publications, pp.143-163.

Butler, R.W. (1995) 'Introduction', in R. Butler and D. Pearce (eds), *Change in Tourism: People, Places, Processes*, London: Routledge, pp. 1-11.

Butler, R.W. and Pearce, D. (1995) *Change in Tourism: People, Places, Processes*, London: Routledge.

Cohen, E. (1979) 'Rethinking the sociology of tourism', *Annals of Tourism Research*, 6 (1), 18-35.

Cohen, E. (1993) 'The study of touristic images of native people: mitigating the stereotype of a stereotype', in D.G. Pearce and R.W. Butler (eds), *Tourism Research: Critiques and Challenges*, London: Routledge, pp. 36-69.

Cooper, C. and Wanhill, S. (1997) *Tourism Development: Environmental and Community Issues*, Chichester: Wiley.

Crompton, J.L. (2005) 'Issues related to sustaining a long-term research interest in tourism', *Journal of Tourism Studies*, 16 (2), 34-43.

Dann, G.M.S. (1993) 'Limitations in the use of "nationality" and "country of residence" variables', in D.G. Pearce and R.W. Butler (eds), *Tourism Research: Critiques and Challenges*, London: Routledge, pp.88-112.

Dann, G.M.S. (1999) 'Theoretical issues for tourism's future development: identifying the agenda', in D.G. Pearce and R.W. Butler (eds), *Contemporary Issues in Tourism Development*, London: Routledge, pp.13-30.

Dann, G.M.S. (2009) 'How international is the International Academy for the Study of Tourism', *Tourism Analysis*, **14** (1), 3-13.

Dann, G., Nash, D. and Pearce, P. (1988) 'Methodology in tourism research', *Annals of Tourism Research*, **15** (1), 1-28.

Eadington, W.R. and Smith, V.L. (1992) 'Introduction: the emergence of alternative forms of tourism', in V.L. Smith and W.R. Eadington (eds), *Tourism Alternatives: Potentials and Problems in the Development of Tourism*, Philadelphia: University of Pennsylvania Press, pp.1-12.

Gartner, W.G. (2005) 'A synthesis of tourism trends', in J. Aramberri and R. Butler (eds), *Tourism Development: Issues for a vulnerable Industry*, Clevedon, Channel View, pp.3-22.

Gartner, W.C. and Hsu, C.H.C. (forthcoming) *A Handbook of Tourism Research*, London: Taylor and Francis.

Getz, D. (2008) 'Event tourism: definition, evolution and research', *Tourism Management*, **29** (3), 403-428.

Gibson, C. (2008) 'Locating geographies of tourism', *Progress in Human Geography*, **32** (3), 407-422.

Gosar, A. (2005) 'The impact of the creation of two nation-states (Slovenia and Croatia) on tourism in Istria', in J. Aramberri and R.W. Butler (eds), *Tourism Development: Issues for a Vulnerable Industry*, Clevedon: Channel View, pp.193-214.

Jenkins, C.L. (1999) 'Tourism academics and tourism practitioners: Bridging the great divide', in D.G. Pearce and R.W. Butler (eds), *Contemporary Issues in Tourism Development*, London: Routledge, pp.52-64.

Jennings, G. R. (2007) 'Advances in tourism research: Theoretical paradigms and accountability', in A. Matias, P. Nijkamp and P. Neto (eds), *Advances in Modern Tourism Research: Economic Perspectives*, Heidelberg: Physica Verlag, pp. 9-35.

Li, L. (2008) 'A review of entrepreneurship research published in the hospitality and tourism management journals', *Tourism Management*, **29** (5), 1013-1022.

Nepal, S. K. (2009) 'Traditions and trends: a review of geographical scholarship in tourism', *Tourism Geographies*, **11** (1), 2-22.

Pearce, D.G. (1993) 'Introduction', in D.G. Pearce and R.W. Butler (eds), *Tourism Research: Critiques and Challenges*, London: Routledge, pp.1-8.

Pearce, D.G. (1999) 'Introduction: issues and approaches', in D.G. Pearce and R.W. Butler (eds), *Contemporary Issues in Tourism Development*, London: Routledge, pp.1-12.

Pearce, D.G. and Butler, R.W. (1993) *Tourism Research: Critiques and Challenges*, London: Routledge.

Pearce, D.G. and Butler, R.W. (1999) *Contemporary Issues in Tourism Development*, London: Routledge.

Pearce, P.L. (1993) 'Fundamentals of tourist motivation' in D.G. Pearce and R. Butler (eds), *Tourism Research: Critiques and Challenges*, London: Routledge, pp.113-134.

Pearce, P.L. (2005) 'Professing tourism: tourism academics as educators, researchers and change leaders', *Journal of Tourism Studies*, 16 (2), 21-33.

Pearce, P.L. and Moscardo, G. (1999) 'Tourism community analysis: Asking the right questions', in D.G. Pearce and R. Butler (eds), *Contemporary Issues in Tourism Development*, London: Routledge, pp.31-51.

Phillimore, J. and Goodson, L. (2004) 'Progress in qualitative research in tourism: Epistemology, ontology and methodology', in J. Phillimore and L. Goodson (eds), *Qualitative Research in Tourism: Ontologies, Epistemologies and Methodologies*, London: Routledge, pp. 3-29.

Ritchie, J.R.B. (1996) 'Beacons of light in an expanding universe: an assessment of the state-of-the-art in tourism marketing/marketing research', *Journal of Travel and Tourism Marketing*, 5 (4), 49-84.

Riley, R.W. and Love, L.L. (2000) 'The state of qualitative tourism research', *Annals of Tourism Research*, 27 (1), 164-187.

Ryan, C. (2005) 'Authors and editors – getting published: context and policy – an editor's view', *Journal of Tourism Studies*, 16 (2), 6-13.

Smith, V.L. and Eadington, W.R. (1992) *Tourism Alternatives: Potentials and Problems in the Development of Tourism*, Philadelphia: University of Pennsylvania Press.

Tribe, J. and Airey, D. (2007) 'A review of tourism research' in J. Tribe and D. Airey (eds), *Developments in Tourism Research*, Oxford: Elsevier, pp. 3-14.

UNWTO (2006a) 'Tourism Market Trends', available from http://unwto.org./facts/eng/ tmt.htm (accessed on 30 October 2009).

UNWTO (2006b) 'Facts & Figures: information, analysis and know-how', available from http://unwto.org./facts/eng/vision.htm (accessed on 30 October 2009).

UNWTO (2009) *World Tourism Barometer*, 7 (3).

Van Scotter, J.R. and Culligan, P.E. (2003) 'The value of theoretical and applied research for the hospitality industry', *Cornell Hotel and Restaurant Administration Quarterly*, 44 (2), 14-27.

Wang, Y and Wall, G. (in press) 'Perspectives on tourism planning in China', in W.C. Gartner and C.H.C. Hsu (eds), *A Handbook of Tourism Research*, London: Taylor and Francis.

Yeoman, I. with the Future Foundation (2008) *Tomorrow's Tourist: Scenarios and Trends*, Elsevier, Amsterdam.

Yoo, J.J-E and Weber, K. (2005) 'Progress in convention tourism research', *Journal of Hospitality and Tourism Research*, 29 (2), 194-222.

Part I

Perspectives on progress in tourism research

2 The real scissors crisis in tourism research

Julio Aramberri

Why and how to

When it comes to discussing tourism the prevailing mood is celebratory. Usually, one provides statistics that show how this modern social phenomenon has become the biggest population movement in history barring times of war. This success narrative has proven correct until recently. Since the turn of the 21st century we have witnessed, among other things, global terrorist attacks (September 11, Bali, and many others), two main international wars (Afghanistan and Iraq), pandemic scares (SARS or the outbreak of the porcine flu), the big tsunami of 2004 and some other minor events that created a less favourable environment for the development of travel and tourism. However, even such a rocky turn of the century only deterred tourism for short periods of time or otherwise redirected flows from some areas of the planet to others. Indeed the current economic crisis presents unexpected and untried challenges that may change this successful course. However, until we know more about its development, we can still expect that the social habit of tourism as well as the industries that cater for it will still be quite resilient (Aramberri and Butler, 2005).

When it comes to theoretical explanations and diagnoses, though, we leave Mardi Gras and enter Ash Wednesday. The present state of theory in tourism research is dismaying. Broadly speaking, academic production comes in two main shapes – *why* and *how to* research. At face value one might think that this distribution overlaps the now classic post-Kuhnian division between basic and everyday science (Lakatos, 1970). The first provides paradigms or solid theoretical constructions that shape a given field of knowledge for a long period of time – epoch-making discoveries that provide a general problematic and sharpen research hypotheses. Everyday science, on its side, gladly accepts the paradigm, works within its framework and solves tiny or sizable problems, following a methodology of research programs (Lakatos, 1978) that strengthens the accepted theoretical framework. It formulates research goals and designs experiments. Everyday science is not a *why* type of knowledge, but it is not *how to* either. Genuine *how to* or applied science is better known under the name of engineering or technology.

My contention is that, on one hand, contemporary tourism research contains plenty of engineering geared, in the tradition of business administration, to tinker with the travel industry (including transportation, hospitality, food and beverage, entertainment, shopping, and other aspects of the offer) and to improve its effectiveness, as well as much social engineering, following the tradition of international bureaucracies, in search of best practices to make the former friendlier and fairer to local providers. These two ways of approaching tourism usually work within the paradigm of modernity, that is, that of the present global capitalist economy (and its social and political formulas) stressing different ways to organize it better, either through more proficient technological or marketing mechanisms or through increased regulation of its workings.

On the other side, a significant amount of literature prefers to address *why* issues. Countless case studies and a few openly theoretical works are designed in such a way that things such as tour packages, airports, beaches, and sundry other attractions fade away from the horizon. They prefer to concentrate on a Husserlian eidetic unity of essences and claim that the paradigm of modernity should be cast aside by reason of its many theoretical shortcomings and its allegedly unpalatable practical consequences. Usually, one notices a stubborn reiteration that economics only offers a biased view of tourism and that it should be replaced by other social sciences, mostly anthropology, that offer a more wholesome view of human intercourse. Economic views of tourism are but another instance of the twisted arrangements created by a societal model that produces, reproduces and sanctions the inequalities that lie at modernity's core between haves and have-nots in the national and international arenas, between genders, between races, between ethnic groups, between cultures. This post-modern or 'pomo' matrix contends that another world is possible or, at least, that consistent evidence shows that the paradigm of modernity does not live up to standard and should be discarded. Whether aware of it or not, tourists and the travel industry play a not minor role in the extended reproduction of domination of the South by the North, or of the powerful over the disempowered. In this way, most *why* approaches in tourism research reflect only one of the possible ways of theorizing about modernity – its radical critique. The *why* mainstream believes that modernity, defined as the conjunction of science/technology, markets and open societies, should be exposed.

In fact, this is nothing new. Similar viewpoints were at the core of the romantic critique of modernity in the 19th century (Berlin, 1999) and pervaded most social sciences. However, the conflict between modernity and its radical critics has become sharper since industrialized societies took a new bend in the road to emerge as mass societies at the end of World War I and to undergo increasing globalization since the end of World War II. In the social sciences, this time has seen a greening of post-romanticism.

It is not surprising that tourism research should reproduce this conflict, as it is a branch of the social sciences. The vexing part, though, is that in our field the pro-modernity tradition has vacated the field. While the *how tos* devote their energies to the improvement of known management techniques or to the formulation of end-less lists of best practices for the industry and the markets, the radical *whys* roam with nary a critique. Both sides seem quite happy with an arrangement that, to use a Cold War acronym, could be labelled as MAD (Mutually Accepted Disinterest). In this way, the *how to* tinkers can proceed with their problem solving without feeling the need to justify their key assumptions. Models and equations are all they care about. One can read, for instance, a cavalier *how to* dismissal of Cohen's typologies of tourists (1972, 1979) because they are not based on empirical research (Sharpley, 1994) and, at the same time, attempts at building a notion of the global tourist by means of psychographic categories with a dubious empirical base (Swarbrooke and Horner, 1999). Examples of this trend abound in the two main encyclopaedias dealing with travel and tourism (Jafari, 2000; Pizam, 2005).

In this way, cultural critics are allowed to occupy the heights of theory *tout court* (Eagleton, 2003) and, with them, the higher moral ground unopposed. They are not even asked to offer any evidence for their foibles. MacCannell (2001), for instance, announced recently the oncoming demise of tourism without showing a single fact for it except his own expert opinion, that is, what wine tasters know as *the nose*. The parish, on its side, tries to haphazardly reconcile both in order to avoid the need for further reflection. On weekdays, they observe the strictures of the *Cornell Hotel and Restaurant Administration Quarterly*; on holy ones, they lament the ways of the world after the latest homily in *Annals of Tourism Research* or other well-known professional journals. If you happen to be an agnostic, you will have to put up with both the churlish moral superiority of the pomos *and* the unbearable conceptual lightness of the engineering crowd.

This condition looks like a genuine scissors crisis of the type that, on a completely different matter, Trotsky announced in Soviet Russia during the 1920s. Industry and agriculture, the countryside and the towns, the peasantry and the urban proletariat could not sustain their growing economic divergences and were bound for a period of conflicts. Possibly this will also be the outcome of the present stage in tourism research. It is difficult to accept that the chasm may go unabated in its present state. One misses the presence of options that defend the achievements of modernity in most areas of human activity including tourism and hospitality.

The present situation of a scissors crisis and its MAD logo seems perfectly endurable, even pleasantly comforting for both sides of present-day academia, especially to the *how tos*. They do not bother to defend their theoretical turf because they know that it is not in real danger. Post-romantic cultural critics have been perfectly unable to offer any tangible alternative to the markets. The problem, however, is that between business administration and post-modern cultural studies, the key issues of modern mass tourism remain unaddressed. This predicament is unsustainable. Bottom liners may ignore the rants of cultural critics, but if the latter could find a way to dispense with markets, commoditization, consumerism and other modern institutions, as is their wont, the former would soon find themselves on the dole.

This state of affairs may not – at least, should not – last. One can feel a degree of discomfort in our homely paradise with the many unsuccessful attempts to ignore the gap between *why* and *how to* approaches (Leiper, 1981, 2000). Different authors have already expressed their opinion that research in tourism has been unable to reach an acceptable level of theorizing (Echtner and Jamal, 1997; Tribe, 1997, 2000, 2009; Franklin, 2004), and that this is the effect of a split between managerial approaches on one side, and cultural critiques on the other (Franklin and Crang, 2001). In a telegraphic manner, the following paragraphs will try to document some unsatisfactory answers to the problems we face.

Dead ends

Jafari, either alone (1987, 1990, 1994, 1997a, 1997b, 2001) or in good company (Jafari and Ritchie 1981; Jafari and Aasar 1988; Jafari and Pizam 1996) has proposed on different occasions a creative solution to steer us clear of the swamp. In his formulation, tourism research has grown through the successive cross-pollination of a number of hypotheses or *platforms*, as he prefers to call them, which paved the way for the scientification of tourism research. He sees the evolution of the discipline starting in the 1960s and travelling from advocacy or uncritical acceptance of tourism as the privileged way to economic development to caution (tourism may rather be a bane than a blessing) to adaptancy (search for new or alternative ways to mass tourism) to a knowledge-based platform (with research leading to a holistic view of tourism and the formation of a shared body of knowledge). Lately, Jafari (2005) has added a fifth or public interest platform. More than a stage in theory, this latest remodelling reflects an increasing pervasiveness of the knowledge-based platform that reverberates in many different social quarters increasing the interest of the public in matters touristic.

Suggestive as it is, Jafari's plastic notion of a succession of platforms in tourism research cannot dispel a few funny things that happened on the way to scientification. For instance, the birth certificate of the new research field provides it with an unexpected facelift, as it takes for granted that academic reflection on tourism started in the 1970s. In fact it was on track much earlier. By the 1970s, the Ecole Hôtelière de Lausanne in Switzerland (founded in 1893) and Cornell's Hotel Department (founded in 1922 to evolve later into today's School of Hotel Administration) had been in business for a long time. Indeed, they had a different way of looking at tourism and hospitality from the 1970s. Both institutions were examples of the *how to* approach. On the throes of César Ritz (Roulet, 1998) or Escoffier (James, 2002), the former saw tourism as the preserve of the affluent and its idea of hospitality was excellent service to this growing elite; the latter would be difficult to understand without the inception of modern mass tourism in the USA. As *how to* revenue management thus became the occupation of a considerable part of academics, tourism research was bereft of general theorizing and its social dynamics were overlooked.

However, those are not compelling reasons to expunge them from the historical record. Delaying the birth of academic tourism research until it became adopted by a group of anthropologists (Smith, 1989; MacCannell 1999; Cohen, 2004) years later only gives a plus of legitimacy to the claim so often touted by the *why* side that tourism can only be roundly understood ignoring or downgrading its economic and managerial aspects.

One can also take issue with Jafari's model on a second level. It is true that tourism research has become more complex and more detailed as mass tourism has followed a path of increasing fragmentation. In this sense, it seems accurate to talk of increasing conceptual sophistication and better understanding of many new trends beyond the mass model that lies at the base of the advocacy platform. However, that today we may know more about many dimensions of tourism does not mean that, at the same time, we have reached a point where alternative paradigms are redundant. In this vein, the postulation that tourism research has already reached a knowledge-based platform may be too optimistic. It is clear that our engineers, following a time-honoured tradition of business schools, shirk from every possible theoretical confrontation, preferring to go about their day-to-day business and defer paradigmatic issues to others. But one should not conclude that we have built a *freischwebende Intelligenz* or detached collective observer (Mannheim, 1936) that overcomes by pure reasoning the conflicting views of what Jafari calls the advocacy and the cautionary platforms. They are still alive.

The new mobilities school (Urry, 2000; Verstraete and Cresswell, 2002; Sheller and Urry, 2004; Hall, 2005) also winds up in a blind alley. For them, today's world has turned people, institutions and societies into a medley of dynamic forces in perpetual motion. Grasping the movement of this changed object requires different analytical tools than those of traditional disciplines. In the past, people took a holiday at a given time and remained at home and in their working places most of the year. Nowadays we are perpetually on the move in such a way that tourism has to be integrated in a vaster continuum that includes the shortest and the longest of trips (Coles *et al.*, 2005b). In this way, the study of mobilities can blaze a new, post-disciplinary trail for tourism studies.

It is too early to say whether mobilities are here to stay or their glitter will shine with the fleeting grace of a flare star. In a brief assessment, however, it is difficult to see what their added value is. Including tourism in a wider circle of changes and ways of consumption together with our brief shopping trips or the permanent migrations of different ethnic diasporas does not seem to help much in understanding their relative specificity.

Which brings us back to square one. Whether tourism should be grouped with other mobilities, such as going shopping or migrations, does not answer some basic questions. Why did modern mass tourism start at a given point in time (around 1950) and not a few centuries before? Why does a homemaker who has to spend a considerable number of hours per week shopping for groceries not consider this chore as pleasant as going on holiday? Can we really say that migrants trying to sneak unacknowledged into the US or the EU engage in the same type of activity as beachcombers, skiers, or city-hoppers? The merits of mobilities (Coles *et al.*, 2005a) seem definitely overstated.

Paradise lost

MacCannell's approach to tourism is the closest thing to a general theory in a field badly lacking them. No surprise, then, that his work is addressed with reverence and profusely quoted. At the same time, it has also been the source of many misguided assumptions that still plague the field. This is not solely his fault. He has been abetted by a number of sycophants that have not paid much attention to his basic meanings and have appropriated him in abridged form. The ecstatic quotes of his work refer mostly to *The Tourist* (MacCannell, 1976, 1999) and even, more often, to only some parts of it. This is unfair. On one side, MacCannell has covered an impressive field of subjects (for a short list see 1989, 1992, 1993, 2002, 2005). On the other, his production has a consistent internal unity aiming at a thorough critique of the market model. He wraps it in mostly anthropological jargon, but in fact his architecture reveals that he really has a theory of tourism development; a theory of demand; and an alternative to the market system.

Let's start with tourism development. He sees tourist attractions as, above all, a relation between a sight and a sightseer or tourist. The relation, though, has another component – the marker that reminds the tourist that this is where he should focus his gaze. The marker is a sign for the attraction and it thus allows us to see tourism's simplest units as part of a universal language that we can decode. MacCannell often acknowledges his debt to what is known as the French deconstructionist school (especially to Lévi-Strauss' unconscious and Barthes' analysis of myth), and in its wake increasingly loses touch with the marker as a spatial pointer. To some extent, we are told, the marker itself not only confirms the attraction, it creates it. A small rock does not usually draw the attention of passers-by; however, if it is exhibited in a museum with a label as a moon rock, the marker makes it different from other common stones. It creates the attraction.

This is a stretch of the imagination. Indeed, tourists need maps, guides, and other markers of what they visit. They may symbolize whatever we want, but above all they are markers for concrete sites and particular ends. *Pace* MacCannell, markers cannot create attractions out of nothing. Behind the colourless moon rock there was the epoch-making space flight of Apollo 11. This, not the marker, is what made the otherwise nondescript rock different from others. MacCannell's confusion of symbols and interests and the primacy he grants to the former amounts to a gratuitous dismissal of facts. Tourist attractions are not developed at will by smart operators that manipulate symbols in spite of – often in opposition to – the needs of the gullible tourist.

He also offers a theory of demand – his so-called authenticity hypothesis. Here he parts ways with the French deconstructionists to meet Goffman. Attractions have a front and a back. Tourists always try to reach the latter, that is, the genuine or authentic aspect that would make them transparent and meaningful. However, they always miss their target. Why? MacCannell's views at this juncture are not clear. At first blush, he sees authenticity as an impossible dream. '[T]he tourist may believe that he is moving in this direction, but often it is very difficult to know for sure if the experience is in fact authentic' (1999: 101). The tourist reflects the structural incapacity of the human mind to successfully separate the grain of authenticity from the chaff of mystification.

However, a bit later, he will see authenticity or the lack thereof as specific to some social forms. He repeats many times that the tourist stands for modern-man-in-general. Accordingly, (in)authenticity appears only or mostly in modern cultures. 'Primitives who live their lives totally exposed to their "relevant others" do not suffer from anxiety about the authenticity of their lives' (MacCannell, 1999: 93). The relation between authenticity and mystification appears to be not structural but historical. MacCannell sees them both as twins joined at the hip in a structural arrangement known to all societies and, at the same time, absent in others. This may look like a conundrum but it will get a relevant role when he addresses his third and most important task – the critique of modernity.

The preternatural doubt whether the quest for authenticity has a shred of plausibility now braces itself for a happy ending. Undaunted by the Goffmanian ghost of backs and fronts and their irrepressible disjuncture, MacCannell offers his own version of economics. 'The dividing line between structure genuine and spurious is the *realm of the commercial*' (MacCannell, 1999: 155). Here, ensconced at the very heart of modern economics, is where the inauthentic reveals itself. Apparently, MacCannell's elusive primitives had no personality pains because they dispensed with commerce and the exchange of values. Such was the paradise forever lost to the moderns. 'The human type that has been put forward as a corporate twenty-first century ideal in the West is "hard-boiled", shallow, acquisitive, uncritical, hedonistic, chauvinistic, selfish and mean' (2002: 151). If we want to recover our own selves and a true sense of community we need to do away with commerce and its foundation – the division of labour. This is what he calls the revolution that will cast greed and markets to the dustbin of history. Unfortunately, he does not seem to have the slightest clue as to how this might come about; at least, he does not share it with his readers. On its side, the small but vocal cottage industry that follows his authenticity cue either joins the master in demurring from describing the process; or revels in an endlessly idle discussion of the merits of objective or existential authenticity (Wang, 2000; Reisinger and Steiner, 2006; Steiner and Reisinger, 2006; Cohen, 2007). In this way, MacCannell has saddled tourism research with a post-romantic view of tourism and of modernity that is deeply misleading.

Liberation theology

Victor Turner viewed the world through a different looking glass (1968, 1974, 1982). His starting point was an assessment of Van Gennep's work on the rites of passage (1961). Each individual life is a series of transitions between stages like birth, puberty, marriage, fatherhood, occupational activities and, finally, death. Societies mark the transition from one to another stage with a number of rites – of separation, of transition and of incorporation.

In *The Ritual Process* (1968), if not his major work at least the best structured, Turner, after having narrated some major rituals of the Ndembu (the ethnic group of his field years), adds a twist. While Van Gennep focused on the social stability provided by rites of passage, Turner stresses its plasticity. Where van Gennep sees stages of social duration, he chooses to focus on the transitional moment between initial and final stages (he calls it liminality). It is at the same time a fluid instance made both of deprivation and riches, of lowliness and sacredness, where the participants enjoy a special bond that ignores past and future, unifying them in the present. They thus become a communitas suffused with a promise of fusion and freedom. Community, more than an instrument of shared humanity that anybody can experience, becomes an unstructured spiritual meeting place for those that decide to leave behind the rigours of structure with its *us vs. them* categories to enjoy the encounter of the *I* and the *thou*, as proposed by Martin Buber.

Indeed, structure and communitas need each other if societies have to grow in a harmonious way. Exaggerated structure may lead to instability, upheavals and even revolutions from a subdued communitarian feeling; on the other hand, exaggerated communitas may mean despotism, hyper bureaucracies or structural rigidification. In his work Turner gives numerous examples of their interplay (the birth and evolution of the Franciscan order; millenarian movements; the hippie communities; the Sahayiha worshippers of Krishna in 16th–17th century Bengal; Mexico's independence; the Hell's Angels and many others).

Turner's is a binary theory of social change that evaporates it. It brings to mind Weber's process of tradition/charisma/bureaucracy. Both in Turner and in Weber, whether in dyadic or triadic form, we know that events happen, but we never grasp their reason. The mediation of what Weber called charisma and Turner communitas thus becomes a *deus ex machina*. Both acknowledge the emergence of change over time, but do not explain where and why it arises. The notion of societal causality, whatever this might be, thus remains unexplored. In fact, other than saying that they were agents of change, he cannot substantiate any real continuity between, for instance, the Franciscans and the hippies. Their goals, their practices, their interests remain mutually alien and we will never know why they had to differ.

Although Turner's influence on tourism research has been less openly acknowledged than MacCannell's, it is not difficult to see his hand on the pervasive notion that tourism represents the realm of the extraordinary as opposed to the predictability of everyday life. From there one can shape a vision of tourism as one of the many ways in which freedom counters necessity. It may be the opposition between the sacred and the profane, as in tourism as pilgrimage; or that between work and leisure as two mutually excluding entities; or tourism as unconstrained enjoyment as opposed to the anomy of social existence; or of the enlightened individual that knows how to enjoy life pleasures that escape the huddled masses. A detailed catalogue of such Turnerian turns of mind would need space beyond the limits of this chapter.

Turner also proposes a theory of modernity. It is deeply optimistic. For him, communitas can thrive in any liminal situation. Suddenly a wind of freedom may blow that shatters existing structures. Bureaucracies try to stand on the way, but they are finally overwhelmed. Modernity, that is, a societal order with a complex division of labour and free markets offers more opportunities for the dawning of liberty than most previous social forms. Those who view tourism as a privileged form of liminality or liminas or any other limen-something celebrate its explosive potential. Tourism can contribute to individual or social liberation, either in a limited way of role reversal while on holiday or blowing the social order into smithereens by way of global mega events or cosmic parties. Thus, he and his followers may come up with all kinds of ideas at no cost. More rituals of role reversal (like carnival or different pride parades); or some cultural capitalism replacing the rigours of the marketplace; or that sex, play, leisure or tourism may do away with the rigidities of social life. The sky is the limit for Shirley Valentine.

Turner and his tourism-research followers place themselves at the antipodes of MacCannell. Unfortunately, as they lack any serious notion of change and of social history, their conception of freedom has no real bearings. History becomes a whimsical pursuit of freedom that some times succeeds while failing at others. We will never know why. Turner's liberation theology remains as deluding as MacCannell's nostalgia for the lost paradise.

Conclusions

These remarks are perforce somewhat epigrammatic. Hopefully, however, they may contribute to a discussion of the present theoretical predicament in tourism research. On one side, in a quadrant mostly populated by economists, tourism, both in its behavioural and industrial dimensions, is but an appendix of microeconomics. A good deal of academic production is solely concerned with the bottom line – how to make it more profitable. The refinements offered in such short-range arguments have grown considerably while the practical totality of their practitioners takes for granted the world as it is; to wit, shaped by market behaviour and performance. They have no further ambition than understanding both a bit better. They make useful contributions to research, but at the same time, seem unable to venture beyond this box. Markets are all they know and they marvel that people might even question their very *raison d'être*.

On the other, one finds a large number of researchers, usually trained in the rest of the social sciences, who see their job as a mission – decrying the institutions that the other side holds holy. Market societies in their deepest recesses follow a limited rationality bound to produce and reproduce exploitation, injustice and domination. This post-romantic streak has been greatly enhanced by an overall critique of modernity that takes its cue from a 1968 motto (*soyons réalistes; démandons l'impossible*) and has become the golden section for many academics. In its pessimistic avatar, tourism, like many other manifestations of modern-man-in-general, compound the rush to the evil side of human nature. Only its wholehearted dismissal, followed, one supposes, by that of all their underlying props (modernity, markets, even the division of labour) might bring mankind back to the right track. There is, indeed, another, sunnier view. For their champions, by hovering between two worlds of determinacy, tourism offers a space for choice that humans can use to get rid of the stasis of everyday life. In the end, people can – and should – use such a wonderful state to opt for everything that would make their lives worth living.

Such, in my view, is the chasm that permeates tourism research at this point in time. Like open scissors, each blade follows a divergent direction and becomes further apart from the other. Most practitioners have opted for MAD (Mutually Accepted Disinterest), so each side tries to ignore the other. The *How tos* feel secure that the markets they probe are here to stay and think it unnecessary to even listen to the arguments of the other side. The *whys* profess a complete distaste for the framework their opponents take for granted and hope that, in the pessimistic persuasion, it may be done away with or, in the optimistic one, plainly ignored.

There have been some attempts to bridge the gap. Jafari's succession of platforms expects that it will go away as research grows and becomes more knowledge-based. From a different point of view, the mobilities school raises the expectation that once tourism is merged with the rest of activities that push people to go from one place to the other (shopping, travelling, migrating), it will be easier to find a single explanation for all such movement. I have tried to explain why both attempts wind up in a blind alley.

So, the scissors crisis not only remains alive; it keeps on growing. At the same time, there seems to be no eclectic or middle way out of this predicament. Should not we discard MAD and start a serious discussion where modernity and its accomplishments (including the practice of tourism) are better explained and defended from its adversaries?

References

Aramberri, J. and Butler, R. (2005) 'Tourism development: vulnerability and resilience', in J. Aramberri and R. Butler (eds), *Tourism Development: Issues for a Vulnerable Industry*, Clevedon: Channel View Publications.

Berlin, I. (1999) *The Roots of Romanticism*, Princeton, NJ: Princeton University Press.

Cohen, E. (1972) 'Towards a sociology of international tourism', *Social Research*, **39**, 64-82.

Cohen, E. (1979) 'A phenomenology of tourist experience', *Sociology*, **13**, 179-201.

Cohen, E. (2004) *Contemporary Tourism: Diversity and Change*, Oxford: Elsevier.

Cohen, E. (2007) '"Authenticity" in tourism studies: aprés la lutte', *Tourism Recreation Research*, **32** (2), 75-82

Coles, T., D.T. Duval and Hall, C.M. (2005a) 'Sobre el turismo y la movilidad en tiempos de movimiento y conjetura posdisciplinar', *Política y Sociedad*, **42** (2), 181-198.

Coles, T., D.T. Duval and Hall, C.M. (2005b) 'Tourism, mobility and global communities: new approaches to theorising tourism and tourist spaces', in W. Theobald (ed.), *Global Tourism: The Next Decade*, 3rd edn, London: Butterworth Heinemann, pp. 463-481.

Eagleton, T. (2003), *After Theory*, New York: Basic Books.

Echtner, C. and Jamal, T. (1997) 'The disciplinary dilemma of tourism studies', *Annals of Tourism Research*, **24** (4), 868-883.

Franklin, A. (2004) *Tourism: An Introduction*, London: Sage.

Franklin, A. and Crang, M. (2001) 'The trouble with tourism and travel theory', *Tourist Studies*, **1** (1), 5-22

Gennep, A. Van (1961) *The Rites of Passage*, Chicago: University of Chicago Press.

Hall, C.M. (2005) *Tourism: Re-thinking the Social Science of Mobility*, Harlow: Prentice-Hall.

Jafari, J. (1987) 'Tourism models: the sociocultural aspects', *Tourism Management*, **8**, 151-159.

Jafari, J. (1990) 'Research and scholarship: the basis of tourism education', *Journal of Tourism Studies*, **1**, 33-41.

Jafari, J. (1994) 'Structure of tourism: three models', in S. Witt and L. Moutinho (eds), *Tourism Marketing and Management Handbook*, 2nd edn, New York: Prentice Hall, pp. 1-7.

Jafari, J. (1997a) 'Tourism and culture: an inquiry into paradoxes', in *Proceedings of a UNESCO Roundtable on Culture, Tourism, Development: Critical Issues for the 21st Century*, Paris: UNESCO.

Jafari, J. (1997b) 'Tourismification of the profession: chameleon job names across the industry', *Progress in Tourism and Hospitality Research*, **3** (3), 175-181.

Jafari, J. (2000) *Encyclopedia of Tourism*, London: Routledge.

Jafari, J. (2001) 'The scientification of tourism', in V. Smith and M. Brent (eds), *Hosts and Guests Revisited: Tourism Issues of the 21st Century*, New York: Cognizant Communication Corporation, pp.28-41.

Jafari, J. (2005) 'El turismo como disciplina científica', *Política y Sociedad*, **42** (1), 39-56.

Jafari, J. and Ritchie, B. (1981) 'Toward a framework for education: problems and prospects', *Annals of Tourism Research*, 8 (1), 13-34

Jafari, J. and Aaser, D. (1988) 'Tourism as the subject of doctoral dissertations', *Annals of Tourism Research*, **15** (3), 407-429.

Jafari, J. and Pizam, A. (1996) 'Tourism management', in M. Warner (ed.), *International Encyclopedia of Business and Management*, London: Routledge, pp. 4903-4913.

James, K. (2002) *Escoffier: The King of Chefs*, London/New York: Hambledon and London.

Lakatos, I. (1970) 'Falsification and the methodology of scientific research programmes', in I. Lakatos and A. Musgrave (eds), *Criticism and the Growth of Knowledge*, Cambridge: Cambridge University Press.

Lakatos, I. (1978) 'History of science and its rational reconstructions', in J. Worrall and C. Gregory (eds), *Philosophical Papers, Vol. 1*, New York: Cambridge University Press.

Leiper, N. (1981) 'Towards a cohesive curriculum in tourism: the case for a distinct discipline', *Annals of Tourism Research*, 8 (1), 69-83.

Leiper, N. (2000) 'An emerging discipline', *Annals of Tourism Research*, **27** (3), 805-809.

MacCannell, D. (1976) *The Tourist: A New Theory of the Leisure Class*, New York: Schocken Books.

MacCannell, D. (1989) 'Faking it: comment on face-work in pornography', *American Journal of Semiotics*, **6** (4), 153-174.

MacCannell, D. (1992) 'Landscaping the unconscious', in M. Francis and R.T. Hester (eds), *The Meaning of Gardens*, Cambridge, MA: MIT Press, pp. 94-102.

MacCannell, D. (1993) 'Democracy's turn: on homeless noir', in J. Copjec (ed.), *Shades of Noir: A Reader*, London and New York: Verso, pp. 279-297.

MacCannell, D. (1999) *The Tourist: A New Theory of the Leisure Class*, Berkeley: University of California Press.

MacCannell, D. (2001) 'The commodification of culture', in V. Smith and M. Brent (eds), *Hosts and Guests Revisited: Tourism Issues of the 21st Century*, New York: Cognizant Communication Corporation, pp.380-390.

MacCannell, D. (2002) 'The ego factor in tourism', *Journal of Consumer Research*, **29** (1), 146-151.

MacCannell, D. (2005) 'Silicon values: miniaturization, speed and money', in C. Cartier and A.A. Lew (eds), *Seductions of Place: Geographical Perspectives on Globalization and Touristed Landscapes*, London and New York: Routledge, pp. 91-102.

Mannheim, K. (1936) *Ideology and Utopia*, London: Routledge.

Pizam, A. (ed.) (2005) *The International Encyclopedia of Hospitality Management*, London/New York: Butterworth Heinemann.

Reisinger, Y. and Steiner, C.S. (2006) 'Reconceptualizing object authenticity', *Annals of Tourism Research*, **33** (1), 65-86.

Roulet, C. (1998) *Ritz : Une histoire plus belle que la légende*, Paris: Quai Voltaire, La Table Ronde.

Sharpley, R. (1994) *Tourism, Tourists and Society*, Huntingdon: Elm.

Sheller, M. and Urry, J. (2004) *Tourism Mobilities: Place to Play, Places in Play*, London: Routledge.

Smith, V. (ed.) (1989), *Hosts and Guests: The Anthropology of Tourism*, Philadelphia: University of Pennsylvania Press.

Steiner, C.R. and Reisinger, Y. (2006) 'Understanding existential authenticity', *Annals of Tourism Research*, **33** (2), 299-318.

Swarbrooke, J. and Horner, S. (1999) *Consumer Behaviour in Tourism*, Oxford: Butterworth Heinemann.

Tribe, J. (1997) 'The indiscipline of tourism', *Annals of Tourism Research*, **24** (3), 638-657.

Tribe, J. (2000) 'Indisciplined and unsubstantiated', *Annals of Tourism Research*, **27** (3), 809-813.

Tribe, J. (2009) 'Philosophical issues in tourism', in J. Tribe (ed.), *Philosophical Issues in Tourism*, Bristol, Buffalo, Toronto: Channel View Publications, pp. 3-23.

Turner, V. (1968) *The Ritual Process: Structure and Anti-Structure*, New York: Aldine de Gruyter.

Turner, V. (1974) *Dramas, Fields and Metaphors: Symbolic Action in Human Society*, Ithaca and London: Cornell University Press.

Turner, V. (1982) *From Ritual to Theatre: The Human Seriousness of Play*, New York: PAJ Publications.

Urry, J. (2000) *Sociology Beyond Societies: Mobilities for the Twenty-First Century*, London: Routledge.

Verstraete, G. and Cresswell, T. (eds.) (2002) *Mobilizing Place, Placing Mobility: The Politics of Identity in a Globalising World*, Amsterdam: Rodopi.

Wang, N. (2000) *Tourism and Modernity: A Sociological Analysis*, Kidlington: Pergamon.

3 A typology of 'theory' in tourism

Stephen Smith and Hoffer Lee

Introduction

'Theory', a common academic term, comes from the Greek, *theoria* (Oxford English Dictionary, 1991). The term traditionally denotes contemplation, speculation, or a world view. Other definitions include a mental scheme or course of action for doing something, a systematic statement of facts or principle on which a body of knowledge is founded, abstract knowledge, or speculation. A frequent academic connotation of the term is that what is presented as theory reflects intellectual sophistication and is therefore superior to the atheoretical. As a result, supervisors of graduate students often expect their students to position their research in a theoretical context. Many journal editors also expect that submissions to their journals contribute to theory (Perdue *et al.*, 2009). Given both the plasticity and import of the word, the purpose of this chapter is to look at how the word 'theory' has been used in tourism, how this use has changed over time, and how it might be expected to be used in the future.

Views on 'theory' in tourism

Interest in theory is long-standing within tourism research. One of the first authors to address the topic was Cohen (1972). Drawing from Schuetz (1944), he developed a typology of tourists' attitudes toward the unknown versus the familiar. He believed these attitudes were reflected in individuals' travel styles. Cohen also suggested several implications arising from his typology. First, his typology illustrated the potential for a middle ground between a 'grand theory' of tourism and idiosyncratic studies. Second, he believed diverse theoretical perspectives should be applied to the study of tourism. Third, Cohen urged that a common approach to investigation be developed to support the development of a detailed, consistent, and theoretically informed understanding of tourism. His urging for 'theories of the middle ground' rather than the creation of a single theory would be repeated three decades later by Franklin and Crang (2001: 18) who observed, *it seems to us that tourism studies does not need to try to find some 'northwest passage' or Big Theory to legitimate itself as a school of thought. It seems very unlikely that one size will fit all.*

Despite such conclusions, other authors including Jovicic (1988), Meethan (2001), and Noy (2007) have called for a single, integrated theory of tourism. But even a quick reflection of the experiences of researchers in other fields suggests that the dream of creating a 'theory of everything in tourism' is naïve, if not egocentric. Despite decades of efforts, neither physics (which has led the charge) nor any other science has an overarching theory that encompasses all phenomena studied within the context of a body of science. If a grand theory is elusive in the natural sciences, surely the complexity and plasticity of the phenomena known collectively as tourism preclude the creation of any sort of comprehensive theory for that subject.

Dann *et al.* (1988) examined the balance between what they called 'methodological sophistication' and 'theoretical awareness in tourism research'. They developed a framework based on two intersecting continua: the degree of theoretical awareness (high to low) and the degree of methodological sophistication (high to low). These axes formed quadrants into which they classified articles from two journals. The authors suggested the quadrant combining high theoretical awareness and high methodological sophistication represented the correct balance for tourism research, but observed that most tourism researchers had not achieved this.

Of more direct relevance to this study, they defined theory as a 'body of logically interconnected propositions [that] provides an interpretive basis for understanding phenomena' (p 4). Moreover, their framework implies theory can be independent of methodology. However, the authors appeared to hold other views on the nature of theory as well. In one passage, they stated the 'evaluation of tourists' motives may only be *post hoc* theorizing by experts who are simply projecting their own choices' (p 11). This implies they saw theory as synonymous with speculation rather than rigorous development and testing of causal models. Elsewhere, they suggested the degree of theoretical awareness could be judged on the basis of 'understanding, prediction, and falsifiability' (p. 10). In other words, it is not clear whether they meant that theory is a subjective lens through which some phenomenon may be interpreted, or that theory should be grounded on empirical evidence.

In 2000, Dann traced six transitions in the sociology of tourism, such as the shift from typological description to a search for understanding of motivations of tourists' behaviours. As part of his review, Dann acknowledged that their earlier characterization of theory (Dann *et al.*, 1988) would not necessarily be accepted by other sociologists, noting some would limit the connotation of theory to 'understanding' only, excluding any connection with causality.

In 2005, Dann undertook a more thorough examination of the state of tourism theory. He identified a number of social scientists whom he believed had made theoretical contributions to tourism, noting, though, their contributions fell short of being truly new theories. Instead, he characterized the contributions as modifications of concepts from outside tourism. Although re-engineering someone else's concepts as a basis for insights into tourism could be criticized as reflecting a lack of creativity, Dann suggested this was evidence that tourism theory was still in a formative stage.

Another critical review of tourism theory was offered by Athiyaman (1997). He looked at tourism demand models to assess the degree to which they built upon or contributed to theory. Athiyaman described the creation of knowledge through research as proceeding through three phases: (1) observation and discovery of important variables; (2) the formation and testing of hypotheses about these variables; and (3) the integration of confirmed hypotheses into theory. A review of published studies resulted in his conclusion that forecasters were ignorant of the process of theory construction and that, as a result, progress in the scientific understanding of tourism was seriously constrained.

Working from a pedagogical perspective, Ritchie et al. (2008) argued tourism curricula should be founded on theories appearing in research literature. While the authors began with a discussion of the nature of theory in the natural sciences, they did not explicitly define the term. However, they implied theory in tourism should be the same as that in the natural sciences – propositions based on substantial empirical evidence and falsifiable hypotheses. They also proposed a model in which they distinguished between core theory – theory specifically developed in the context of tourism – and foundational theory, which refers to theories from other fields and applied to tourism.

Working from a focus on knowledge management, Hallin and Marnburg (2007) reviewed empirical research published in hospitality journals. They examined these from a variety of perspectives including 'research quality of contributions', by which they meant how well the original authors of the studies met 'theory-of-science criteria': whether the results were empirically tested and whether the findings could be generalized to other situations. The authors concluded that the great majority of knowledge management research studies in hospitality were 'inconclusive and mostly descriptive, focusing on anecdotal and one-off case studies' (p. 379).

Toward a typology of 'theory'

To examine in greater detail how 'theory' is used by tourism researchers, we conducted a content analysis of articles from *Annals of Tourism Research* (*ATR*), *Journal of Travel Research* (*JTR*), and *Tourism Management* (*TM*), Articles were selected from two lustra representing the first five years of the International Academy for the Study of Tourism (1989–93) and the five most recent years (2004–08). The search was limited to individual papers that could reasonably be considered to represent 'research' such as full-length articles and research notes. Book reviews, conference reports, and other non-research pieces were excluded.

Each paper's title, abstract, and key words were used as search fields with 'theor*' as the search term to identify papers for examination. One limitation to this scan is the possible omission of articles in which 'theory' is a fundamental perspective but does not appear in the search fields. Another limitation to our approach is, of course, the focus on just three Anglophone journals and two time periods. This reflected the pragmatic need to limit the scope of data collection. While we believe that this sampling frame provides a reasonable picture of how the term 'theory' has been and is being used by Anglophone researchers, we acknowledge that the use of additional journals, additional time periods, and, especially, other languages might have resulted in different conclusions.

Each article captured by the search was reviewed to ascertain whether:

1   A specific theory was named.
2   The theory was explicitly grounded in a discipline or referenced other studies using that theory.
3   The form of the theory: mathematical/statistical, verbal, graphic.
4   The article presented hypotheses or research propositions/questions.
5   Any hypotheses or research propositions/questions were empirically tested.
6   Conclusions relevant to the development or testing of theory were explicitly identified.

The content of each article with respect to these issues was then annotated in a matrix for each journal and for each lustrum. The annotations were reviewed iteratively, each time looking for more general patterns on which to base a tentative typology of types of theory. The final typology consists of seven categories, generically labelled 'Theory of the nth type'. A brief description of each type is provided in Table 3.1; this is followed by a fuller discussion of each type.

Table 3.1: Typology of 'theory'

Category	Brief description
Theory of the first type	'Traditional theory' of the form found in the natural sciences
Theory of the second type	Theory is synonymous with an a priori, usually empirical, model
Theory of the third type	Theory is equated with statistical analysis
Theory of the fourth type	Theory is an untested/untestable verbal or graphic model
Theory of the fifth type	Epistemology as theory
Theory of the sixth type	Grounded theory
Theory of the seventh type	Theory as an ungrounded label or adjective

Types of theory

Theory of the first type is theory as normally understood in economics or the natural sciences: well-tested, capable of producing new and significant falsifiable predictions, and conceptually linked to other theories that provide an integrated understanding of some aspect of reality. The theory is well-established in literature and represents an integral part of a discipline. Such theory typically is articulated in equations or graphs that have broad applicability to different manifestations of a subject. It is based on successfully meeting repeated tests; if hypotheses that emerge logically from the theory fail to be supported, the theory is incorrect or, at least, incomplete.

An example of a Type 1 Theory is Wie's (2005) application of Nash open-loop equilibrium drawn from game theory, to decision-making in the cruise industry. Wie characterized the cruise industry as 'an oligopoly where a finite number of cruise lines compete to maximize their profits over a fixed planning horizon' (p. 204). In other words, he viewed the industry as a game involving a small number of players operating in a perfectly competitive market place (there are many buyers and each of them will buy) to maximize their share of total revenues. For modelling purposes, Wie made a number of assumptions, such as that cruises are functionally homogeneous and that the firms compete in a single market. He then constructed a model to predict the optimal number of berths available in the cruise industry for the period in question. His solution involved a set of theorems that provided the basis for his five-step solution. After applying numerical data and solving his formulation, he identified managerial implications arising from his findings.

Theory of the second type is not as consistently supported by empirical evidence and may not be linked to other theories as is theory of the first type. However, Type 2 theories do reflect some form of prior testing. These theories can often be considered as synonymous with 'models'. Type 2 Theory generates falsifiable predictions; however, these tests may show only limited support for the theory due to complexities or irregularities in the phenomenon being studied. Because the studied phenomenon may involve elements not fully accounted for in the theory, failure to generate an accurate prediction is not seen as sufficient for rejecting the theory. As a result, two or more theories describing the same phenomenon may co-exist. Theories of human behaviour or social dynamics from anthropology, community development, human geography, planning, political science, psychology, and sociology often are theories of the second type.

An example can be seen in Lee and Back (2008). In a study of how potential participants decide whether to attend an association meeting, the authors drew on two models from social psychology: the theory of reasoned action (TRA) and its extension, the theory of planned behaviour (TPB). TRA and TPB are well-established models in social psychology and provided the authors with concepts on which to develop and test their own model of meeting participation.

TRA hypothesizes a set of variables that influence how a person makes decisions about her actions. TPB extends TRA to include variables related to how she might perceive certain involuntary controls on her actions. Lee and Back proposed a further elaboration of TPB through their development of a 'meeting participation model' (MPM). Each model was empirically specified and tested using structural equation modelling (SEM). The results of all three models were judged to provide an adequate representation of decisions regarding meeting participation. However, the results of the TPB were viewed to be superior to those of TRA, and those of MPM as superior to TPB. The authors concluded their study with a discussion of the 'theoretical implications' of each model.

Theory of the third type refers to statistical models that test speculative causal relationships among variables but without an *a priori* model. A common example of this type of theory would be a structural equation model whose results are presented as 'theoretical insights' although the SEM is not founded on an existing conceptual model. The models may be couched in the context of a larger framework such as branding, market segmentation, consumer decision-making, or destination marketing, but they are classified as belonging to the third type if they lack ties to an explicit, formal theory.

Lee *et al.* (2007) examined the motivations and experiences of visitors on tours of the Demilitarized Zone between North and South Korea. The authors asked visitors about their perceptions of the value of their satisfaction with the tour. Proposed relationships among measures of value and satisfaction were tested using an SEM that the authors positioned as a 'theoretical model'. However, the hypothesized relationships and variables were not based on either a Type 1 or Type 2 theory. The results were generally supportive of the hypothesized relationships, so the authors concluded the model had implications for 'theories' relating satisfaction and perceived value.

Theory of the fourth type is similar to Type 2 Theory in that it represents a conceptual model used for description or explanation; it differs from the second type in that the models are not falsifiable. These models tend to be verbal, but may be supported by graphic representations. Relationships among key elements of the model as well as implications for some larger phenomenon are described but, again, the propositions are not testable.

Potter and Coshall (1988) provide an example of theory of the fourth type. The authors were interested in demonstrating the utility of a method known as repertory grid analysis to identify the principal dimensions by which individuals perceive destinations. They grounded their analysis in the notion of personal construct theory, which they characterized as 'a well-articulated theory' (p. 64).

Theory of the fifth type is epistemology presented as theory. It is a formal, prescriptive way of collecting and interpreting the data. As do theories of the fourth type, theories of the fifth type lack falsifiable hypotheses. Indeed, Type 5 theories can overlap those of Type 4 in that epistemologies may include propositions that form the basis for subjective research designs such as feminist theory. These designs include assumptions that indicate which questions are permissible, information that may be collected, and how observations are to be interpreted. However, the findings of such research cannot be independently verified because the analysis is not empirical. Different researchers observing the same phenomena may come to very different conclusions, depending on their personal perspectives.

An example of this approach, using 'post-colonial theory', is Caton and Santos' (2007) examination of photographs taken by university students on a field trip to former colonies of Western nations. The authors were interested in whether the photographs taken by the students reflected Western stereotypes of the residents of the countries visited. The photographs were treated as 'text' and coded in terms of their portrayal of binary themes such as 'centre/periphery'. Using the vocabulary of post-colonial theory, the authors concluded '[t]he analyzed photographs . . . [completed] a circle of representation that is inscribed with socio-cultural ideologies of Western power and dominance' (p. 7).

Theory of the fifth type thus is a filter through which a researcher selects and interprets data. Rather than suggesting hypotheses that can be empirically tested, Type 5 theory prescribes a set of values and propositions that shape the questions a researcher is permitted to ask. As a result, the application of Type 5 theory tends to be self-perpetuating. For example, a conflict theorist views social interactions as a struggle between unequal powers. If the premise of conflict theory is accepted, then data are always viewed as evidence of unequal power struggles.

Theory of the sixth type is so-called grounded theory. Grounded theory is not a single theory, per se, but represents the derivation of conclusions in the form of themes or patterns based on a structured, iterative, subjective coding of interview transcripts. It begins with the development of codes in a source of data, typically an interview transcript, and then proceeds systematically to a set of statements about the topic under study. Unlike theories of the first and second type, the findings of grounded theory cannot be generalized beyond the specific context of the research. These findings may have the potential to be translated into falsifiable propositions although, in practice, this is rarely done. As with theory of the fifth type, different researchers observing the same phenomena may come to different conclusions based on their world views.

Decrop and Snelders (2003) used grounded theory in their examination of vacation decision-making processes. Employing in-depth interviews to elicit information on vacation decision-making, behaviours, motives, and plans and intended destinations, the authors felt they were able to obtain insights into the contexts, complexities, and dynamics of decision-making. Transcripts of the interviews were reviewed and coded using the standard approach of grounded theory. The results, based on 25 Belgian households, were interpreted by the authors as representing six different vacation styles that they described as being useful for 'both theoretical and segmentation purposes' (p. 121).

Theory of the seventh type represents diverse uses of 'theory'. The unifying characteristic of this type of theory is that the term 'theory' is used uncritically, casually, or without substantive foundation. Findings may be claimed to be theoretical but they are not based on either testable propositions or an *a priori* model. *Post hoc* empirical results may be presented, although these usually are descriptive only. In other words, theory of the seventh type includes the description of research results as offering 'theoretical insights' but with no justification for the claim.

Kim *et al.* (2005) employed multidimensional scaling to examine how the Korean golf market viewed different destinations. Data were obtained from a questionnaire designed to elicit perceptions of countries popular as golf destinations. Questions also elicited socio-demographic and trip preference data. A series of perceptual maps comparing the selected destinations to each other were developed as well as correlations between socio-demographic variables and trip preferences. The authors described their results, including the strengths and weaknesses of each country, as offering 'theoretical and managerial implications' (p. 905), but without explicitly identifying a theory or even a model as a context for the discussion of their findings.

Another version of theory of the seventh type is to label an analytical method as 'theory'. In their study of attendees' needs and service priorities in an American convention centre, Breiter and Milman (2004) employed a method known as importance–performance assessment (or analysis) (IPA). They positioned the method, not just as an assessment tool, but as 'importance-performance theory'. IPA is a potentially useful tool but it cannot be meaningfully characterized as a theory or even as a model.

Articles that attempt to position themselves as an application of an existing theory but just use the theory analogically also are classified as Type 7. Chaos theory is a common metaphor that has been invoked in a wide variety of contexts ranging from the movie, *Jurassic Park*, to entrepreneurship in tourism development. This latter example comes from a paper by Russell and Faulkner (2004). The authors proposed chaos theory as a perspective to examine different types of entrepreneurship under conditions of unpredictability in the tourism marketplace.

The appeal of chaos theory as an analogue for describing complex systems is understandable, but chaos theory is not simply an analogy. Russell and Faulkner illustrate the intellectual appeal and allude to the potential strengths of the theory when they observe:

> *[w]hile the principles of the deterministic, reductionist, top-down analysis established by Newton and Descartes centuries ago may remain applicable to phenomena characterized by stable systems and linearity, they do not explain the true nature of many systems that are inherently more unstable and non-linear (p. 559).*

However, just noting the limitations of deterministic or even stochastic models and invoking phenomena associated with chaos theory, as Russell and Faulkner do:

> *[s]ome of the more pertinent features of chaotic systems that are particularly relevant to the examination of destination development are 'edge-of-chaos phenomena', 'self-organizing behavior', the 'butterfly effect', 'lock-in effect', 'self-similarity' and 'bifurcation' (p. 557)*

does not constitute an application of chaos theory. Chaos theory is a formal, sophisticated mathematical modelling, much of which depends on the use of ultra-high speed computers. We are unaware of any valid application of chaos theory in its scientific form in tourism.

Let us now briefly consider the relative frequency of each type of theory and how this has changed over time. Table 3.2 summarizes the frequencies of the appearance of each type of theory for the two time periods and journals examined.

Table 3.2: Frequency of types of 'theory' by journal and lustrum

	Type 1	Type 2	Type 3	Type 4	Type 5	Type 6	Type 7	Total Theory	Total Articles
1989 – 1993									
ATR	3	2	2	6	4	0	0	17	645
	17.6%	11.8%	11.8%	35.3%	23.5%	0.0%	0.0%	2.6%[a]	
JTR	1	1	1	1	0	0	0	4	165
	25.0%	25.0%	25.0%	25.0%	0.0%	0.0%	0.0%	2.4%	
TM	0	0	0	0	0	0	0	0	219
	0.0%	0.0%	0.0%	0.0%	0.0%	0.0%	0.0%	0.0%	
Sub-Total	4	3	3	7	4	0	0	21	1,029
	19.0%	14.3%	14.3%	33.3%	19.0%	0.0%	0.0%	2.0%	
2004 – 2008									
ATR	1	7	4	5	3	4	11	35	510
	2.9%	20.0%	11.4%	14.3%	8.6%	11.4%	31.4%	6.8%	
JTR	0	13	16	9	1	12	8	59	270
	0.0%	22.0%	27.1%	15.3%	1.7%	20.3%	13.6%	21.9%	
TM	2	26	5	6	3	3	20	65	465
	3.0%	40.0%	7.7%	9.2	4.6%	4.6%	30.8%	14.0%	
Sub-total	3	46	25	20	7	19	39	159	1,245
	1.9%	28.9%	15.7%	12.6%	4.4%	11.9%	24.5%	12.8%	
Total	7	49	28	27	11	19	39	180	2,274
	3.9%	27.2%	15.6%	15.0%	6.1%	10.6%	21.7%	7.9%	

Note: a = percent of total articles

As can be gleaned from the table, the use of 'theory' (and its variants) as a term has increased dramatically over the last 20 years. In terms of absolute numbers, the occurrence of these terms rose from 21 articles between 1989 and 1993, to 159 articles between 2004 and 2008. This might reflect increased attention to theoretical issues over the 20 years, although we suggest the trend more likely reflects researchers explicitly positioning their research as being 'theoretical' without necessarily being rigorous in their use of the term. Still, 'theor*' remains a relatively infrequent term. It occurred in less than 3 per cent of all articles published in two of the three journals in the first lustrum, and not at all in the third. Its incidence rose in the most recent lustrum, but still occurred in less than one-quarter of articles (and in only one in 15 articles in one journal).

In the three journals examined, no article using Types 6 or 7 theory appeared in the first lustrum. Twenty years later, over 10 per cent of articles used Type 6 and over 20 per cent used Type 7. Indeed, Type 7 (the ungrounded use of 'theor*') was the second most common application of the term. Type 4 theory was the predominant use of 'theory' in the first lustrum. It should be noted, though, that all but one of the occurrences of Type 4 theory was in one journal. Type 2 theory dominated the use of the term in the most recent five-year period. Type 1 theory occurred in about one in five articles in the first lustrum, but dropped to one in 25 articles in the second. The rise in Type 7 versus the fall in Type 1 indicates that the term, 'theor*', is increasingly used in ways in which the term has no substantive meaning. In contrast, Type 1 theory is becoming increasingly rare in tourism research.

Conclusions

Our review of the use of 'theory' demonstrates a substantial and increasingly inconsistent use of the word. Seven different uses of 'theory' have been identified, ranging from traditional scientific theory to the casual and uncritical use of the term.

Theory in the traditional scientific sense (Type 1) is becoming much less common in tourism research. Nearly one in five of the articles examined in the first lustra were deemed to be of Type 1. Twenty years later, less than one in 50 used Type 1 theory. In contrast, Type 2 theories have doubled their rate of appearance, from about one in seven articles to two in seven. Types 6 and 7 did not appear in any articles in the first five-year sample, but had become common in the most recent five-year period. Indeed, Type 7 – the causal (and we suggest largely meaningless) use of 'theory' – appears in nearly one in four articles. The rise of Type 6 theory, so-called grounded theory, arguably reflects not only the growing popularity of this method, but of other subjective research designs in tourism.

So, are we going to suggest a single correct use of 'theory' in tourism research? The fecundity of English vocabulary, especially in the context of developing new or diverse meanings for words, is well-documented (Hitchings, 2008). Still, in the context of scholarship, some consistency in the use of terms that are as meaning-laden as 'theory' is desirable. Clarity and precision in scholarly language facilitates communication. Divergent meanings of words by scholars impede communication and become a source of pedantic debate.

Recognizing the English language does not have its equivalent of the *L'Académie française*, and that there is pressure on authors to position their work as 'theoretical', a continuing creep in the meaning of 'theory' is likely. Still, we suggest that 'theory', in a published research context, should be limited to Type 1 and Type 2 theory. In other words, 'theory' is most appropriately used in the context of models that are based on substantial empirical evidence and that produce falsifiable predictions.

For other uses, including subjective speculation, 'theory' can be replaced by 'model', 'concept', 'method', 'paradigm', or 'epistemology'. For the specific case of grounded theory, the name itself is misleading in that grounded theory is not, in our view, theory in any sense, but, rather, a method involving a type of coding and drawing themes out of interview transcripts. Thus, it might be more accurately called sequential or hierarchical coding.

The diverse uses of 'theory' can lead not only to miscommunication but misrepresentation of how a model or findings are positioned in the canon of tourism research. There are important distinctions that need to be maintained between an author's speculations and subjective musings, and empirically supported results (e.g. hypotheses that have been subjected to falsifiable testing). Blurring this distinction through the increasingly indiscriminate use of 'theory' does our field a disservice. More honesty, precision, and clarity in researchers' vocabularies would facilitate understanding and communication, and help support future progress in the social scientific understanding of the nature, structure, and dynamics of tourism.

References

Athiyaman, A. (1997) 'Knowledge development in tourism: tourism demand research', *Tourism Management*, **18** (4), 221-228.

Breiter, D. and Milman, A. (2004) 'Attendees' needs and service priorities in a large convention centre: application of the importance-performance theory', *Tourism Management*, **27** (6), 1364-1370.

Caton, K. and Santos, C. (2007) 'Closing the hermeneutic circle? Photographic encounters with the other', *Annals of Tourism Research*, **35** (1), 7-26.

Cohen, E. (1972) 'Towards a sociology of international tourism', *Social Research*, **39**, 164-182.

Dann, G. (2000) 'Theoretical advances in the sociological treatment of tourism', in S. Quah and A. Sales (eds), *The International Handbook of Sociology*, London: Sage, pp. 367-384.

Dann, G. (2005) 'The theoretical state of the state-of-the-art in the sociology and anthropology of tourism', *Tourism Analysis*, **10**, 3-15.

Dann, G., Nash, D. and Pearce, P. (1988) 'Methodology in tourism research', *Annals of Tourism Research*, **15** (1), 1-28.

Decrop, A. and Snelders, D. (2003) 'A grounded typology of vacation decision-making', *Tourism Management*, **26** (2), 121-132.

Franklin, A. and Crang, M. (2001) 'The trouble with tourism and travel theory', *Tourist Studies*, **1** (1), 5-22.

Hallin, C. and Marnburg, E. (2007) 'Knowledge management in the hospitality industry: a review of empirical research', *Tourism Management*, **29** (2), 366-381.

Hitchings, H. (2008) *The Secret Life of Words: How English Became English*, New York: Farrar, Straus, and Giroux.

Jovicic, Z. (1988) 'A plea for tourismological theory and methodology', *Revue de Tourisme*, **43** (3), 2-5.

Kim, S., Chun, H. and Petrick, J. (2005) 'Positioning analysis of overseas golf course destinations by Korean golf tourists', *Tourism Management*, **26** (6), 905-917.

Lee, C-K., Yoon, Y-S. and Lee, S-K. (2007) 'Investigating the relationships among perceived value, satisfaction, and recommendations: the case of the Korean DMZ', *Tourism Management*, **28** (1), 204-214.

Lee, M. J. and Back, K-J. (2008) 'Association meeting participation: a test of competing models', *Journal of Travel Research*, **46**, 300-310.

Meethan, K. (2001) *Tourism in Global Society*, Basingstoke: Palgrave.

Noy, C. (2007) *A Narrative Community: The Voices of Israeli Backpackers*, Detroit, MI: Wayne State University Press.

Oxford English Dictionary (1991) Available from http://db.uwaterloo.ca/OED/search/ oed-local/lookup.cgi (accessed on 3 November 2008).

Perdue, R., Meng, F. and Courtney, J. (2009) 'Publishing in the *Journal of Travel Research*: an assessment of manuscript acceptance and rejection', *Journal of Travel Research*, **47**, 267-275.

Potter, R. and Coshall, J. (1988) 'Sociopsychological methods for tourism research', *Annals of Tourism Research*, **15** (1), 63-75.

Ritchie, J.R.B, Sheehan, L. and Timur, S. (2008) 'Tourism sciences or tourism studies?', *Téoros*, **27**, 33-41.

Russell, R. and Faulkner, B. (2004) 'Entrepreneurship, chaos, and the tourism area lifecycle', *Annals of Tourism Research*, **31** (3), 556-579.

Schuetz, A. (1944) 'The stranger: an essay in social psychology', *American Journal of Sociology*, **49**, 499-507.

Wie, B.-W. (2005) 'A dynamic game model of strategic capacity investment in the cruise industry', *Tourism Management*, **26** (2), 203-217.

4 Tourism and development: looking back and looking ahead – more of the same?

David Harrison

Introduction

Since the Second World War, mass international tourism has become immensely significant to the world economy and is now established globally as a tool for development, making a major contribution to the world economy, especially to developing countries, even though they take but a small proportion of the world's tourists, and most particularly small states and island societies (UNWTO, 2008: 1). As a consequence, mass international tourism has increasingly attracted the attention not only of governments and a plethora of aid agencies and national and other international institutions, but also of scholars of 'development'. Indeed, while social change and 'progress' have been the major concern of social science since the Enlightenment, 'development' as a separate concept, along with 'development studies' as a self-conscious sub-discipline, emerged only after 1945, and it was thus inevitable that, from the beginnings of mass international tourism, it would be linked with development, and would reflect the changing priorities of development studies.

From the 1960s until the 1980s, the trajectory of tourism in developing countries was largely conceptualised through the competing lenses of pro-capitalist Modernisation (bourgeois) Theory (MT) or anti-capitalist Underdevelopment (UDT) (Neo-Marxist, Dependency or World Systems) Theory (Telfer, 2002). In so far as these represented different 'paradigms', they tended to focus, respectively, on the advantages and disadvantages of tourism as a form of development, as purportedly seen from the perspective of the developing countries.

However, by the 1980s (especially after the fall of the Berlin Wall) the positions occupied by adherents of these competing perspectives were no longer considered theoretically adequate, empirically justified or politically appropriate in a world where old ideologies were being subjected to new questioning and found wanting. Globalisation theory emerged, denoting a process where 'constraints of geography on social and cultural arrangements recede and in which people become increasingly aware that they are receding' (Waters, 1995: 3). Although divisions between those favouring state intervention (statists) and others wishing to give a free rein to the market (neo-liberals) continued, globalisation theory incorporated the internal economic and socio-cultural factors prioritised by MT and the external and systemic linkages of UDT, *along with* the increasingly pressing concerns of environmentalism.

Inevitably, such changes in theoretical perspectives were reflected in approaches to tourism, development, and over the last decade tourism scholars have started to focus on tourism's role in the interplay of local destinations with global processes (Sofield, 2001; Wahab and Cooper, 2001; Munar, 2007; Sharpley, 2009). And with the decline of the old ideologies and 'grand theories' of tourism's role in development came a more pragmatic, empirical focus on what was happening 'on the ground'. It was less important to know who (and of what persuasion) said what, than to know if there was empirical evidence for their assertions.

In the context of this new and more empirically-orientated environment, the focus of this chapter is, first, the current state of tourism development studies, its descriptive and prescriptive elements, and the role of international organisations. It then moves to the need for further empirical research on the role of the state, and the ways different economic institutions, including TNCs and SMEs, and different kinds of tourism, including domestic tourism, influence tourism development. Finally, a brief agenda for the future is suggested, focusing on: the theoretical understanding of tourism's role in the context of climate change; closer relationships with, and understanding of, other stakeholders involved in using tourism as a development tool; comparative studies of tourism development in developing societies *and* developed societies and, finally, the impacts of different *kinds* of tourism in reducing poverty and bringing about 'development'.

The current state of tourism development studies

The less ideological approach just described enables and entails a greater element of cross-disciplinary co-operation. Geography, sociology, anthropology, political science, history and social psychology, for example, can all legitimately add the suffix 'of tourism development', as can a raft of physical sciences, which together contribute to our understanding of the tourism 'system'. Such a notion, which is neither new nor subject to consensus (Hall, 2008: 76-80), is a conceptual construct that recognises tourism occurs in a highly complex global, biophysical, social, cultural and economic environment. As conceived here (Figure 4.1), the tourist 'system' is similar to the 'Comprehensive Tourism System' of Farrell and Twining-Ward (2003: 279), which 'includes significant social, economic, geological and ecological components'. The system's processes, viewable from a variety of perspectives, are geared to the movement of tourists to and from generating societies in a shifting international context, continuously linking the changing cultures and

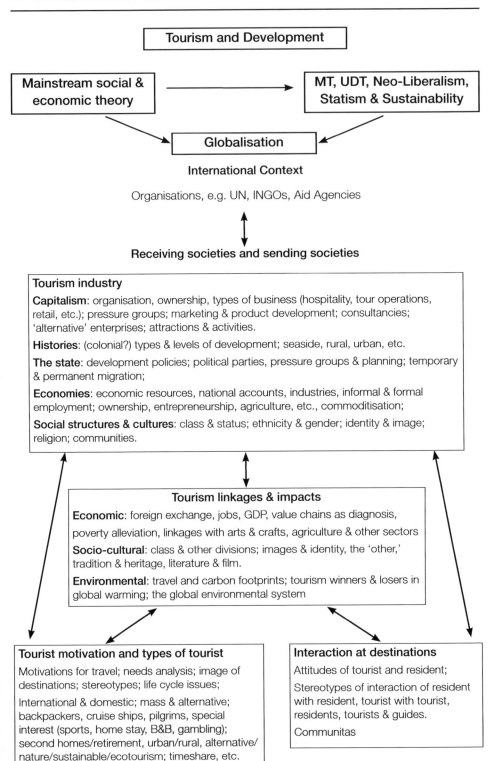

Figure 4.1: Theoretical perspectives informing approaches to tourism and development

social and economic structures of generating and destination regions according to external and local factors, including the numerous resources in destination areas described by Sharpley (2009: 159) as 'tourism destination capitals'. These socio-cultural and economic processes both affect and are affected by wider environmental considerations, as seen, for example, in the debate about tourism's relationship to climate change (Becken and Hay, 2007).

Not surprisingly, such a framework incorporates research on a wide variety of topics, including tourist motivation, geographies of tourist movement over time and space, the rise and fall of tourism destinations, and the images associated with them, tourism organisations, carrying capacity and detailed case studies of what occurs at specific destinations, and the local, national, regional and international significance of tourism and the *processes* that link changes in developed societies to what is going on in developing societies.

The breadth of approaches in tourism is also reflected in the emergence of sub-sectors of tourism studies which, though often concentrated on developed societies, are equally relevant to developing societies. Studies of events and festivals, their significance and impact, or of varieties of heritage tourism, for example, are not restricted to urban areas in the West; they are equally relevant to developing societies, which continually seek new attractions, even new 'traditions', to bring people to their destinations.

Such interest, fuelled and sustained by the growth of tourism and awareness of its many impacts, has led to a burgeoning of academic courses and the expansion of tourism studies into planning, management and marketing of what is now a major global 'industry'. Debates continue over the extent to which 'tourism studies' is a discipline in its own right (Tribe, 2000), but 'it' is undoubtedly being studied and practised the world over.

Any review of tourism development studies is unavoidably selective, and at least partly dependent on the disciplinary orientation of the analyst, but some features of tourism development studies over the period under review seem especially noteworthy.

First, with the growth of international tourism, simply *describing* what is happening (and changing) in international tourism, and dealing with the ramifications on a day-to-day basis, is a major task for everyone with a stake in the travel and tourism 'industry'. In particular, though, the role of the UNWTO in compiling and correlating statistics and reports has become crucial in quantifying tourism's significance to the global economy.

Second, there is a general consensus that tourism brings economic benefits (Sinclair and Stabler, 1997). There may be qualifying caveats from some quarters, but nowhere has there been a serious move to reverse the process. There is also widespread agreement, among academics and practitioners alike, that it also has social and cultural effects, but – and it is an important caveat – there is major *disagreement* about what these are and how they should be assessed (Harrison, 1992: 19-34). Indeed, since MacCannell first suggested that tourists from developed countries sought authenticity (1976), and Greenwood accused tourism authorities in Spain of selling tourism 'by the pound' ([1978]1989), the linked topics of authenticity and commoditisation have been ubiquitous in discussions of tourism's impacts, though extensive studies of tourist motivation and wide recognition that authenticity is an *emergent* and negotiated property have made these debates largely redundant (Wang, 2000). Similarly, wrangles about tourism's alleged 'demonstration effects', especially on apparently vulnerable women and youth, and the linked accusation that tourism has untoward effects on (apparently static) 'tradition' (McKean, 1978; Fisher, 2004) have probably been the subject of increasingly diminishing returns (Cohen, 1988; Kim and Jamal, 2007). In fact, over the decades numerous lists of tourism's negative and positive impacts have been produced, reflecting, as Wood suggests (1993: 48-49), not so much any available empirical evidence, or even the perceptions of residents in tourist destination areas, as the prejudices of the writer.

Nevertheless, in the 1980s, disillusionment with mass tourism, coupled with the general shift in development studies, led to increasing support for types of tourism that were perceived to be more beneficial to communities in destination areas (Fennell, 1999; Telfer, 2002). Alternative tourism, ecotourism, community-based tourism and 'pro-poor tourism' were added to already-extensive tourist typologies and became a major focus of academic research. In addition, they were enthusiastically adopted by many international organisations, including the United Nations, where the key tourism player is the UNWTO. While its main role is to promote tourism generally, it has a specific 'development' focus through its Sustainable Tourism – End Poverty (ST-EP) Initiative, which is linked to the UN's eight Millennium Development Goals (MDGs). Other UN organisations, for example, ILO, UNESCO, UNDP and UNEP, while not having tourism as their *central* concern, also play major roles in funding and promoting tourism development, as even a cursory search at their respective websites reveals. UNEP's tourism programme, for example, links tourism to the environment, often cooperating with other partners from the UN, including UNWTO and UNESCO (where there is a mutual interest in world heritage) and with such non-profit-making organisations as the International Ecotourism Society and the Rainforest Alliance (www.unep.fr/pc/tourism: accessed on 6 August 2007).

Other international organisations involved in tourism development projects include the International Bank of Reconstruction and Development (World Bank) and IMF (Mowforth and Munt, 2003: 263; Hawkins and Mann, 2007), regional development banks, regional trading blocs, and government departments, or their agents, that fund overseas aid programmes with a tourism component. Invariably, the focus of all these international organisations has been 'alternative' tourism. Indeed, from 1990 until 2007 the UNDP alone funded more than 700 such projects, all of which could be somewhat vaguely categorised as ecotourism or community-based tourism (http://sgp.undp.org/index: accessed on 6 August 2007).

Over four decades, then, academic studies of tourism have established a major body of literature, including numerous journals devoted to aspects of travel and tourism (Law *et al.*, 2006), at which anyone first studying tourism as a tool for development in (say) the 1970s can only marvel. Furthermore – and worryingly for anyone reviewing the state of tourism development studies – many of those making major contributions would not be generally considered as writing on tourism and development, but of focusing primarily on what is happening in *developed* societies (Mac-Cannell, 1976, 1989,1992; Urry, 1990, 1992; Rojek and Urry, 1997). It is grounds for suggesting that, as at the start of Western social science, any study of social change is ultimately about 'development'.

More of the same...?

Again, suggestions as to where existing literature can be improved upon are selective and subjective, but perhaps the major criticism that can be made of how tourism development studies has developed is that there has been a dearth of consistency. Like development studies generally, it has succumbed to the vagaries of academic fashion; as a consequence, there has almost invariably been a failure to substantiate theories and/or findings over time and place.

Take, for example, the role of the state in tourism development (Harrison, 2001: 23-46). Adherents of all theoretical perspectives have examined its role, though, inevitably their emphasis varies. For political scientists favouring UDT, it is an agent (or mediator) of capitalist development, often prioritising transnational over local capital, and ensuring that the former is a beneficiary of tourism development plans (Britton, 1989; Bianchi, 2002). By contrast, those implicitly or explicitly taking a modernisation perspective focus on the extent to which government is active or passive in promoting specific forms of tourism development (Jenkins and Henry, 1982).

However, the state's *success* in carrying out any of these functions is conditioned by external influences, as well as political, economic and cultural realities (Bianchi, 2002: 289). In the Caribbean, for example, promoting international tourism has long been a racially sensitive issue (Mitchell, 1972; Crick, 2002; McDavid and Ramajeesingh, 2003), whereas institutions geared at environmental protection and cultural heritage promotion in Greece were facilitated by local awareness of environmental issues (Tsartas, 2003: 126). However, there are few detailed empirical studies of the role of any *actual* state in promoting tourism development (Clancy, 2001), the extent to which it is *efficient* in doing so, or (perhaps more important) the degree it is actually *committed* to furthering the welfare of its citizens. As Lockwood (2005) notes, if such a commitment is absent, development is not going to occur.

A similar point can be made about our understanding of the major economic actors in tourism development (Sinclair and Stabler, 1997: 58-94). Transnational companies (TNCs), for example, are frequently portrayed as the 'bad guys' of tourism capitalist development by neo-Marxists (oddly, though, more in developing than developed societies), who accuse them, *inter alia*, of perpetuating uneven development and neo-colonialism, incurring high leakages and producing correspondingly low income multipliers; distorting economies through concentration and seasonality; reducing control over local resources; exacerbating social inequality; prompting alienation; increasing crime rates; keeping workers in servile positions, and polluting and destroying the environment (Dunning and McQueen, 1982; Britton, 1987; Brohman, 1996).

However, the case against TNCs is far from proven (Sinclair and Stabler, 1997: 124-142). Statistics of high leakages and low multipliers are misleading (Mitchell and Ashley, 2007); poor linkages with other sectors, especially agriculture, are hardly unique to international hotels, and little account is taken of a region's natural and human resources. Despite relatively high leakages, TNCs attract more tourists than smaller, independent operators, bring in more foreign exchange, create more capital and jobs than smaller establishments, and offer a higher range of facilities and services (Sinclair and Stabler, 1997: 137; Meyer, 2003: 58), which explains why governments of developing societies want more rather than less TNC participation in tourism (Endo, 2006: 601). They are also more likely to pay better than local companies, have better training schemes and working conditions, and support, albeit for publicity purposes, many local charities and community causes.

In the face of such differing interpretations, the natural recourse is to seek the evidence in from detailed studies of specific tourism TNCs. However, these are not to be found!

Similarly, relatively little is known about tourism SMEs that occupy the lower end of the economic spectrum in the formal and informal sectors of developing societies. They contribute to poverty reduction and help reduce unemployment and leakages (Go and Appelman, 2001; Harrison and Schipani, 2007) but, again, much will depend on the level of tourism development at a destination. Intensive capital investment could reduce the number of SMEs, though marginal enterprises may continue to offer products and services of no commercial interest to international companies, or provide goods and services as dependent partners of the bigger tourism players (Dahles, 1999: 1-19).

Available evidence suggests some patterns. First, colonial and post-colonial tourism development tends to mirror pre-tourism structures, enabling an established capitalist class to exploit new opportunities (Bianchi, 2004: 503; Harrison, 2003: 5-7). Second, tourism opens up new opportunities for women and young people, increasing their independence, with important and often deep effects on family structures (Peake, 1989: 210-220; Apostolopoulos et al., 2001). Third, entrepreneurs may occupy structurally marginal positions (Nunez, 1989: 268-270) and in some cases are ethnic minorities, unhampered by constraining norms and values of other residents (Harrison, 1992: 23) and, fourth, some are known to have been former employees of international hotels (Ghodsee, 2005: 115-150). Finally, some entrepreneurs may be less concerned with financial profitability than with expanding their *social* capital (de Burlo, 2003: 76; Harrison, 2003: 19). In such cases, financial 'failure' may be offset by social success, a situation possibly widespread even in developed societies.

An equally important topic is the economic and socio-cultural impacts of different kinds of tourism. Even at the level of common sense, it is evident that cruise ship visitors, retirees, backpackers, hotel guests patronising differently starred establishments, sex tourists of various types, conference delegates and 'special interest' tourists – to name but a few – will have radically different impacts at both interactional and institutional levels in destination societies. And yet, as Cohen (1984: 379) noted two decades ago, despite decades of studies of tourism and development, and a plethora of typologies of tourists, except for some work in Indonesia (Hampton, 2005) few efforts have been made to document the economic and other impacts of different types of tourists, *including* the wide variety of alternative tourists in developing society destinations.

In the case of TNCs, entrepreneurs and the differential impact of types of tourist, then, much work remains to be done. The same might also be said for domestic tourism, the importance of which has been consistently underrated. Accurate statistics are scarce, but in 1995 domestic tourism was estimated to be ten times international tourism (Gee and Fayos-Solá, 1997: 24), and the ratio is unlikely to have changed since then. In some parts of Europe, for example, it contributes more than international tourism to GDP (Schmidt, 2002: 2). Less data exist for developing countries, but if 'domestic tourism' is considered to include pilgrimages and visits to religious and other festivals, as well as VFR (which is almost impossible to estimate), it is *vastly* in excess of international tourism (Ghimire, 2001: 1-29). In China in 2002, for example, there were an estimated 878 million domestic tourists, accounting for 90 per cent of tourist movement and 70 per cent of revenue from tourism in China (JustChina, 2004). And yet, despite its importance, it has been subject to very little research.

More generally, while there has been a relatively recent tendency to discuss tourism's role in globalisation (Sofield, 2001), as both cause and effect, there have been few efforts to theorise or empirically compare local *responses* to globalisation processes. Indeed, as MacNaught (1982) noted a while ago, tourism's critics often assume that cultures in developing country destinations are helpless and hapless in the face of tourist incursions. However, such an assumption is unwarranted while, at the opposite end of the spectrum, there has been no research at all on outward acculturation, which refers to cultural changes in *tourists* and their home countries that result from the tourist experience.

Looking ahead...

So far, I have suggested that 'balance sheets' of tourism's impacts in developing societies are of doubtful value, and that more might be gained by focusing on the negotiated aspects of tourist–resident interaction and perception as it occurs over time and place. I have also argued the need for research on the impacts on destination areas of different kinds of tourist, on the role and commitment of the state in tourism in different developing societies, on the various economic actors involved in tourism destinations, and that investigation of the articulation of the global with the local in developing society tourism is urgently required. To some extent, all these themes are found in existing tourism literature, but in embryonic form. However, they need now to be the subject of sustained and *comparative* attention.

Several other priorities, of both theoretical and empirical significance, emerge as a result of this brief review. The first centres on theories of tourism. As indicated earlier, globalisation theory was less ideological than its predecessors, but as it became more comprehensive and less divisive, it arguably also led to a loss of focus. At the same time, the incorporation of the physical environment into globalisation theory made its scope even wider, and arguably exacerbated the process. Yet climate change is a pressing issue of theoretical and practical relevance, and tourism is a key player in the global system (Viner, 2006; Becken and Hay, 2007). This has been recognised by Farrell and Twining-Ward (2005: 119), who call for a renewed and wider focus on 'complex adaptive systems, natural ecosystems, co-evolution, a more inclusive tourism system, integrated social-ecological systems, and non-linear science'. Such a clarion summons, necessitated by the dominant challenge of our time, might not be popular, but they may be right.

Second, an intensely practical and political imperative, and the *major* priority for the future, is the need for closer links between academics working in tourism development studies and other tourism stakeholders, most notably international agencies, aid organisations, NGOs and consultants. Currently they operate in different and largely distinct spheres, and most published outputs (and outlets), of which there are a plethora (Mitchell and Ashley, 2007), remain solidly within their respective walls. They are indeed central to the literature on tourism and development, but they vary widely in quality and have rarely been subjected to rigorous objective review. Indeed, where outsiders *have* conducted their own assessments, the evidence has been decidedly mixed (Sofield, 2003: 189). As it stands, this division, which amounts to an academic/practitioner apartheid, is unproductive and unhealthy and needs to be broken down. Rather, for tourism to be an effective tool for development, we need to carry out detailed research on the roles of other stakeholders involved in tourism development and to be prepared to co-operate with them to ensure that tourism benefits are spread widely.

Third, there is a need to attend more to comparative histories of tourism in *developed* countries. The past *is* another country, and can demonstrate, *inter alia*, how changes in one region may directly affect another, including the social foundations of tourist motivation, and how tourism's impacts – and people's perceptions of them – change over time and place. As yet, though, few have recognised such a need (Walton, 2005, 1-2; Butler, 2006: 25-26), and there is little interchange among scholars working on tourism in developed and developing societies.

Three decades ago, de Kadt (1979) asked if tourism was a 'passport to development', a question of theoretical and practical significance, and a query as valid now as then. We also need to ask, with Seers (1977), what we mean by 'development'. If, with him, we consider it includes a reduction in poverty, unemployment, inequity and dependence, everyone involved in tourism development, and not just advocates of 'pro-poor tourism' (Harrison, 2008), should focus not only on small-scale, donor-assisted and community-based tourism, which have little overall effect on human welfare (Goodwin, 2006), but also on *mass* tourism, which is clearly hugely influential, but which (amazingly) has been relatively ignored by tourism researchers. Only if this reorientation occurs will we really begin to understand how far tourism really is 'a tool for development'.

References

Apostolopoloulos, Y., Sönmez, S. and Timothy, D.J. (eds) (2001) *Women as Producers and Consumers of Tourism in Developing Regions*, Westport, CT: Praeger.

Becken, S. and Hay, J. (2007) *Tourism and Climate Change, Risks and Opportunities*, Clevedon: Channel View Publications.

Bianchi, R. (2002) 'Towards a new political economy of global tourism', in R. Sharpley and D. Telfer (eds), *Tourism and Development, Concepts and Issues*, Clevedon: Channel View Publications, pp. 265-299.

Bianchi, R. (2004) 'Tourism restructuring and the politics of sustainability: a critical view from the European periphery', *Journal of Sustainable Tourism*, **12** (6), 495-529.

Britton, S. (1987) 'Tourism in Pacific Island states, constraints and opportunities', in S. Britton and W. Clarke (eds), *Ambiguous Alternatives, Tourism in Small Developing Countries*, Suva: University of the South Pacific, pp. 113-139.

Britton, S. (1989) 'Tourism, Dependency and Development, a mode of analysis', in T.V. Singh, H.L. Theuns and F.M. Go (eds), *Towards Appropriate Tourism, the Case of Developing Societies*, Frankfurt and Berne: Peter Lang, pp. 93-110.

Brohman, J. (1996) 'New directions in tourism for third world development', *Annals of Tourism Research*, **23** (1), 48-70.

Burlo, C. de (2003) 'Tourism, conservation, and the cultural environment in rural Vanuatu', in D. Harrison (ed.), *Pacific Island Tourism*, New York: Cognizant, pp. 69-81.

Butler, R. (2006) 'The origins of the TALC', in R.W. Butler (ed.), *The Tourism Area Life Cycle, Vol. l, Applications and Modifications*, Clevedon: Channel View, pp. 13-26.

Clancy, M. (2001) *Exporting Paradise, Tourism and Development in Mexico*, Oxford: Pergamon.

Cohen, E. (1984) 'The sociology of tourism, approaches, issues, and findings', *Annual Review of Sociology*, **10**, 373-392.

Cohen, E. (1988) 'Authenticity and commoditization in tourism', *Annals of Tourism Research*, **15** (3), 371-386.

Crick, A.M. (2002) 'Smile, you're a tourism employee, managing emotional displays in Jamaican tourism', in I. Boxill, O. Taylor and J. Maerk (eds), *Tourism and Change in the Caribbean and Latin America*, Kingston: Arawak Publications, pp. 162-178.

Dahles, H. (1999) 'Tourism and small entrepreneurs in developing countries, a theoretical perspective', in H. Dahles and K. Bras (eds), *Tourism and Small Entrepreneurs, Development, National Policy, and Entrepreneurial Culture, Indonesian Cases*, New York: Cognizant, pp. 1-19.

Dunning, J.H. and McQueen, M. (1982) 'Multinational corporations in the international hotel industry', *Annals of Tourism Research*, **9** (1), 69-90.

Endo, K. (2006) 'Foreign direct investment in tourism – flows and volumes', *Tourism Management*, **27** (4), 600-614.

Farrell, B.H. and Twining-Ward, L. (2003) 'Reconceptualizing tourism', *Annals of Tourism Research*, **31** (2), 274-295.

Farrell, B.H. and Twining-Ward, L. (2005) 'Seven steps towards sustainability: tourism in the context of new knowledge', *Journal of Sustainable Tourism*, **13** (2), 109-122.

Fennell, D. (1999) *Ecotourism, an Introduction*, London: Routledge.

Fisher, D. (2004) 'The Demonstration effect revisited', *Annals of Tourism Research*, **31** (2), 428-446.

Gee, C.Y. and Fayos-Solá, E. (1997) *International Tourism: A Global Perspective*, Madrid: World Tourism Organization.

Ghimire, K.B. (ed.) (2001) *The Native Tourist, Mass Tourism within Developing Countries*, London: Earthscan.

Ghodsee, K. (2005) *The Red Riviera, Gender, Tourism, and Postsocialism on the Black Sea*, Durham, NC: Duke University Press.

Go, F.M. and Appelman, J. (2001) 'Achieving global competitiveness in SMEs by building trust in interfirm alliances', in S. Wahab and C. Cooper (eds), *Tourism in the Age of Globalisation*, London: Routledge, pp. 184-197.

Goodwin, H. (2006) 'Community-based tourism, failing to deliver?', *id21 Insights*, **62**, 1-3.

Greenwood, D. ([1978] 1989) 'Culture by the pound, an anthropological perspective on tourism as cultural commoditization', in V.L. Smith (ed.), *Hosts and Guests, the Anthropology of Tourism*, Philadelphia: University of Pennsylvania Press, pp. 171-185.

Hall, C.M. (2008) *Tourism Planning: Policies, Processes and Relationships*, 2nd edn, Harlow: Pearson.

Hampton, M. (2005) 'Heritage, local communities and economic development', *Annals of Tourism Research*, **32** (3), 735-759.

Harrison, D. (1992) 'Tourism to less developed countries, the social consequences', in D. Harrison (ed.), *Tourism and the Less Developed Countries*, London: Belhaven, pp. 19-34.

Harrison, D. (2001) 'Tourism and less developed countries, key issues', in D. Harrison (ed.), *Tourism and the Less Developed World, Issues and Case Studies*, Wallingford: CAB International, pp. 23-46.

Harrison, D. (2003) 'Themes in Pacific island tourism,' in D. Harrison (ed.), *Pacific Island Tourism*, New York: Cognizant, pp. 1-23.

Harrison, D. (2008) 'Pro-poor tourism, a critique,' *Third World Quarterly*, **29** (5), 851-868.

Harrison, D. and Schipani, S. (2007) 'Lao tourism and poverty alleviation', *Current Issues in Tourism*, **10** (2-3), 194-230.

Hawkins, D.E. and Mann, S. (2007) 'The World Bank's role in tourism development', *Annals of Tourism Research*, **34** (2), 348-363.

Jenkins, C.L. and Henry, B.M. (1982) 'Government involvement in tourism in developing countries', *Annals of Tourism Research*, **9** (4), 499-521.

JustChina (2004) *Chinese Tourism Industry*, China Knowledge Press, available from http://store.justchina.com/chtoin.html (accessed on 13 July 2007).

Kadt, E. de (1979) *Tourism, Passport to Development?*, New York: Oxford University Press.

Kim, H. and Jamal, T. (2007) 'Touristic quest for existential authenticity', *Annals of Tourism Research*, **34** (1), 181-201.

Law, R., Lam, T. and McKercher, R. (2006) 'A case for rating tourism journals', *Tourism Management*, **27** (6), 1235-1252.

Lockwood, M. (2005) *The State they're in, an Agenda for International Action on Poverty in Africa*, Bourton-on-Dunsmore: ITDG Publishing.

MacCannell, D. (1976) *The Tourist, A New Theory of the Leisure Class*, London: Macmillan.

MacCannell, D. (1989) *The Tourist, A New Theory of the Leisure Class*, 2nd edn, London: Macmillan.

MacCannell, D. (1992) *Empty Meeting Grounds: The Tourist Papers*, London: Routledge.

MacNaught, T.J. (1982) 'Mass tourism and the dilemmas of modernization in Pacific island communities', *Annals of Tourism Research*, **9** (3), 359-381.

McDavid, H. and Ramajeesingh, D. (2003) 'The state and tourism, a Caribbean perspective', *International Journal of Contemporary Hospitality Management*, **15** (3), 180-183.

McKean, P.F. (1978) 'Towards a theoretical analysis of tourism: economic dualism and cultural involution in Bali', in V.L. Smith (ed.), *Hosts and Guests: The Anthropology of Tourism*, 1st edn, Oxford: Blackwell, pp. 93-107.

Meyer, D. (2003) 'The UK outbound tour operating industry and implications for pro-poor tourism', *PPT Working Paper No. 17*, London: Overseas Development Institute.

Mitchell, J. and Ashley, C. (2007) '"Leakage" claims, muddled thinking and bad for policy', *Opinion*, June, London: Overseas Development Institute.

Mitchell, J.F. (1972) 'To hell with paradise, A new concept in Caribbean tourism', in J.F. Mitchell (1989), *Caribbean Crusade*, Vermont: Concepts Publishing, pp. 177-182.

Mowforth, M. and Munt, I. (2003) *Tourism and Sustainability, Development and New Tourism in the Third World*, 2nd edn, London: Routledge.

Munar, A.M. (2007) 'Rethinking globalization theory in tourism', *Tourism, Culture, Communication*, **7** (2), 99-115.

Nunez, P. (1989) 'Touristic studies in anthropological perspective', in V.L. Smith (ed.), *Hosts and Guests: The Anthropology of Tourism*, 2nd edn, Philadelphia: University of Pennsylvania Press, pp. 265-274.

Peake, R. (1989) 'Tourism and Swahili identity in Malindi Old Town, Kenyan coast', *Africa*, **59** (2), 209-220.

Rojek, C. and Urry, J. (1997) *Touring Cultures: Transformations of Travel and Theory*, London: Routledge.

Schmidt, H-W. (2002) How Europeans go on holiday, *Statistics in Focus*, Industry, Trade and Services, Theme 4:15 February.

Seers, D. (1977) 'The new meaning of development', *International Development Review*, **19** (3): 2-7.

Sharpley, R. (2009) *Tourism, Development and the Environment: Beyond Sustainability*, London: Earthscan.

Sinclair, M.T. and Stabler, M. (1997) *The Economics of Tourism*, London: Routledge.

Sofield, T. (2001) 'Globalisation, tourism and culture in Southeast Asia', in P. Teo, T.C. Chang and K.C. Ho (eds), *Interconnected Worlds, Tourism in Southeast Asia*, Oxford: Elsevier Science, pp. 103-120.

Sofield, T. (2003) *Empowerment for Sustainable Development* Amsterdam: Pergamon.

Telfer, D.J. (2002) 'The evolution of tourism and development theory', in R. Sharpley and D.J. Telfer (eds), *Tourism and Development, Concepts and Issues*, Clevedon: Channel View, pp. 35-78.

Tribe, J. (2000) 'Indisciplined and unsubstantiated', *Annals of Tourism Research*, **27** (3): 809-813.

Tsartas, P. (2003) 'Tourism development in Greek insular and coastal areas, socio-cultural changes and crucial policy issues', *Journal of Sustainable Tourism*, **11** (2/3), 116-132.

UNTWO (2008) *Tourism Highlights, 2008 Edition*, Madrid: United Nations World Tourism Organization.

Urry, J. (1990) *The Tourist Gaze, Leisure and Travel in Contemporary Societies*, London: Sage.

Urry, J. (1992) 'The tourist gaze and the environment, *Tourism, Culture and Society*, **9** (3), 1-26.

Viner, D. (ed.) (2006) 'Special issue, tourism and its interactions with climate change', *Journal of Sustainable Tourism*, **14** (4).

Wahab, S. and Cooper, C. (eds.) (2001) *Tourism in the Age of Globalisation*, London: Routledge.

Walton, J. (2005) *Histories of Tourism, Representation, Identity and Conflict*, Clevedon: Channel View.

Wang, N. (2000) *Tourism and Modernity, A Sociological Analysis*, Amsterdam: Pergamon.

Waters, M. (1995) *Globalization*, London: Routledge.

Wood, R.E. (1993) 'Tourism, culture and the sociology of development', in M. Hitchcock, V.T. King and M. Parnwell (eds), *Tourism in South-East Asia*, London: Routledge, pp. 19-70.

5 Carrying capacity in tourism: paradox and hypocrisy?

Richard W. Butler

Introduction

Carrying capacity is a well established concept in tourism and recreation, as in many other elements of society. One might have expected, with the growth of sustainable development and the inextricable links of that concept to limits, and, by implication, the capacity of resources, that carrying capacity of tourist resources would be of increasing importance in current research and literature. In fact, somewhat the opposite is the case. In previous decades carrying capacity was a major focus in tourism and recreation research (Burton and Jackson, 1989) and a bibliography of over 3000 references on this topic (Vaske, 1992) was published. The topic is still mentioned, almost without exception, in major text books on tourism and merits specific attention in several others (e.g. Jenkins and Pigram, 2003; McCool, 2003). The concept is one of the basic foundations of the Tourism Area Life Cycle Model (Butler, 1980), the most widely used and cited model in tourism for the past three decades, and the term is found in many reports and policies relating to tourism planning and development. With this considerable pedigree, it is puzzling to note that in the 21st century this concept has virtually disappeared from the tourism research literature and is barely mentioned in the recreation resource management literature, where it was once a mainstream concept. At a meeting of the International Academy for the Study of Tourism in 1995 this author (Butler, 1997: 13) noted an earlier decline in research on this topic and argued that this trend would

> serve destination areas poorly in the long run, especially those areas which are most dependent upon natural characteristics for their attractiveness and appeal, [and]... has left destination areas potentially exposed to overuse.... inevitable radical change and possibly ultimate despoliation.

Given that over the intervening decade and a half since those words were written tourist numbers have continued to rise both globally and in almost every region of the world (WTO, 2008), visitor pressure on resources and destinations has increased rather than remained stable or decreased. This has meant that because destinations are experiencing increasing numbers of visitors they are witnessing ever more severe impacts upon the destination environments, both ecological and human. At a time when most tourism destination countries have 'signed up' to the principles of sustainable development, and by implication, sustainable tourism, this represents both a great paradox and considerable hypocrisy.

Carrying capacity is not alone in being an area of research in tourism which has experienced a rise and fall in interest and involvement. Similar traits can be seen in the research literature on approaches to visitor management, which peaked in the 1980s (see for example, Stankey *et al.*, 1985), and has similarly declined in interest since then, as has research on resort morphology and concepts such as the Recreation Business District (Stansfield and Rikert, 1970), which also are no longer discussed in the tourism journals. Whether these patterns are the result of changing academic 'fashions', maturation of the topic, or perceived irrelevancy of the subject is open to interpretation and returned to later in the discussion. This chapter continues with a brief review of the concept of carrying capacity and discusses its initial application in recreation and tourism. It then considers the reasons why the concept has declined as a focus of research interest and the implications of this decline. The chapter concludes with a short discussion on what that might involve for tourism in the future.

Carrying capacity: definition and origins

Carrying capacity is inextricably linked to limits, normally limits on resource exploitation, which may take a variety of forms, including numbers, volumes, interactions relating to negative impacts. The concept is age-old, as noted in an anonymous poem from the sixteenth century:

> But now the sport is marred,
> And wot ye why?
> Fishes decrease,
> For fishers multiply.

(Anon, 1598)

While today that lament may apply with more force to commercial than recreational fish stocks, it reflects well the basic premise of the concept, namely, that overuse (over extraction, over pollution) of a resource beyond its natural ability to recover will result in diminishing returns and perhaps ultimately the disappearance of that resource. Most of the best examples of use at levels beyond the carrying capacity of the resource relate to wildlife consumption, including the extinction of the dodo, the carrier pigeon and almost the North American bison, all resources thought to be inexhaustible and hunted beyond their natural recovery levels. Ignorance over the level and quantity of resources can explain those examples, but other forces also affect the level of use.

Perhaps the most significant of these is the placing of individual benefit ahead of the well being of the community to which the individual belongs. This behaviour has been well described by Hardin (1968) in his now classic paper 'The tragedy of the commons', and applied to tourism by Healy (1994) and Briassoulis (2002). The 'tragedy' for Hardin was the inevitability of the ruination of the commons (community grazing lands) because in the short term, with an absence of assigned responsibility, it was to every individual's benefit to overuse the resource. Only with regulation and control could the common resource be protected from overuse. The short-term gain for individuals behaving in a selfish manner is almost immediate and obvious, while the loss to the community is longer term and less obvious for a considerable period of time, often not appearing until the opportunity for restoration may have passed. The analogies for tourism are clear, especially for those destinations which rely on common resources such as the sea and lakes, wildlife, wild lands, scenery and amenity in particular. In the case of tourism, however, there is another element to carrying capacity, relating to the effect of too many visitors on local residents and on visitors themselves. This involves both the quality of life of residents of destinations and the quality of the visitor experience in those locations.

Most definitions of carrying capacity incorporate statements that suggest that it is the level of use beyond which irreparable damage occurs to the environment under consideration (Tivy, 1973). What is important in such definitions are two essential points, the first is the level of use, and the second is the irreparable nature of the damage. Every use of a resource has an impact and causes 'damage' of some kind and to some extent; what is important from the resource management perspective is the significance of that damage and whether the effects can be prevented or reversed.

The first studies of carrying capacity in recreation and tourism that feature in the literature date back to the 1960s, although references to over development and over use are found much earlier (Butler, 2006). The reason for such a relatively late start to research on carrying capacity in the leisure context lies in the fact that until this time, overuse and overdevelopment of recreation and tourism destinations had rarely occurred. The expansion in outdoor recreation and tourism in modern times began in the boom years after the Second World War, and it is then that the first signs of potential problems from numbers were recognised (Clawson, 1959). The first significant studies on carrying capacity were those done by scientists working for the US Forest Service concerned about the potential impacts of rapidly rising visitor numbers on the wildlands under their management. The pioneering work of Lucas (1964a, b) and Wagar (1964), in particular, provided clear evidence that it was possible to identify critical levels of use, beyond which negative impacts occurred and which could, if not controlled, threaten the existence and permanent quality of the resource involved. Lucas (1964a) demonstrated two vitally important facts, first, that human opinions on crowding varied with the type of use in the same setting, and second, that one could derive numbers that could be used to identify maximum use levels. These early works were conducted in wilderness areas in which there was no permanent population, thus removing the economic sector and part of the human interaction sector from consideration. This made the identification of limits much less complicated, as did the fact that the environments and the types of use being studied were generally similar.

These situations were much closer to the settings found in the range land studies from which carrying capacity research originated. In these studies of the 1930s it was relatively simple to calculate the carrying capacity of similar environments for one 'user', cattle. In general, studies of the sustainable yield of wildlife populations have been successful in identifying the levels of extraction which can be imposed on wildlife in order to maintain the stock at desired levels. Such knowledge is essential in the case of hunting and fishing, where the price for renting shooting proper-ties (e.g., deer and grouse moors in the United Kingdom) or fishing rights (e.g. for salmon) is based on the 'bag sizes' or the numbers of animals and fish which can be taken in any season (O'Dell and Walton, 1962). In such cases, human intervention is normally involved also, in terms of improving resource quality such as increas-ing river flow and water quality, and improving habitat for young birds and deer. Numbers of fishermen and 'guns' are precisely calculated and a made condition of leases of such properties, to ensure that consumption is in line with a sustainable population. Capacity is an integral element in such calculations and has been so for many centuries. This view matches that of O'Reilly (1986) who argued that the concept was useful for the way in which it could make the case for environmental planning and support the precautionary principle in tourism development. The situ-ation is relatively simple, in most such cases there is one type of visitor, engaging in one activity, and consuming one resource, and the type of visitor is expected to, and normally does, abide by the limits agreed.

In the case of tourist destinations in general, however, the situation is more com-plicated, no destination is identical to another (not in setting, in facilities, in local population, nor in tourists) thus one has to deal with variations in several criteria. Thus carrying capacity in the case of tourism has been discussed in terms of three broad sectors, as in the case of the impacts of tourism (Mathieson and Wall, 1982), namely; ecological, human (social-cultural), and economic. It has been recognised that the levels of carrying capacity, in terms of visitor numbers, may be different for each sector, depending on the specific location involved. This is similar to the case of sustainable development where it is acknowledged that factors are site-specific and while general indicators may be identified, they need to be refined and often changed at individual sites (Miller and Twining-Ward, 2005). In the case of tourism carrying capacity it can be argued that there are more than the three sectors noted above. A key element in many settings where man-made structures are involved is safety, e.g., on golf courses, where sufficient distance has to be maintained between groups of players. Another relevant factor, again relating to man-made structures, is the physical capacity of a structure, e.g., spaces in a car park, berths in a marina, or gates for aircraft at an airport, or the related human capacity in operations, e.g., numbers of passport control officers or security screening personnel at airports. An important difference exists between these latter two sectors and the first three, particularly the environmental sector. This is that the capacity of man-made struc-tures and the human operating levels can be increased to meet demand (or create demand) through investment of funds, whereas it is difficult if not impossible to alter the carrying capacity of the environment without altering its natural state.

Abandonment and replacement: the decline in use of the concept

The initial interest in carrying capacity research in the 1960s spread beyond that conducted by the US Forest Service to other areas (An Forbas Forbatha (1966) in Ireland and Tivy (1973) in Scotland). Writers such as Clawson (1963) and Wolfe (1964, 1966) discussed the implications of rapidly rising visitor numbers on destinations and resources and the concept began to appear in many books on tourism as an area of relevance. In the wider context, Rachel Carson's *Silent Spring* (1962), Hardin's *Tragedy of the Commons* (1968) and Meadows *et al.*'s (1972) *Limits to Growth* drew attention to human impacts on the environment at levels beyond the capacity of the environment to recover. Pollution concerns such as Love Canal, mercury levels in fish, and acid rain also raised concerns among the public about the ability of the environment to withstand human exploitation. By the 1970s, in the tourism literature, articles such as those by Doxey (1975) and Plog (1974) focused particularly on the issue of over use and too many visitors, and led to the key role of carrying capacity in the Tourism Area Life Cycle Model (Butler, 1980), where it was argued that without intervention, destinations would inevitably be subject to over development, loss of appeal and eventual fall in visitor numbers and expenditure, creating a vicious cycle of decline.

With such continued interest in carrying capacity, in tourism and beyond, the fact that research on the topic has almost disappeared is puzzling to say the least. In tourism research the impacts of tourism began to receive major attention in the 1970s and 1980s, beginning with the work of Bryden (1973), De Kadt (1973) and Young (1973), culminating in the seminal and defining work on the topic by Mathieson and Wall (1982). The responsibility for the abandonment of interest in carrying capacity can probably be assigned to the group of researchers responsible for its appearance in the first place, those in the US Forest Service. They (Lime, McCool, Moisley, Stankey and others) began to shift emphasis from searching for a specific number of visitors who could be accommodated satisfactorily in an area to attempting to identify alternative approaches, often based on the change in environment and setting that could be tolerated by managers and visitors alike. The classic example of this is the model of Limits of Acceptable Change (Stankey *et al.*, 1985), which has provided the basis for a number of subsequent resource management models, including the Recreation Opportunity Spectrum, the Tourism Opportunity Spectrum, the Visitor Impact Management Programme and Visitor Activity Management Programme.

The rationale behind the abandonment of carrying capacity as a research focus is based on the fact that to find a realistic and acceptable figure to represent the total number of visitors permissible for a destination is probably unrealistic if not impossible (Washbourne, 1982). Lucas' early research (1964b) showed that the perceptual capacity of visitors varied with their activity, and when this is added to the variety of tourist destinations, the range of preferences of visitors and varying policies on degrees and nature of development of destinations, it is clear that a maximum acceptable number of visitors is extremely difficult to derive, let alone defend politically. As well, it is clear that for the same reasons, the nature and severity of impacts is not dependent solely or simplistically on numbers of users, and so the focus shifted to what change was acceptable in destinations. This frequently has been based primarily, or in part, on the levels of use deemed acceptable by managers and visitors (Graefe *et al.*, 1984; Stankey *et al.*, 1985; Shelby and Heberlein, 1986). The logic behind this is deceptively simple, in that if managers and users agree what change is acceptable, then the managers need only to monitor change in the environment and in user satisfaction, or in some cases, only the latter, to be managing the resource appropriately. This assumes, however, that visitor, if not manager, norms remain static, thus allowing the resource to be maintained at a certain quality, but if some users find the use levels too high and do not return, they will likely be replaced by visitors who find the increased use levels acceptable. If such a process continues, the use levels perceived by visitors as acceptable will continue to increase as those with less tolerance of higher levels are replaced by those with a higher tolerance. In such a scenario, ultimately numbers are likely to rise as there will be little or no noticeable visitor reaction to increasing numbers. By the time the effect of increased numbers on resources is noted, it may be too late to reverse this effect on the environment and on the image of the destination. Despite this, the search for numbers has been replaced in most management circles by varying forms of the models noted above that focus on norms and preferences (Manning, 1999).

There is a further complicating factor, and that is politics. It is extremely difficult to find a way to limit numbers that is acceptable to many segments of the public and the tourism industry. Tourism, unlike recreation in wilderness settings, has a major economic element, and while absolute numbers alone may not determine total expenditure, there is a relationship between numbers and expenditure generated. Thus decision-makers face a difficult choice in limiting numbers (Ryan, 2002). Few destinations and fewer private sector players in tourism would support such a restriction. Whenever numbers decline, the automatic response of destination development agencies is to increase marketing to restore or increase numbers to or beyond previous levels. Such an attitude pervades many public sector agencies which may be dependent on the income generated by admission charges or on political support which is also contingent on public support as expressed by visitor numbers (Keenan, 1970, personal communication). These attitudes continue despite widespread support for the concept of sustainable development, in part at least related to the fact that that concept is so vague and imprecise, with a large number of interpretations, that it is virtually meaningless (Butler, 1991).

The present role of carrying capacity in tourism research

It is quite amazing that the widespread adoption of sustainable tourism by so many agencies has not resulted in increased interest and commitment to the study of carrying capacity of tourism destinations (Saarinen, 2006). Sustainable development involves meeting the needs of the present without compromising the needs of future generations (WCED, 1987). Implicit in the application of the concept is the idea of living within the limits of the earth and its atmosphere, avoiding irreparable loss of resources. The comparison with carrying capacity is inescapable and unavoidable, and indeed, carrying capacity was one of eight tools listed in the context of sustainable tourism by Mowforth and Munt (1998). Yet the idea of imposing limits on tourism and tourist numbers is still not widely practised. A few destinations and specific sites have limited numbers in a variety of ways, but even where clear limits have been set, e.g., in the Galapagos Islands National Park, they have not been adhered to (Weaver, 2009) because of economic and political pressures. Bramwell (2007: 80) notes, in the context of a carrying capacity study conducted for the island of Malta:

> *The carrying capacity study highlights the need to consider the complex political economy and governance issues that lie behind tourism growth management policies and also the requirement to reflect on the full implications of these policies across diverse and variously connected economic, social and environmental domains.*

Increasing numbers of visitors have meant increasing impacts and demands on destinations and their resources and populations, and the need for limits to be recognised and applied is becoming ever more obvious and critical. The failure to 'bite the bullet' is similar and related to the failure of most jurisdictions to actually implement the sustainable tourism policies they have created (Dodds and Butler, 2009). Gossling *et al.* (2009: 2-3) note:

> *Inevitably, market driven expansion fostered ecological, sociocultural, and economic problems in many locations, and within the sea–sand–sun destinations of the Third World pleasure periphery in particular.*

The acceptance of sustainable principles implies the need to determine appropriate limits or carrying capacity of destinations. In discussing the sustainability of ski resorts, for example, Eydol (2004) noted that 'research is important to understanding the environmental and social processes that underpin the social and environmental carrying capacity related to the ski resort's operation' (cited in Del Matto and Scott 2009: 139).

The failure to conduct such research and act on the findings has seen an ever increasing number of destinations being developed beyond the point of acceptability in terms of quality of environment and visitor satisfaction with subsequent results as noted below:

the falling numbers of inbound tourists not only underpins the argument that Eilat has long passed its optimal carrying capacity, but are also indicative of the fact that its life-cycle as a seaside resort is probably, as Mansfield (2001) correctly foresaw, reaching its end.

(Shoval and Cohen-Hattab, 2007: 243)

It is interesting to note, however, that in at least one of the newly emerging tourism destinations, China, research on carrying capacity is being undertaken. The potentially enormous pressures on resources and destinations resulting from both its own already very large domestic tourism industry and a rapidly growing foreign market has meant that Chinese tourism researchers are examining ways of avoiding overuse and irreparable damage to popular tourist areas. Li and Zhang (2009) have proposed a modified version of the traditional carrying capacity model, focusing particularly on seasonal 'overloading' and suggesting a new theoretical base for tourism development and environmental quality. Wu (2009: 79) notes that in a study of residents in an ecotourism destination the respondents were aware of the problems of overuse and suggested what he describes as 'a moderate tourism capacity' for the destination. Other researchers (Song and Zhong, 2009) have applied the Opportunity Spectrum Approach to adventure tourism destinations in order to improve management of such areas and avoid the problems of overuse. The greater ability in much of China to control the use of areas and to manage the human element suggests such approaches may have greater success in applying the concept of carrying capacity than has occurred in western destinations.

Conclusions and implications for the future

If one assumes that, after the current economic depression and swine flu outbreaks have run their respective courses, tourism will continue to grow, and also that the current support for sustainable tourism remains a political reality in theory, if less so in practice, then the lack of attention in research to carrying capacity of destinations will become even more of a major problem for many areas. Alternatives such as the LAC and related models will not stem the ever increasing pressure on resources and the accompanying symptoms of over-use and loss of attractiveness, nor will they achieve sustainability on a long-term basis.

Underlying support for the concept of carrying capacity does exist. Hunter (1995: 66) concludes that it is 'an inherently attractive concept for those concerned with the environmental impacts of tourism and for those seeking a rationale for interventionist management'. But as Sharpley and Telfer (2002: 254) note:

a disjuncture evidently exists between the new and merging paradigm of environmental management and post-positivist ecological theory (based on notions of non-linearity), and the essentially positivist approach to environmental control implicit in land-use planning.

They go on to cite Sneddon (2000) in the context of the appreciation of the difficulty, if not impossibility, of managing ecological systems. However, it can be argued that what is needed is not necessarily the management of the ecological system, desirable if divisive that may be, but rather the management and control of one (of possibly many) external forces acting on that system, in this case, tourism. A rare recent article (Jovicic and Dragin, 2009) also stresses the crucial need to manage the effects of tourism in destinations through the carrying capacity concept.

One problem is that carrying capacity is what is known as a 'messy problem', complex and complicated because it is both a theoretical and an applied issue. It is clearly multi-disciplinary, in that it involves several fields of study: ecology (environmental sector), economics (economic sector), geography (interaction of humans and the physical world), politics (decision making), and psychology and sociology (visitor experience, resident attitudes, visitor perceptions). The concepts involved are both theoretical and abstract as well as having direct management implications. It is a classic example of how research can be conceptual and applied, and can serve as an encouraging example of how academic research can assist in solving a real world problem.

Research on carrying capacity needs to incorporate multiple disciplinary viewpoints using an integrative and holistic approach. This applies equally to research on sustainable development and explains in part why that concept has not been implemented effectively (Dodds and Butler, 2009). It is difficult to identify a research topic which better typifies the eclectic nature of tourism itself than carrying capacity, but this complexity perhaps explains why few individual researchers have successfully pursued the topic. However, for academics to ignore the problem now is even more depressing than when this author reviewed this problem in 1995. In avoiding this problem, we are both ignoring a valid academic issue and failing those involved in the management of destination areas, and thus abrogating the right to criticise destinations on the grounds of over-development and managers for failing to protect valued resources from impacts resulting from excessive visitation. If one has to answer the question posed by McCool and Lime (2001: 372), whether carrying capacity is 'tempting fantasy or useful reality', one has little choice but to respond that it is not only a useful but also an awkward and unavoidable reality.

References

An Foras Forbatha (1966) *Planning for Amenity and Tourism*, Dublin.

Anon (1598) cited in Brougham, J.E. (1972) *An evaluation of the impact of crowding upon the quality f recreational experience*, Unpublished master's thesis, London, Canada: University of Western Ontario.

Bramwell, B. (2007) 'Complexity, interdisciplinarity and growth management: the case of Maltese resort tourism', in S. Agarwal and G. Shaw (eds), *Managing Coastal Tourism Resorts A Global Perspective*, Clevedon: Channel View, pp. 73-89.

Briassoulis, H. (2002) 'Sustainable tourism and the question of the commons', *Annals of Tourism Research*, **29** (4), 1065-1085.

Bryden, J. (1973) *Tourism and Development: A Case Study of the Caribbean*, Cambridge: Cambridge University Press.

Burton, T.L. and Jackson, E. (1989) *Understanding Leisure and Recreation*, State College, PA: Venture Publishing.

Butler, R.W. (1980) 'The concept of a tourist area cycle of evolution: implications for the management of resources', *Canadian Geographer*, **24** (1), 5-12.

Butler, R.W. (1991) 'Tourism, environment and sustainable development', *Environmental Conservation*, **18** (3), 201-209.

Butler, R.W. (1997) 'The concept of carrying capacity for tourism destinations: dead or merely buried?', in C. Cooper and S. Wanhill (eds), *Tourism Development Environmental and Community Issues*, Chichester: Wiley, pp. 11-22.

Butler, R.W. (2006) 'The origins of the tourism area life cycle', in R.W. Butler (ed.), *The Tourism Area Life Cycle, Volume 1, Applications and Modifications*, Clevedon: Channel View, pp. 13-26.

Carson, R. (1962) *Silent Spring*, Boston: Houghton Mifflin.

Clawson, M. (1959) *The Crisis in Outdoor Recreation*, Washington, DC: Resources for the Future.

Clawson, M. (1963) *Land and Water for Recreation – Opportunities, Problems and Policies*, Chicago: Rand McNally.

De Kadt, E. (1973) *Tourism – Passport to Development?*, New York: Oxford University Press.

Del Matto, T. and Scott, D. (2009) 'Sustainable ski resort principles', in S. Gossling, C.M. Hall and D.B. Weaver (eds), *Sustainable Tourism Futures*, London: Routledge, pp. 131-151.

Dodds, R. and Butler, R.W. (2009) 'Inaction more than action: barriers to the implementation of sustainable tourism policies', in S. Gossling, C.M. Hall and D.B. Weaver (eds), *Sustainable Tourism Futures*, London: Routledge, pp. 43-57.

Doxey, G.V. (1975) 'A causation theory of visitor–residents irritants, methodology, and research inferences', in *The Impact of Tourism Proceedings of the Travel Research Association, 6th Conference*, San Diego, pp. 195-198.

Eydal, G. (2004) 'The development of a sustainability management system for ski areas', unpublished master's thesis, Burnaby, BC: Simon Fraser University.

Gossling, S., Hall, C.M. and Weaver, D.B. (2009) 'Sustainable tourism futures: perspectives on systems, restructuring and innovations', in S. Gossling, C.M. Hall and D.B. Weaver (eds), *Sustainable Tourism Futures*, London: Routledge, pp. 1-18.

Graefe, A.R., Vaske, J.J. and Kuss, F.R. (1984) 'Social carrying capacity', *Leisure Sciences*, **6** (4), 395-431.

Hardin, G. (1968) 'The tragedy of the commons', *Science*, **62**, 1248.

Healy, R.G. (1994) 'The "common pool" problem in tourism landscapes', *Annals of Tourism Research*, **21** (3), 596-611.

Hunter, C. (1995) 'Key concepts for tourism and the environment', in C. Hunter and H. Green (eds), *Tourism and the Environment: A Sustainable Relationship?*, Issues in Tourism Series, London: Routledge, pp. 52-92.

Jenkins, J.M. and Pigram, J.J. (eds) (2003) *Encyclopedia of Leisure and Outdoor Recreation*, London: Routledge.

Jovicic, D. and Dragin, A. (2009) 'The assessment of carrying capacity – a crucial tool for managing tourism effects in tourist destinations', *Turizam*, 1 (1), 4-11.

Li, J. and Zhang, Y. (2009) 'Regulation and improvement of the model of tourism environment carrying capacity – Shuanglong Scenic Area as an example', paper presented at 2009 International Forum on Ecotourism, August, Xining, China.

Lucas, R.C. (1964a) 'The recreational carrying capacity of the Quetico-Superior area', *USDA Forest Service Research Paper*, LS-15, St Paul: USDA.

Lucas, R.C. (1964b) 'Wilderness perception and use: the example of the Boundary Waters Canoe Area', *Natural Resources Journal*, 3 (3), 394-411.

Manning, R. E. (1999) 'Crowding and carrying capacity in outdoor recreation: from normative standards to standards of quality', in E. Jackson and T.L. Burton (eds), *Leisure Studies: Prospects for the Twenty-First Century*, State College, PA: Venture Publishing, pp. 323-334.

Mansfield, Y. (2001) 'Acquired tourism deficiency syndrome: planning and developing tourism in Israel', in A. Apostolopoulos, P. Loukissas and L. Leontidou (eds), *Mediterranean Tourism: Facets of Socioeconomic Development and Cultural Change*, New York: Routledge, pp. 159-178.

Mathieson, A. and Wall, G. (1982) *Tourism: Economic, Physical and Social Impacts*, New York: Longman.

McCool, S. (2003) 'Carrying capacity', in J.M. Jenkins and J.J. Pigram (eds), *Encyclopedia of Leisure and Outdoor Recreation*, London: Routledge, pp. 42-44.

McCool, S.F. and Lime, D.W. (2001) 'Tourism carrying capacity: tempting fantasy or useful reality?', *Journal of Sustainable Tourism*, 9 (5), 372-388.

Meadows, D.H., Meadows, D.L., Randers, J. and Behrens, W.W. (1972) *Limits to Growth*, New York: Universal Books.

Miller, G. and Twining-Ward, L. (2005) *Monitoring for a Sustainable Tourism Transition: The Challenge of Developing and Using Indicators*, Wallingford: CAB International.

Mowforth, M. and M. Munt, I. (1998) *Tourism and Sustainability*, London: Routledge.

O'Dell, A.C. and Walton, K. (1962) *The Highlands and Islands of Scotland*, London: Nelson.

O'Reilly, T. (1986) 'Tourism carrying capacity: concepts and issues', *Tourism Management*, 8 (2), 254-258.

Plog, S.C. (1974) 'Why destination areas rise and fall in popularity', *Cornell Hotel and Restaurant Administration Quarterly*, 14, 55-58.

Ryan, C. (2002) 'Equity, management, power sharing and sustainability – issues of the "new tourism"', *Tourism Management*, 23 (1), 17-26.

Saarinen, J. (2006) 'Traditions of sustainability in tourism studies', *Annals of Tourism Research*, **33** (4), 1121-1140.

Sharpley, R. and Telfer, D.J. (2002) *Tourism and Development Concepts and Issues*, Clevedon: Channel View.

Shelby, B. and Heberlein, T.A. (1986) 'A conceptual framework for carrying capacity determination', *Leisure Sciences*, **6** (4), 433-451.

Shoval, M. and Cohen-Hattab, K. (2007) 'The role of the state and the rise of the Red Sea resorts in Egypt and Israel', in S. Agarwal and G. Shaw (eds), *Managing Coastal Tourism Resorts A Global Perspective*, Clevedon: Channel View, pp. 235-249.

Sneddon, C. (2000) '"Sustainability" in ecological economics, ecology and livelihoods: a review', *Progress in Human Geography*, **24** (4), 521-549.

Song Z. and Zhong, L. (2009) 'Research on ATOS methods of adventure tourism resource–product conversion suitability: a case study of Sanjiangyuan Region in Qinghai Province', paper presented at 2009 International Forum on Ecotourism, August, Xining, China.

Stankey, G., Cole, D.N., Lucas , R.C., Peterson, M.E., and Frissel, S.S. (1985) 'The limits of acceptable change (LAC) systems for wilderness planning', *USDA Forest Service General Technical Report aINT-176*, Ogden, Utah: Intermountain Forest and Range Experiment Station.

Stansfield, C.A . and Rikert, J.E. (1970) 'The recreational business district', *Journal of Leisure Research*, **2** (4), 213-225.

Tivy, J. (1973) *Recreational Carrying Capacityi*, Perth: Countryside Commission for Scotland.

Vaske, J.J. (1992) *VIMDEX*, Durham, NH: University of New Hampshire.

Wagar, J. A. (1964) 'The carrying capacity of wildlands for recreation', *Forest Science Monograph No. 7*, Washington, DC: Society of American Foresters.

Washbourne, R.F. (1982) 'Wilderness recreation carrying capacity: are numbers necessary?', *Journal of Forestry*, **80**, 726-728.

WCED (1987) *Our Common Future*, World Commission on Environment and Development, Oxford: Oxford University Press.

Weaver, D.B. (2009) 'Reflections on sustainable tourism and paradigm change', in S.Gossling, C.M. Hall and D.B. Weaver (eds), *Sustainable Tourism Futures*, London: Routledge, pp. 33-42.

Wolfe, R.I. (1964) 'Perspective on outdoor recreation a bibliographical summary', *Geographical Review*, **54**, 203-238.

Wolfe, R.I. (1966) 'Recreational travel: the new migration', *Canadian Geographer*, **10** (1), 1-14.

WTO (2008) *Tourism Statistics*, Madrid: World Tourism Organization.

Wu, H. (2009) '"Residents" perception of ecotourism and attitude for ecotourism development – a case study on Xuxhou Huancheng National Forest Park', paper presented at 2009 International Forum on Ecotourism, August, Xining, China.

Young, G. (1973) *Tourism – Blessing or Blight?*, Harmondsworth: Penguin.

Part II

Advances in research on the business of tourism

6 Measuring and interpreting the economic impact of tourism: 20-20 hindsight and foresight

Douglas Frechtling and Egon Smeral

Measuring the economic consequences of tourism activities for national and sub-national (regional) areas has provided valuable input for rationally addressing issues of importance to four key stakeholder groups: public officials, business owners and managers, employees of tourism establishments, and other residents of host communities (Frechtling, 2008). It seems appropriate at the time of commemorating the twentieth anniversary of the founding of the International Academy for the Study of Tourism to review developments in measuring such economic contributions over the last two decades and to suggest future developments in the field.

Before we address our topic, it is essential to define it. We had thought that standard English usage over the last three decades was pretty well established. As Reece (forthcoming) reaffirms, the economic impact of tourism comprises 'changes in regional employment, incomes, tax payments, and other measures of economic activity . . . that result from a region's tourism development' (p. 50), except that we understand this to apply to nations as well as regions. Reece follows a long train of authors who have defined 'tourism economic impact broadly' (e.g. Frechtling, 1994; Smith, 2000; Goeldner and Ritchie, 2003; Mason, 2003). Some now claim that reliable 'tourism economic impact' measures only result from complex economic equilibrium models (Dwyer *et al.*, 2008), a clear break with tradition and the ways the term is commonly used in tourism research today.

According to the tradition of tourism economic studies, the 'economic impact of tourism' is a term that covers one, some or all of the following economic changes resulting from the presence of visitors in an area, their activities or their expenditures:

♦ Business receipts
♦ Value added contribution to gross domestic or regional product
♦ Employment (jobs, persons employed)
♦ Labour earnings

- Other factor earnings (dividends, interest, rent, profits)
- Government tax revenue
- Other government revenue (e.g. user fees, fines, receipts of government enterprises)
- Distribution of income
- Government spending
- Externalities and public goods
- Multiplier effects on transactions, output, income, employment or government revenue
- New business formation
- Real property and other asset values
- Business investment in plant and equipment
- Price levels
- Interest rates on borrowed funds and return on capital
- Foreign exchange rates
- Imports and exports
- International balance of payments.

The way we were – 1988

Serious research interest in measuring aspects of the economic impact of tourism dates back more than 75 years (Mathieson and Wall, 1982: 35). In the post World War II period, a landmark study of the current and future demand for outdoor recreation in the US (Clawson and Knetsch, 1966) implicitly addressed tourism spending and suggested a number of aspects of measuring visitor economic impact on a local area. In 1969, an official of the US Bureau of the Census proposed a model to estimate domestic tourism expenditures, and this model was implemented within five years (Frechtling, 1974). About the same time, a study was published of national economic impacts of tourism for a collection of small island economies in the Caribbean (Bryden, 1973). This study focused on the costs and benefits of international tourism development on these 'small "open" developing economies' and policy recommendations for obtaining favourable national impacts (Bryden, 1973: 56). Then in 1975, the World Tourism Organization (UNWTO) held its first conference on measuring domestic tourism and its economic effects (Frechtling, 1975). That same year, the first economic model designed to estimate the value of visitor spending and its impact on employment, labour income and tax revenue at sub-national levels across a country was published and applied (Frechtling and Muha, 1975).

Direct economic impacts

The first book-length treatment of the economic consequences of international and domestic tourism in the English language was Mathieson and Wall's (1982) *Tourism: Economic, Physical and Social Impacts*. In addressing the economic side, the authors used the term, 'economic impact' broadly to indicate the primary and secondary impacts, costs and benefits of tourists on destination areas (pp. 6, 12). They defined 'impact' as 'the form of altered human behaviour that stems from interactions between agents of change and sub-systems on which they impinge' (p. 14). The authors identified the economic benefits documented in the literature as (p. 52):

1. Foreign exchange earnings and balance of payments

2. Generation of income

3. Generation of employment

4. Improvement of economic structures

5. Encouragement of entrepreneurship.

By 1988, the research on measuring and interpreting the economic effects of tourism activities had blossomed. Most of this research was focused on measuring the economic benefits of tourism to a national or regional (i.e., sub-national) area (Frechtling, 1987). Studies published measuring the economic impact of special events were relatively few (Frechtling, 1987; Getz, 1994).

Most economic impact studies concentrated on measuring the gross benefits of visitors to an area, driven by their expenditures while in the area (Frechtling, 1987). Most attention was focused on who derived economic benefits from visitors to the area, and who bore the costs (Frechtling, 1987). Models were developed and applied that simulated domestic visitor expenditures and their direct effects on business receipts, employment, labour earnings and tax revenue (Frechtling, 1987; Rovelstad, 1987).

These efforts were driven by various techniques of estimating visitor spending in a country or sub-national region (Frechtling, 2006). Surveying visitors onsite by probability sampling techniques was the most popular approach, but data from household surveys were also employed to estimate spending at the state or provincial level.

Multiplier effects

The approaches discussed so far estimated the direct or primary effects of visitor spending on business receipts, employment, labour earnings and tax revenue in an area. In addition, there are secondary effects as other businesses buy and sell from one another to supply the visitor, and as the employees of these establishments spend their earnings in the area (Frechtling, 1987). The sum of these secondary effects fuels the computation of various multipliers or ratios of the ultimate (i.e. sum of primary plus secondary effect) measures of sales, output, earnings, employment or government revenue to the initial injection of visitor expenditures into the area. There were three methods employed in published studies to estimate such multiplier effects: the economic base model, the ad hoc model and the Input–Output model (Frechtling, 1987).

As applied to visitor impact, economic base models required determining for each industry in the study area the volume of sales to visitors, a form of export revenue. The sum across all export industries constitutes the denominator of a sales multiplier. The numerator is the total sales of all industries located in the area. Then, all one needs to do is to estimate visitor spending for the period and multiply it by the sales multiplier to get total (primary plus secondary) sales generated by visitors. With some simple modelling, income and employment multipliers can be derived. While straightforward, the approach assumes all economic growth in an area is export-driven, and the distribution of the visitor spending (such as percentages for food service, accommodation, local transportation, shopping) does not change over time.

Archer (1977) developed an ad hoc multiplier model that applied the principles of the Keynesian multiplier to regional tourism analysis. This model consisted of a multiplicand of visitor spending that remains in the study area after first round leakages and the direct and indirect income this generates, and a multiplier that represented the induced effects of visitor spending on the economy.

Input–output analysis

The most prevalent approach to estimating the direct and secondary effects of visitor spending in the 1980s and 1990s was the Input–Output model, and this method is still popular today (Reece forthcoming). The use of Input–Output analysis in the classical sense allows calculating the direct, indirect and induced value-added effects resulting from visitor spending (Fletcher, 1989). Direct value added is value added that can be attributed to the productive activities directly serving visitors. Indirect value added is value created in the goods and services industries that supply the industries that directly serve visitors. In other words, indirect value added is generated in industries that supply goods and services to businesses that produce the final goods and services purchased before, during and after a visit.

Finally, the induced effect is value added generated by industries providing goods and services to consumers who gain income from the direct and indirect processes noted above. Direct, indirect and induced effects are summed for a destination to produce total economic impact. Multipliers can be derived by dividing the total impact measure for a variable (e.g. business receipts, income, and employment) by the initial visitor spending.

Input–Output analysis is a general equilibrium approach to determining the results of a marginal change imposed on an economic system, such as visitor spending, new investment in plant and equipment, withdrawal of a productive establishment or a catastrophic shock.

The technique of Input–Output analysis comprises two stages (Fletcher, 1989, 2000). First there is the construction of an inter-industry transactions, or supply and use, table. This table details the transactions that take place between industries within the economy as they buy and sell from one another. The inter-industry transactions table provides information to planners, managers and policy-makers in pointing out the economic structure of the destination and demonstrates the direct economic effects associated with any change in final demand.

The second stage of the analysis involves the conversion of the table into an Input–Output model (Fletcher, 1989, 2000). This requires dividing the value contained in each cell by the corresponding column total. This process results in a table of coefficients where the vertical columns show the production functions of each industry, and where the sum of each column is one. This coefficient table is then subjected to the Leontief inversion routine, which produces the total effects table calculating indirect economic impacts associated with any change in final demand.

Input–Output analysis produces estimates of economic multiplier values relating to transactions, output, income, employment and government revenues as well as an estimate of the import requirements as a consequence of any change in final demand.

The application of Input–Output analysis produces useful estimates for measuring the multiplier effects of visitors to an area. However, in interpreting these results, the restrictive assumptions of the Input–Output model must be considered (Fletcher and Archer, 1991). These restrictive assumptions have generated interest in computable general equilibrium (CGE) models as discussed below.

Current state of affairs in measuring tourism's economic impact

Computable General Equilibrium (CGE) models

In reaction to the limiting and possibly unrealistic assumptions of Input-Output analysis, it has become a fashion in recent years to use computable general equilibrium (CGE) models for measuring the economic impact of a change in tourism demand or an event (Dwyer and Forsyth, 1997; Dwyer et al., 2003, 2004, 2005; Narayan, 2004). After early CGE modelling performed in the 1970s, the first impact analysis of tourism was carried out in the late 1980s. CGE models have three general characteristics (Adams and Parmenter, 1995; Dixon and Parmenter, 1996):

1. The assumption of competitiveness in CGE models. This describes a competitive world that includes utility maximization in consumption, cost minimization in production, zero pure profits, and market clearing (Zhou *et al.*, 1997).

2. CGE models simulate an economy with efficient markets. In the CGE world, each market has an equilibrium solution for a set of prices and levels of production.

3. The core database of a CGE model is usually a set of Input-Output accounts showing the flows of commodities and factors between industries, households, governments, importers and exporters. These tables are normally supplemented by numerical estimates of various elasticity parameters.

CGE models go beyond Input-Output models by linking industries via economy-wide constraints. With these constraints in place, the economy-wide implications of stimulating one industry can be negative and a positive impact for some industries may be generated at the expense of others. For example, contrary to Input-Output analysis, CGE models do not assume that resources, such as labour, land and capital, flow freely to tourism-related industries, and they generally include feedback effects from other markets.

CGE models are sometimes criticised as being too time-consuming to build and too complicated to use (Dwyer *et al.*, 2004). It is also argued that CGE analyses are quite expensive compared to simpler techniques such as Input-Output analysis.

It is also questionable whether CGE models describe economic reality. As one observer has pointed out, 'most empirical exercises confront theory with numbers . . . . CGE models, by contrast, put numbers to theory' (*The Economist*, 2006: 69). In some cases the parameters of CGE models are calibrated by values not derived from valid statistical processes related to the variable. For example, current data on consumption in a country may be lacking, so consumption coefficients from other countries are substituted. Moreover, in contrast to Input-Output modelling, the equations representing the structure of the CGE model are not revealed, even in lengthy technical reports on specific elaborations of the CGE approach (e.g. Dwyer *et al.*, 2004). This prevents scholars from examining the assumptions, relationships and data vintage of the models, precluding the peer review, testing and reproducibility that is the hallmark of the scientific method (Godfrey-Smith, 2003). Furthermore, such 'opacity risks bringing a useful analytical tool into disrepute' (*The Economist*, 2006: 69).

Several studies are available on the assessment of the economic impact of a demand shock that compare the results of CGE and Input-Output analysis (Dwyer and Forsyth, 1997; Dwyer *et al.*, 2005; Zhou *et al.*, 1997). All these studies found that Input-Output estimates of impact are greater than CGE estimates, but fail to evaluate these results in a more general economic context that considers factor availability and the degree of market efficiency. In other words, the finding that Input-Output analysis overestimates impact is based on the lower CGE results as benchmarks, but no evidence is presented showing CGE estimates represent reality.

The Tourism Satellite Account

Over much of the last two decades, the World Tourism Organization and other international economic organizations have developed the Tourism Satellite Account (TSA) to measure the impact of visitor consumption expenditures on Gross Domestic Product and employment in a country. In 2008, two key documents defining the structure and elaborating the data sources for the TSA were accepted by the United Nations Statistical Commission (United Nations Statistics Division et al., 2008; World Tourism Organization, 2008). Seventy countries have elaborated at least one annual TSA in the last 15 years (Libreros et al., 2006).

The TSA is limited to dealing with 'tourism', defined by UNWTO as 'specific types of trips: those that take a traveller outside his/her usual environment for less than a year and for a main purpose other than to be employed by a resident entity in the place visited' (United Nations Statistics Division et al., 2008: 12). 'Usual environment' is defined as 'the geographical area (though not necessarily a contiguous one) within which an individual conducts his/her regular life routines' (United Nations Statistics Division et al., 2008: 13). So the TSA deals only with the activities of 'visitors' in a country, including both residents of the country and non-residents, who leave their usual environment for any purpose but to be employed by an organization in the places visited.

The TSA is a 'satellite' to a larger body, in this case the System of National Accounts (hereafter 'SNA 1993'). It is subordinate to and dependent upon the concepts, definitions, structure, and compilation rules of SNA 1993 (Commission of the European Communities et al., 1993).

Finally, at its core, the TSA is an 'account', that is, a table or set of tables 'which records, for a given aspect of economic life, the uses and resources or the changes in assets and the changes in liabilities and/or stock of assets and liabilities existing at a certain time' (Commission of the European Communities et al., 1993: 26). This recording is based on recorded observations of economic variables. This is in contrast to the economic impact measurement methods described above, which are 'models', that is, 'simplified description(s) of a system, process, etc., put forward as a basis for theoretical or empirical understanding' (Trumble and Stevenson, 2002: 1805).

When a country undertakes to develop a TSA, it necessarily defines tourism characteristic products: those that are sold directly to visitors. It also designates a set of industries conventionally defined as 'tourism industries'. The results are estimates of tourism's direct contribution to Gross Domestic Product for the specific country (Dwyer et al., 2008).

There is considerable interest in extending the TSA to subnational levels, such as states, provinces and major metropolitan areas. UNWTO is considering approving such extensions (Frechtling, 2008, 2009).

Tourism economic impact studies for the next decade

Contrary to the main research thrust of the last two decades, focusing on the general impact of tourism and later on the impact of small events, future research on tourism economic impact should concentrate on the impact of large-scale or 'mega events' since their importance for regional development has become of considerable political interest. A steady supply of festivals and similar small events in many destinations over time has turned such marketing tools into standard features of many destination products, so that they no longer offer competitive advantages.

Impacts of mega events

The economic significance of mega events and their impact on tourism need to be seen from several angles. Planned events typically provide sufficient motivation for people to travel to a given destination country or subnational area. Further, the construction of event facilities and related infrastructure (e.g. for international expositions) often has a considerable economic impact, since such direct investments create income and employment in the short-run and improve a destination's long-term competitiveness.

There can also be negative economic impacts. Planned mega events can produce environmental degradation, overcrowding and traffic congestion that impose significant economic costs on the local residents. In contrast to such events, unscheduled events such as manmade disruptions and natural catastrophes typically have negative economic impacts, requiring crisis management. It appears that the negative economic impacts of unscheduled events such as financial and economic crises, terrorist attacks, violent demonstrations, earthquakes, and the row over Russian gas supplies to Europe, will need to come under more careful scrutiny for evidence of adding to economic instabilities (Bram *et al.*, 2004; Enders, 2004).

For measuring event impacts, future research will concentrate first on capturing the size of the events with the help of modern time series econometrics (Song and Witt, 2000; Smeral and Wüger, 2000, 2008). It is essential to identify the size of an event – i.e. in expenditure terms – before impact measurement methods can be applied, because it is only by having unbiased measures of the event shock that we can produce unbiased impact estimates.

Identifying the magnitude of an event was formerly done mostly through heuristic methods. These approaches begin by assessing the number of attendees, the duration of their stay and their average expenditure per day in order to arrive at a measure of expenditure to calculate the direct, indirect and induced impacts (Hultkrantz, 2000). It can be argued that heuristic approaches are unreliable tools for isolating pure event-related factors from other factors such as business cycles, trends, prices, influences of seasonal and calendar effects or unknown outliers. Nor do they allow statistical inference, making it impossible to be statistically confident of their results, i.e. to ascertain whether or not they exceed normal levels of random variation.

Given these limitations of the heuristic approaches, we expect economists in the future to make more use of applied times series intervention models to accurately measure impacts of mega events.

Intervention models

In the 1970s, Box and Jenkins (1976) developed so-called auto-regressive, integrated moving average or 'ARIMA' models to analyse time series, where they attempted to explain time series movements based on their intrinsic dynamics (autoregressive terms and moving averages). Since economic time series are usually influenced by events, such additional information must be accounted for in modelling a time series. This can be done through intervention models, which are extensions of the ARIMA models (Box and Tiao, 1975; Box and Jenkins, 1976).

Since data in economic time series frequently are impaired by changes in recording methods and faulty reporting, and since the process to generate data for tourism time series can be affected quite substantially by factors such as exchange rate fluctuations, disasters, media reports and unknown events, it is advisable to make use of outlier detection methods when estimating the model, especially since often no information is available on the timing of such events. Such methods use an iterative approach to test whether any of the observed values of a time series are unknown outliers within the data generation process (Smeral and Wüger, 2005, 2006).

Categories of outliers are defined in advance: additive outlier (events that influence a time series at a single point in time), level shifts (permanent changes in the data generation process), innovational outliers (innovations in the data generation process) and temporary changes (effects of an event decaying in accordance with a damping factor). The model parameters of the data generation process and the outlier effects are estimated simultaneously and the three steps – identifying outliers, adjusting outliers and estimating parameters based on the corrected series, repeated until outliers are no longer found.

By accounting for such unknown outliers, it is possible to quantify their effects and thereby improve the parameter estimates of the overall model, since outliers may distort estimates of the model parameters through their impact on them. This also ensures that the effect of an event and an assessment of its significance are given a more solid foundation than when an intervention model is estimated without outlier adjustment (Liu, 2005).

The technical aspects of intervention models can be summarized as follows (Smeral and Wüger, 2008). These models distinguish three components in a time series of visits, expenditures, employment or other economic impact measure: (1) the intervention variables that represent the effects of the event; (2) outlier adjustments to filter out the effects of other unknown special influences; and (3) the standard ARIMA elements capturing the other factors in the time series (such as trend, business cycles, season) influencing the data generation process for the tourism variables being analysed.

Future research directions

Accurate measurement of the effects of planned and unplanned events on economic activity is complicated by:

- Delays in obtaining data measuring the activities
- Need to apply *ex ante* and *ex post* perspectives to discern the additions or subtractions due to the event
- Markets reacting inefficiently to unexpected shocks
- Human behaviour failing to follow the maximization principles of neoclassical economic theory.

In addition, assessment of the impacts of unplanned events faces the constraints of:

- Lack of detailed *ex ante* assessments of the activities affected
- The results of these complications may be unacceptably long intervals between the event and accurate measurement of its effects.
- Probabilities of structural changes in national or regional economies.
- Asymmetric behaviour of price and income elasticities in unexpected downturns versus periods of uninterrupted growth.

These concerns may be dealt with in the future through:

- Systems instituted to provide forecasts of relevant economic activities over three- to five-year periods for nations and regions to define normal trends and levels
- Meta-analysis of event impact studies to identify ranges of impact to be expected from events (e.g. Teigland, 1996; Smeral and Wüger, 2000, 2008)
- Research distinguishing short-lived impacts on economic activities (Spilling, 2000) from long-term or structural changes in an economy due to the event.

We recommend the development of an accessible database of studies of the impact of planned and unplanned events on various national and regional tourism activities, organized by type of impact, duration of the event, type of event (its planned or unplanned nature), and scope of impact (direct or secondary impacts). Researchers and policy officials could access these studies to better simulate the potential effects of events and their measurable effects after they occur.

References

Adams, P. and Parmenter, B. (1995) 'An applied general equilibrium analysis of the economic effects of tourism in a quite small, quite open economy', *Applied Economics*, **27**, 985-994.

Archer, B. (1977) *Tourism Multipliers: The State of the Art*, Cardiff: University of Wales Press.

Box, G. and Jenkins, G. (1976). *Time Series Analysis: Forecasting and Control*, 2nd edn, San Francisco: Holden Day.

Box, G. and Tiao, G. (1975) 'Intervention analysis with applications to economic and environmental problems', *Journal of the American Statistical Association*, **70** (349), 70–79.

Bram, J., Haughwout, A. and Orr, J. (2004) 'Has September 11 affected New York City's growth potential', in Y. Okuyama and S.E. Chang (eds), *Modeling Spatial and Economic Impact disasters*, Berlin: Springer, pp. 53-73.

Bryden, J. (1973) *Tourism and Development: A Case Study of the Commonwealth Caribbean*, Cambridge: Cambridge University Press.

Clawson, M. and Knetsch, J. (1966) *Economics of Outdoor Recreation*, Baltimore: Johns Hopkins Press.

Commission of the European Communities, International Monetary Fund, Organization for Economic Cooperation and Development, United Nations and World Bank (1993) *System of National Accounts 1993*, United Nations.

Dixon, P. and Parmenter, B. (1996) 'Computable general equilibrium modelling for policy analysis and forecasting', in H. Aman (ed.), *Handbook of Computational Economics, Vol. 1*, Amsterdam: Elsevier Science, pp. 4-85.

Dwyer, L. and Forsyth, P. (1997) 'Impacts and benefits of MICE tourism: a framework for analysis', *Tourism Economics*, **3** (1), 21-38.

Dwyer, L., Forsyth, P., Spurr, R. and Van Ho, T. (2008) 'Tourism's economic contribution versus economic impact assessment: differing roles for satellite accounts and economic modelling', in A. Woodside and D. Martin (eds), *Tourism Management: Analysis, Behaviour and Strategy*, Wallingford: CAB International, pp. 459-469.

Dwyer, L., Forsyth, P. and Spurr, R. (2004) 'Evaluating tourism's economic effects: new and old approaches', *Tourism Management*, **25** (3), 307-317.

Dwyer, L., Forsyth, P. and Spurr, R. (2005) 'Estimating the impacts of special events on a economy', *Journal of Travel Research*, **43** (4), 351-359.

Dwyer, L., Forsyth, P., Spurr, R. and Vanho, T. (2003) 'Tourism's contribution to the state economy: a multi-regional general equilibrium analysis', *Tourism Economics*, **9** (4), 431-448.

Economist, The (2006) 'Big questions and big numbers', *The Economist*, **380** (8486), 67-69.

Enders, W. (2004) *Applied Econometric Time Series*, New York: John Wiley & Sons.

Fletcher, J. (1989) 'Input-Output analysis and tourism impact studies', *Annals of Tourism Research*, **16** (4), 514-529.

Fletcher, J. (2000) 'Input-Output-Analysis', in J. Jafari (ed.), *Encyclopedia of Tourism*, New York: Routledge, pp. 310-312.

Fletcher, J. and Archer, B. (1991) 'The development and application of multiplier analysis', in C. Cooper and A. Lockwood (eds), *Progress in Tourism, Recreation and Hospitality Management, Vol. 3*, London/New York: Belhaven Press, pp. 28-47.

Frechtling, D. (1974) 'A model for estimating travel expenditures', *Journal of Travel Research*, **12** (4), 9-12.

Frechtling, D. (1975) 'Definition and measurement of domestic tourism', *Travel Research Journal*, World Tourism Organization, pp. 21-28.

Frechtling, D. (1987) 'Assessing the impacts of travel and tourism – measuring economic benefits', in J. Ritchie and C. Goeldner (eds), *Travel, Tourism, and Hospitality Research: A Handbook for Managers and Researchers*, New York: John Wiley & Sons, pp. 333-351.

Frechtling, D. (1994) 'Assessing the impacts of travel and tourism – introduction to travel impact estimation', in J. Ritchie and C. Goeldner (eds), *Travel, Tourism, and Hospitality Research*, 2nd edn, New York: John Wiley & Sons, pp. 359-365.

Frechtling, D. (2006) 'An assessment of visitor expenditure methods and models', *Journal of Travel Research*, **45** (1), 26-35.

Frechtling, D. (2008) 'Measurement and analysis of tourism economic contributions for sub-national regions through the tourism satellite account', paper presented to the International Tourism Conference on Knowledge as a Value Advantage for Tourist Destinations, World Tourism Organization, Malaga, Spain..

Frechtling, D. (2009) 'Clarifying and extending the TSA brand', paper presented to the Fifth World Tourism Organization International Conference on Tourism Statistics, Bali, Indonesia.

Frechtling, D. and Muha, S. (1975) *Travel Economic Impact Model, Volume I: Final Economic Analysis Methodology*, Washington DC: US Travel Data Center.

Getz, D. (1994) 'Event tourism: evaluating the impacts', in J. Ritchie and C. Goeldner (eds), *Travel, Tourism, and Hospitality Research, A Handbook for Managers and Researchers*, 2nd edn, New York: John Wiley & Sons, pp. 437-450.

Godfrey-Smith, P. (2003) *Theory and Reality: an Introduction to the Philosophy of Science*, Chicago: University of Chicago Press.

Goeldner, C. and Ritchie, J. (2003) *Tourism: Principles, Practices, Philosophies*, New York: John Wiley & Sons.

Hultkrantz, L. (2000) 'Event economics: top down approaches', in L. Mossberg (ed.), *Evaluation of Events: Scandinavian Experiences*, Elmsford, NY: Cognizant Communication Corporation, pp. 104-121.

Libreros, M., Massieu, A. and Meis, S. (2006) 'Progress in tourism satellite account implementation and development', *Journal of Travel Research*, **45** (1), 83-91.

Liu, L. (2005) *Time Series Analysis and Forecasting*, Champaign: University of Illinois Press.

Mason, P. (2003) *Tourism Impact, Planning and Management*, London: Butterworth-Heinemann.

Mathieson, A., and Wall, G. (1982) *Tourism: Economic, Physical and Social Impacts*, Harlow: Longman.

Narayan, P. (2004) 'Economic impact of tourism on Fiji's economy: empirical evidence from the computable general equilibrium model', *Tourism Economics*, **10** (4), 419-434.

Reece, W. (2010) *The Economics of Tourism*, Upper Saddle River, NJ: Pearson Prentice Hall.

Rovelstad, J. (1987) 'Model building and simulation', in J. Ritchie and C. Goeldner (eds), *Travel, Tourism, and Hospitality Research: A Handbook for Managers and Researchers*, pp. 449-458.

Smeral, E. and Wüger, M. (2000) 'Use of intervention models to assess the effects of the EU presidency on revenues from international tourism', *Tourism Economics*, **6** (1), 61-72.

Smeral, E. and Wüger, M. (2005) 'Does complexity matter? Methods for improving forecasting accuracy in tourism', *Journal of Travel Research*, **44** (1), 100-110.

Smeral, E. and Wüger, M. (2006) 'Improving marketing efficiency through the implementation of advanced forecasting methods: a short-term approach', in P. Keller and T. Bieger (eds), *Marketing Efficiency in Tourism – Coping with Volatile Demand*, Pontresina, Switzerland: AIEST Conference, pp 183–192.

Smeral, E. and Wüger, M. (2008) 'Methods for measuring the effects of EU presidency on international tourism', *Tourism Economics*, **14** (2) 313-324.

Smith, S.L.J. (2000) 'New developments in measuring tourism as an area of economic activity', in W. Gartner and D. Lime (eds), *Trends in Outdoor Recreation, Leisure and Tourism*, New York: CAB International, pp. 225-234.

Song, H. and Witt, S. (2000) *Tourism Demand Modelling and Forecasting*, Oxford: Pergamon.

Spilling, O. (2000) 'Beyond intermezzo? On the long term industrial impacts of mega-events – the case of Lillehammer 1994', in L. Mossberg (ed.), *Evaluation of Events: Scandinavian Experiences*, Elmsford, NJ: Cognizant Communication Corporation, pp. 122-147.

Teigland, J. (1996) *Impacts on Tourism from Mega-Events: The Case of Winter Olympic Games*, Sogndal, Norway: Western Norway Research Institute.

Trumble, W. R. and Stevenson, A. (eds) (2002) *The New Shorter Oxford English Dictionary on Historical Principles*, Oxford University Press.

United Nations Statistics Division, Statistical Office of the European Communities, Organisation for Economic Co-operation and Development and the World Tourism Organization (2008) *2008 Tourism Satellite Account: Recommended Methodological Framework*, World Tourism Organization.

World Tourism Organization (2008) *2008 International Recommendations for Tourism Statistics*, World Tourism Organization.

Zhou, D., Yanagida, J., Chakravorty, U. and Leung, P. (1997) 'Estimating economic impacts from tourism', *Annals of Tourism Research*, **24** (1), 76-89.

7 Tourism SMEs: changing research agendas and missed opportunities

Gareth Shaw and Allan M. Williams

Introduction

Work on SMEs (small and medium enterprises) within tourism has become a major focus of research activity during the last 30 years, reflecting the numerical importance of SMEs in tourism and across a range of differing economies (OECD, 2005). This is reflected both in the volume of publications and more significantly in the range of themes being studied (see Thomas, 1998; Morrison *et al.*, 1999; Shaw, 2003; Thomas, 2004). Surprisingly, despite a proliferation of research activities, progress has been uneven, with Thomas commenting that some key themes have only received very limited attention where research 'remains relatively shallow' (Thomas, 2004: 1). Research also remains unevenly distributed in terms of national economies, tourism economic environments, and sub-sectors, and institutional economics remains poorly specified in tourism SME research (Shaw and Williams, 2004: Chapter 3).

The aim of this chapter is to review the changing research agendas associated with tourism SMEs with a focus on developed economies and the UK in particular. In doing so we will briefly review the key themes to have emerged from past research before examining in more detail some significant areas of emerging research. In terms of the latter, particular attention is focused on: innovation, knowledge networks and knowledge management, the importance of sustainability as framed within the notions of environmental responsibility, family-owned business practices and institutions, and the research–policy interface. In drawing out retrospective and emerging research agendas, our sub-text is that two or more decades of exciting progress have been matched, almost step by step, with missed opportunities. Missed opportunities are manifested in two interrelated contexts. First, there has been a persistent failure amongst tourism researchers to fully engage with wider debates in the literature on SMEs (Holt and Macpherson, 2006), to the detriment of both. This has resulted to a large extent in two very different, and parallel rather than engaged, literatures. Second, these missed opportunities have also impacted on the policy field, with this research parallelism contributing to the relative marginalisation of tourism in SME policy domains in many countries. The most obvious implications of this are that some of the specificities of tourism production and consumption, such as the strongly temporal nature of demand and the importance of the supply chain as opposed to in-house R&D as a source of innovation, have often been ignored in wider policy initiatives to support SMEs. This represents a missed opportunity in terms of both informing and engaging critically with policies.

The uneven evolution of tourism SME research

During the last 30 years the increasing interest in SMEs within tourism has seen a number of emergent themes, including research on entrepreneurship and motivations (particularly notions of lifestyle entrepreneurs), the contribution of small firms to tourism economies, and the dynamics of SME development and business performance. In part these themes overlap with some of the research agendas identified by Thomas (2004), and although of course neither list is inclusive, they reflect the broad distribution of English language publications. While considered separately here, in order to simplify the discussions, these themes are of course invariably inter-woven.

The nature and characteristics of small firm entrepreneurship in tourism was an early research focus. Stallinbrass' (1980) pioneering work on SMEs in the coastal resort of Scarborough (England) was followed by Shaw and Williams (1987) who identified the lack of business experience amongst owners of small tourism enterprises in coastal resorts in Cornwall, England. These studies also emphasised that many entrepreneurs had non-economic motives for establishing such businesses and many depended on informal sources of capital. That such studies were all focussed on English coastal resorts helped to highlight some of the difficulties faced by the local economies of such destinations (Shaw and Williams, 1997). As we have argued elsewhere (Shaw and Williams, 2004), subsequent studies of entrepreneurship in tourism have identified a range of entrepreneurial cultures. These vary from a preoccupation with economic maximisation goals through to those mainly interested in non-economic factors, with 'lifestyle' being of critical importance; in practice, however, we increasingly understand that such goals may be blurred, and shift over time, as well as being contested amongst the owners/managers of enterprises (which we return to in discussing family businesses).

There is nothing unique about the role of lifestyle in tourism SMEs. Many surveys of SMEs across a range of sectors have highlighted the importance of 'being your own boss' as a motivation (Storey, 1996; Cosh *et al.*, 2008). Indeed, Morrison *et al.* (1999: 13) argue that the 'majority of small firms in the UK can be termed life-style businesses', since they are largely motivated by maintaining a particular way of life. More significantly, Dewhurst and Horobin (1998) attempted to incorporate many of the non-economic motives, revealed by studies of tourism SMEs, into a strategic management model. In turn they sought to use motives and goals to develop a taxonomy of small business entrepreneurs. This and other studies drew attention to the complexity of interactions between economic and non-economic motives. In part such complexities are linked to the interplay between tourism consumption and production identified by Williams *et al.* (1989). The blurring of boundaries between consumption and production amongst small business entrepreneurs was termed travel stimulated entrepreneurial migration by Snepenger *et al.* (1995), whilst Ateljevic (2000) conceptualised such processes as interrelated consumption and production circuits.

There is a double specificity in much of the early research on tourism entrepreneurship, focusing on coastal resorts and on (largely English speaking) developed countries. The same applied to the conclusions drawn about the limitations of these entrepreneurship models in relation to local economic development (Shaw and Williams, 1997). In contrast, studies of rural economies have tended to draw more positive conclusions, highlighting the importance of institutional specificity (Ateljevic and Dorne, 2000; Komppula, 2004: 139). Thus, Keen's (2004) research in New Zealand highlighted the role of small business in providing 'a unique and enjoyable experience' as a key development factor. Furthermore, she claims that social or community entrepreneurs, of the types initially identified by Ateljevic and Dorne (2000), are the main facilitators of development. Morrison *et al.* (2008) also argue that negative discourses on small firms are more than countered by positive evidence from a range of studies as to their evidence (Getz and Carlsen 2000; Koh 2002; Hollick and Braun, 2005). However, as Morrison *et al.* (2008: 12) point out, the contributions of tourism SMEs are contradictory, and there is a need to go beyond the simplistic 'dichotomy of negative and positive discourses'.

Turning to firm dynamics, most studies of tourism SMEs have focused on conditions of entry and paid very limited attention to business development and growth processes (Shaw, 2004). In contrast, the mainstream literature on SMEs has increasingly emphasised pathways of development. Morrison *et al.* (1999), along with Hill *et al.* (2002), review this literature but do not significantly add to our detailed knowledge of the tourism sector. A number of life-cycle stage models exist as shown in Table 7.1 but unfortunately few, if any, have been utilised or tested within tourism. Yet these can provide a framework for understanding the options facing SMEs over time and how entrepreneurs respond to changing situations (Hill *et al.*, 2002). This in turn links to the need to understand the determinants of such responses, both at the individual level, and the institutional (e.g. availability of capital, regulations). The importance of understanding the dynamics of growth and failure, as well as the usual focus on start-ups, is emphasised by UK annual sample surveys of all SMEs which have identified unusually high failure rates amongst tourism-related businesses in their first three years of operation (Cosh *et al.*, 2008). This clearly has implications in terms of understanding innovation and knowledge management, one of the themes that we address in the discussion of emerging research agendas.

Table 7.1: Selected SME (small and medium enterprise) life cycle models. Source: authors

Authors	Model characteristics
Greiner (1972)	Five-phase growth model based on evolutionary and revolutionary stages, with an organisational management perspective
Churchill and Lewis (1983)	Five-stage growth model linked to small business development, branding-based perspective
Tyebjee et al. (1983)	Four-stage growth model initially based on IT manufacturers, uses a marketing perspective
Scott and Bruce (1987)	Five-stage growth model for small businesses developed from Greiner's work: management-based perspective
Hanks et al. (1993)	Uses cluster analysis to identify six clusters of growth types based on a range of variables, including firm size and age
Dodge et al. (1994)	Two-stage model based on levels and types of competition in SMEs

Finally, we note that most research on SMEs within tourism has drawn on small businesses of less than nine employees, or micro firms. This is not surprising given that such firms tend to be dominant, at least in terms of the size distribution of enterprises; for example, in the UK they account for around 87 per cent of hospitality businesses (Thomas, 2000) which are considered to be micro businesses. Indeed, there are a range of early definitions of SMEs (Thomas, 1998). In this chapter we follow the more accepted definitions of small enterprises being less than 50 employees whilst medium-sized firms have 50–250 employees. There has been relative neglect of medium-sized enterprises, those that employ between 50–250 employees according to some definitions, which comprise only 0.1 per cent of hospitality businesses in the UK. This is a critical weakness in analyses which seek to identify the sources of growth and innovation, with important implications for effective policy making; themes we return to later in the chapter.

From our brief review of tourism SME research over the last 30 years, a number of recurrent themes emerge including:

♦ The importance of a range of goals, including lifestyle orientation, although these must be understood as context specific.

♦ Relatively low entry requirements and low business survival rates.

♦ Contradictory evidence over the role of SMEs in the development of different local economies.

♦ A lack of understanding of the growth stages of individual businesses.

Emerging research agendas: mainstreaming the study of tourism SMEs

The previous emphasis on the significant but uneven progress in SME research implicitly suggests that the last three decades have also been a period of missed opportunities, emanating in part from the distancing of tourism research from what may be termed generic or mainstream SME research. Here we focus on what we consider to be four key emergent research agendas, namely; innovation and knowledge management; sustainability and environmental responsibility; the distinctiveness of family-run businesses; and the interface between research and policy.

The first is somewhat complex, being comprised of three interlinked areas of research, those associated with innovation, knowledge management, including knowledge transfer (Cooper, 2006; Shaw and Williams, 2009) and business networks and value chains. One of the problems for tourism SMEs is that in many academic and policy discourses, they are often not considered to be entrepreneurial or innovative (Shaw and Williams, 1998). This is a feature that they share with consumer services in general. Nevertheless, it is notable that recent work by NESTA (2008) on innovation in services served to highlight the relative paucity of innovations in the tourism sector, as represented by hotels and restaurants and measured by the UK Community Innovation Survey. Despite the limitations of this data source, the perceived weakness of innovation in tourism is striking even when compared to other forms of services. The failure of both academic research and of statistical data to reflect the actual levels of innovation in the service sector is countered by NESTA's (2007, 2008) recognition of four main types of so-called 'hidden innovation' (Table 7.2). This is an implicit statement of the fact that the service sector model of innovation differs significantly from that identified in manufacturing (NESTA 2008: 6). These differences include:

◆ The importance of organisational changes as key drivers of innovation in services – this includes management techniques and new business models.

◆ Service firms are less dependent on R&D but rely more on innovation in the supply chain.

◆ A creative and knowledge-based workforce are key elements to innovation in the service sector.

◆ Service firms, particularly tourism enterprises, are more likely to innovate around consumer needs.

Not all of these findings are relevant to tourism SMEs and even less so to many small businesses. However, emerging evidence in this field suggests that many of these are of significance although further research is needed to help establish the scale and type of 'hidden innovations' within tourism SMEs. At present this represents a missed opportunity to engage with significant research and policy-based debates.

Table 7.2: Main types of hidden innovations. Source: NESTA (2008: 5)

Types	Characteristics
1	Innovation similar to that measured along traditional indicators (based around new technologies)
2	Innovation based on new organisational forms or business models
3	Innovation based around the novel use of combinations of existing technologies and processes
4	Small-scale, locally-based innovations that are often deeply hidden and associated with individuals in a particular activity

Recent work on innovations in tourism (Hjalager, 2002; Hall and Williams, 2008; Hjalager *et al.*, 2008) has increased research awareness in this field, although attention to tourism SMEs has still tended to lag. Decelle (2004), reporting on the French National Tourism Board study on Tourism and Innovation, provides a wide ranging view of types of innovation. More important, he addresses tourism SMEs in the context of their inadequate 'know-how' or tacit knowledge. He identifies two distinctive problems: a lack of propensity to innovate, often associated with unstable economic environments, and a 'form of limited rationality' (p.12), linked with a lack of training. These difficulties tend to be related to firm size and here we need to draw a distinction between small and medium-sized enterprises. By and Dale (2008) highlight firm size in terms of the importance of developing entrepreneurial culture around innovation and creativity through the processes of change management. Their research on visitor attraction SMEs recognises eight critical factors for managing change in tourism, including adaptability and flexibility, communication and support, along with formal business strategies. A significant challenge facing SMEs is the changing role of innovations associated with IT and e-marketing (Tiessen *et al.*, 2001). The adoption of such innovations is linked to the mechanisms of how tacit knowledge is transferred and absorbed by SMEs, and combined with codified knowledge (e.g. in the form of technology). Much still remains to be researched in this context both in terms of the significance of communities of practice, boundary spanners (leadership) and aspects of co-production (Brown and Duquid, 2000; Braun, 2005).

Learning processes and the ability to absorb new knowledge particularly concerning innovations is critical to small firm competitiveness (Deakins and Freel, 1998) while the significance of knowledge management and knowledge transfer are increasingly important within tourism (Shaw and Williams, 2009). Hallin and Marnburg's (2008) review of current empirical progress in this field in the hotel industry is particularly useful in highlighting the importance of knowledge sharing, knowledge capture and aspects of organisational learning. Yang and Wan (2004) and Yang (2007) have explored in detail the flow of knowledge amongst hotel employees along with the obstacles encountered. Whilst such ideas have not fully been explored within SMEs, especially small and micro tourism firms, some important inroads are being made. Thus, Kyriakidou and Gore's (2005) qualitative study of tourism SMEs has suggested that benchmarking organisation cultures can help knowledge transfer. This approach stresses the importance of SMEs identifying knowledge gaps along with assessing which new knowledge to acquire; although, as Hallin and Marnburg (2008) argue, it is often too difficult for small firms to undertake such a benchmarking process without assistance. Some of these difficulties can of course be overcome through collaboration.

The increasing importance of collaboration and networks has been an important strand of generic research on SMEs (Brunetto and Wharton, 2007; Street and Cameron, 2007) and increasingly on tourism SMEs (Morrison *et al.*, 2004; Braun, 2005; Grängsjo and Gummerson, 2006; Novelli *et al.*, 2006). Deakins and Freel (1998) in their study of SME growth and entrepreneurial learning identified the ability to network as a critical factor for successful growth, arguing that SMEs need to 'network in their sector at an early stage' (p.148). The creation of such networks is another area requiring more attention within tourism research. Novelli *et al.* (2006) have highlighted the importance of the local state in cluster formation, in a study of a Health Lifestyle Tourism Cluster of SMEs in the UK, but there is still limited knowledge of inter-firm collaboration at the SME level. As Braun (2005: 2) points out, 'tourism networks are complex structures, yet there are relatively few studies of tourism networks', which is particularly important in an industry where networking amongst firms is relatively weakly developed. In terms of operational factors two critical areas of research concern the nature of leadership in clusters and how 'sticky tacit' knowledge is transferred around such SME networks. Morrison (2003) has started to address the notion of leadership development, Weidenfeld *et al.* (2010) have analysed knowledge flows, co-operation and competition in clusters of (SME) tourism attractions, and Zschiegner (2008) has researched notions of network leadership in SMEs.

Our second major research agenda concerns environmental sustainability and the increasing focus on the role of SMEs in this context (ENSR, 2002; Flash Eurobarometer, 2007). Despite considerable interest in issues of sustainable tourism there is limited information on the environmental practices of tourism SMEs and as such they are not as prominent as they should be in research on environmental sustainability. This is partly due to disconnection between research fields, and Moscardo (2007), for example, calls for a radical rethinking of tourism sustainability to embrace innovation and knowledge management as links to wider policy debates. We would go further and stress the need for more research focused on the barriers and drivers of environmental action with tourism SMEs along with a closer synergy with generic debates on innovation.

In seeking a way forward, Parker *et al.* (2009) provide an agenda for possible future research in this area, centred on developing a typology of SMEs based on environmental behaviour. They identify four basic types, namely; profit, advantage, compliance and environment-driven SMEs. This framework can be used to test how different types of SMEs respond to specific policy interventions, and which policy actions are most effective. Such a typology has not been applied to tourism SMEs and this offers useful research possibilities, particularly when combined with Halme's (2001) exploratory work on learning networks based around public–private initiatives on sustainability. This, in turn, highlights the importance of knowledge transfer and management as critical research agendas within environmental sustainability.

Third, given that many small tourism businesses are family-run firms, it is surprising that tourism research has not drawn more fully on the family business literature or the sociology of the family. Clearly there are exceptions, such as the work of Morrison and Teixeira (2004), who examine agent and structure in small tourism businesses. However, considerable scope exists for applying ideas from the family business literature to tourism SMEs, particularly the conceptualisations of family entrepreneurship (Heck *et al.*, 2008).

Within the context of business management and family-owned firms, Danes *et al.* (2008) have drawn attention to the Sustainable Family Business Theory (SFBT) model. This postulates that there is a strong interplay between the business and the family. As Danes *et al.* (2008: 399) point out, 'resources and interpersonal transactions from the business or family may facilitate or inhibit family business sustainability'. SFBT is based around five key propositions and a series of family adjustment strategies (Table 7.3). This, and other conceptual models, such as family embeddedness perspectives (Heck *et al.*, 2008), may also help to develop our understanding of the dynamics of firm growth in tourism SMEs. The interweaving of family and business demands has been largely neglected in tourism research and yet it may provide important conceptual frameworks to aid our understanding of business survival rates in an industry where family firms are significant.

Table 7.3: Propositions of sustainable family business theory (SFBT) and family adjustment strategies. Source: Modified from Danes et al. (2008)

Proposition	Author
Family is a rational system vs. an irrational system	Stafford et al. (1999)
Systems interact by exchanging resources at their boundaries during times of disruption	Fitzgerald et al. (2001)
Families manage family and business resources together to meet overlapping needs	Paul et al. (2003)
Family or business can be destroyed if boundaries are too diffuse	Stafford et al. (1999)
Conflicts arise when there is a mismatch between demands and resources	Danes (2006)
Adjustment strategies	
1. Personal time reallocation	Miller et al. (2000)
2. Obtaining additional help	Fitzgerald et al. (2001)
3. Adjusting family resources	Miller et al. (1999)
4. Adjusting business resources	Miller et al. (1999)
5. Intertwining tasks	Fitzgerald et al. (2001)

The final research theme relates to the need, and value, of engagement with the policy implications for tourism SMEs. Despite their numerical importance, tourism SMEs have been neglected by policy makers, relative to SMEs in other sectors, in many countries. To some extent this is due to the poor representation of tourism in official statistics (Thomas, 2000), which itself originates in the composite nature of the tourism product (Wanhill, 2004: 53). There are, of course, some important policy developments at the local, regional and national levels (Hall and Jenkins, 2004), as well as the EU level (Wanhill, 2004). Alongside this, there are major generic policies to stimulated entrepreneurship and innovation in SMEs. For example, in the UK the government report on *Enterprise: Unlocking the UK's Talent* (BERR, 2008) embraces the strategy of 'making the UK the most enterprising economy in the world' (p. 5). Much of this strategy is based around developing an enterprise culture through increasing the numbers of SMEs and business start-ups. This in turn is linked to increased levels of entrepreneurship and innovation along with other so-called enterprise enablers (Table 7.4). The strategy document highlights the two-way relationships between innovation and enterprise pointing out that 'innovative small businesses are more likely to achieve growth, while small businesses which have experienced recent growth are more likely to introduce new or improved products and services' (BERR, 2008: 19).

Table 7.4: Enterprise enablers and UK government strategies towards SMEs (small and medium enterprises). Source: Modified from BERR (2008)

Enabler	UK government strategy
Enterprise culture	Unlocking talent and providing entrepreneurial opportunities across different social groups
Knowledge and skills	Ensure businesses have access to develop knowledge and skills to support their growth
Access to finance	Enable businesses to have access to finance and advice
Regulatory framework	Reduction of unnecessary regulatory burdens on SMEs
Business innovation	Strengthen the role of innovation as a driver of enterprise and entrepreneurial activity

One of the failings of tourism research is its failure to engage with these wider policy agendas, and this in part represents its unconvincing engagement, until comparatively recently, with key generic debates in this area. Research on SMEs does contribute to defining what constitutes the key issues in tourism and in this sense forms part of – to borrow Foucault's (1991) term – the 'governmentality' of tourism. It is recognition that power is not as such concentrated in governments but widely distributed across society through practices and discourses that produce knowledge. The emerging research agendas we have outlined above will help tourism researchers to engage with these broader policy debates. That is important in two ways. First and most obviously, in giving tourism a voice at the top table in policy circles and a greater call on state resources. Second, it will enrich tourism research because the performance of tourism policies is integral to how tourism is constituted as a set of economic and social practices.

Conclusions

This short review of changing research agendas in tourism SMEs has identified a number of key issues. These initially related to research themes that stressed the 'uniqueness' of tourism SMEs, particularly as exemplified by the work on 'lifestyle entrepreneurship'. Such perspectives in part led to a dislocation of the research on tourism SMEs from wider SME studies. In turn this rather marginalised the effort of tourism researchers in relation to both the rapidly moving frontier of social science research in these areas, as well as in related policy fields.

Emergent agendas on tourism SMEs have started to rectify some of these difficulties and re-integrate tourism studies into wider debates. This is especially the case in terms of innovation, knowledge management and networks, along with policy issues of environmental sustainability. This is not to argue that tourism does not have distinctive features of consumption and production, and the way that these are interwoven, but rather than both generic and tourism-specific theoretical and empirical research in this field will benefit significantly from bridging such a gap. At the same time, it will create opportunities to contribute to critical social theory debates relating to the relationships between SMEs, policies and social outcomes. That, we believe, provides an exciting future for research on SMEs in tourism.

Acknowledgements

The authors would like to thank the support provided by the UK's Economic and Social Research Council for this research via the Advanced Institute of Management.

References

Ateljevic, I. (2000) 'Circuits of tourism: stepping beyond the production/consumption dichotomy', *Tourism Geographies*, 2 (4), 369-388.

Ateljevic, I. and Doorne, S. (2000) 'Staying within the fence: lifestyle entrepreneurship in tourism', *Journal of Sustainable Tourism*, 8 (5), 378-392.

BERR (2008) *Enterprise: Unlocking the UK's Talent*, Department for Business, Enterprise and Regulatory Reform.

Braun, P. (2005) 'Creating value to tourism products through tourism networks and clusters: uncovering destination value chains', OECD meeting, Gwangju, Korea.

Brown, J. and Duguid, P. (2000) *The Social Life of Information*, Boston, MA: Harvard Business School Press.

Brunetto, Y. and Farr-Wharton, R. (2007) '"The moderating role of trust in SME owner/managers" decision-making about collaboration', *Journal of Small Business Management*, 45 (3), 362-397.

By, R.T. and Dale, C. (2008) 'The successful management of organisational change in tourism SMEs: initial findings in UK visitor attractions', *International Journal of*

Tourism Research, **10**, 305-313.

Churchill, N.C. and Lewis, V.L. (1983) 'The five stages of small business growth', *Harvard Business Review*, May/June, 30-49.

Cooper, C. (2006) 'Knowledge management and tourism', *Annals of Tourism Research*, **33** (1), 47-64.

Cosh, A., Hughes, A., Bullock, A. and Milner, I. (2008) *Financing UK Small and Medium – sized Enterprises: The 2007 Survey. A Report from the Centre for Business Research*, University of Cambridge.

Danes, S.M. (2006) 'Tensions within family business – owning couples over time', *Stress, Trauma and Crisis*, **9**: 227-246.

Danes, S.M., Loy, J.J. and Stafford, K. (2008) 'Business planning practices of family-owned firms within a quality framework', *Journal of Small Business Management*, **46** (3), 395-421.

Deakins, D. and Freel, M. (1998) 'Entrepreneurial learning and the growth process in SMEs', *The Learning Organizationi*, **5** (3), 144-155.

Decelle, X. (2004) 'A conceptual and dynamic approach to innovation in tourism', OECD.

Dewhurst, P. and Horobin, H. (1998) 'Small business owners', in R. Thomas (ed.), *The Management of Small Tourism and Hospitality Firms*, London: Cassell.

Dodge, H.R, Fullerton, S. and Robbins, J.E. (1994) 'Stages of the organizational lifecycle and competition as mediators of problem perception for small business', *Strategic Management JournalI*, **15**, 121-135.

ENSR (2002) *European SMEs and Social and Environmental Responsibility*, Observatory of European SMEs No4. EC, Luxembourg.

Fitzgerald, M.A., Winter, M., Miller, N.J. and Paul, J. (2001) 'Adjustment strategies in the family business: implications for gender and management roles', *Journal of Family and Economic Issues*, **22**, 265-291.

Flash Eurobarometer (2007) *Observatory of European SMEs*, Luxembourg.

Foucault, M. (1991) 'Governmentality', in G. Burchell, C. Gordon and P. Miller (eds), *The Foucault Effect*, London: Harvester Wheatsheaf.

Getz, D. and Carlsen, J. (2000) 'Characteristics and goals of family and owner-operated businesses in the rural tourism and hospitality sectors', *Tourism Management*, **21**, 547-560.

Grängsjö, Y. and Gummersson, E. (2006) 'Hotels networks and social capital in destination marketing', *International Journal of Service Industry Management*, **17** (1), 58-75.

Greiner, L. E. (1972) 'Evolution and revolution as organizations grow', *Harvard Business Review*, July–August, 37-46.

Hall, C. M. and Jenkins, J. (2004) 'Tourism and public policy', in A. A. Lew, C. M. Hall and A. M. Williams (eds), *A Companion to Tourism*, Oxford: Blackwell, pp 525-40.

Hall, M. and Williams A.M. (2008) *Tourism and Innovation*, London: Routledge.

Hallin, C.A. and Marnburg, E. (2008) 'Knowledge management in the hospitality industry: a review of empirical research', *Tourism Management*, **29** (2), 366-381.

Halme, M. (2001) 'Learning for sustainable development in tourism networks', *Business Strategy and the Environment*, **10**, 100-114.

Hanks, S.M, Watson, C.J., Jansen, E. and Chandler, G. N. (1993) 'Tightening the life-cycle construction: a taxonomic study of growth stage configurations in high-technology organizations', *Entrepreneurship, Theory and Practice*, **18**, 5-29.

Heck, R., Hoy, F., Poutziouris, P.Z. and Steier, L. (2008) 'Emerging paths of family entrepreneurship research', *Journal of Small Business Management*, **46** (3), 317-330.

Hill, J., Nancarrow, C. and Wright, L.T. (2002) 'Lifecycles and crisis points in SMEs – a case study approach', *Marketing Intelligence and Planning*, **20** (6), 361-369.

Hjalager, A.M. (2002) 'Repairing innovation defectiveness in tourism', *Tourism Management*, **23** (5), 465-474.

Hjalager, A. M., Huijbens, E. H., Björk, P., Nordin, S., Flagestad, A. and Knútsson, Ö. (2008) *Innovation Systems in Nordic Tourism*, Oslo: Nordic Innovation System.

Hollick, M. and Braun, P. (2005) 'Lifestyle entrepreneurship: the unusual nature of the tourism entrepreneur', *Proceedings of the Second Annual AGSE International Entrepreneurship Research Exchange*, Melbourne, Australia: Swinburne Press.

Holt, R. and Macpherson, A. (2006) *Small Firms Learning and Growth*, London: AIM Research.

Keen, D. (2004) 'The interaction of community and small businesses in Rural New Zealand', in R. Thomas (ed.), *Small Firms in Tourism*, Oxford: Elsevier, pp. 139-152.

Koh, K. (2002) 'Understanding community tourism entrepreneurship: some evidence from Texas', in G. Richards and D. Hall (eds), *Tourism and Sustainable Community Development*, London: Routledge, pp. 205-218.

Komppula, R. (2004) 'Success and growth in rural tourism micro-business in Finland: financial or life-style objectives', in R. Thomas (ed.), *Small Firms in Tourism*, Oxford: Elsevier, pp. 115-138.

Kyriakidou, O. and Gore, J. (2005) 'Learning by example: benchmarking organizational culture in hospitality, tourism and leisure SME's', *Benchmarking: An International Journal*, **12** (3), 192-206.

Miller, N.J., Fitzgerald, M.A., Winter, M. and Paul, J. (1999) 'Exploring the overlap of family and business demands: household and family business manager's adjustment strategies', *Family Business Review*, **12** (3): 253-268.

Miller, N.J., Winter, M., Fitzgerald, M.A. and Paul, J. (2000) 'Family micro-enterprises: strategies for coping with overlapping family and business demands', *Journal of Developmental Entrepreneurship*, **5** (2), 87-113.

Morrison, A. (2003) 'SME management and leadership development: market reorientation', *Journal of Management Development*, **22** (9), 796-808.

Morrison, A. and Teixeira, R. (2004) 'Small business performance: a tourism sector focus', *Journal of Small Business and Enterprise Development*, **11** (2), 166-173.

Morrison, A., Rimmington, M. and Williams, C. (1999) *Entrepreneurship in the Hospitality, Tourism and Leisure Industries*, Oxford: Butterworth-Heineman.

Morrison, A., Lynch, P. and Johns, N. (2004) 'International tourism networks', *International Journal of Contemporary Hospitality Management*, **16**, 187-202.

Morrison, A., Carlsen, J. and Weber, P. (2008) 'Lifestyle orientated small tourism (LOST) firms and tourism destination development', CAUTHE Conference paper, Goldcoast, Australia: Griffiths University.

Moscado, G. (2007) 'Sustainable tourism innovation: challenging basic assumptions', *Tourism and Hospitality Research*, **8**, 4-13.

NESTA (2007) *Hidden Innovation: How Innovation Happens in Six 'Low Innovation' Sectors*. http://www.nesta.org.uk/assets/features/hidden_innovation

NESTA (2008) *Taking Services Seriously: How Policy can Stimulate the 'Hidden Innovation' in the UK's Services Economy*. http://www.nesta.org.uk/

Novelli, M., Schmitz, B. and Spencer, T. (2006) 'Networks, clusters and innovation in tourism: a UK experience', *Tourism Management*, **27** (6), 1141-1152.

OECD (2005) 'Global tourism growth: a challenge for SMEs', paper presented at conference on Global Tourism Growth at Gwanaju, Korea, 6-7 September.

Parker, C., Redmond, J. and Simpson, M. (2009) 'A review of interventions to encourage SMEs to make environmental improvements', *Environment and Planning C: Government and Policy*, 1-21. http://www.envplan.com

Paul, J.J., Winter, M., Miller, N.J. and Fitgerald, M.A. (2003) 'Cross-institutional norms for timing and sequencing and the use of adjustment strategies in family affiliated and family-owned businesses', *Marriage and Family Review*, **35** (1/2), 167-191.

Scott, M. and Bruce, R. (1987) 'Five stages of growth in small business', *Long Range Planning*, **20** (3), 45-52.

Shaw, G. (2004) 'Entrepreneurial cultures and small business enterprises in tourism', in M. Hall, A. Lew and A.M. Williams (eds), *A Companion to Tourism (Blackwell Companions Geography)*, Oxford: Blackwell pp. 122-34.

Shaw, G. and Williams, A.M. (1987) 'Firm formation and operating characteristics in the Cornish tourism industry', *Tourism Management*, **8**, 344-348.

Shaw, G. and Williams, A.M. (1997) 'The private sector: tourism entrepreneurship – a constraint or resource?', in G. Shaw and A.M. Williams (eds), *The Rise and Fall of British Coastal Resorts*, London: Mansell, 122-134.

Shaw, G. and Williams, A.M. (1998) 'Entrepreneurship, small business culture and tourism development', in D. Ioannides and K.D. Debbage (eds), *The Economic Geography of the Tourism Industry*, London: Routledge, 235-255.

Shaw, G. and Williams, A.M. (2004) 'From lifestyle consumption to lifestyle production: changing patterns of tourism entrepreneurship', in R. Thomas (ed.) *Small Firms in Tourism*, Oxford: Elsevier, pp. 99-114.

Shaw, G. and Williams, A.M. (2009) 'Knowledge transfer and management in tourism organizations: an emerging research agenda', *Tourism Management*, **30**, 325-335.

Stafford, K., Duncan, K.A., Danes, S.M. and Winter, M. (1999) 'A research model of sustainable family business', *Family Business Review*, **12** (3): 197-208.

Stallinbrass, C. (1980) 'Seaside resorts and the hotel accommodation industry', *Progress in Planning*, **13**, 103-174.

Storey, D.J. (1996) *Understanding the Small Business Sector*, London: Routledge.

Snepenger, D.J., Johnson, J.D and Rasker, R. (1995) 'Travel-stimulated entrepreneurial migration', *Journal of Travel Research*, **34**, 40-44.

Street, C.T. and Cameron, A.-F. (2007) 'External relationships and small business: a review of small business alliance and network research', *Journal of Small Business Management*, **45** (2), 239-266.

Thomas, R. (ed.) (1998) *The Management of Small Tourism and Hospitality Firms*, London: Cassell.

Thomas, R. (2000) 'Small firms in the tourism industry: some conceptual issues', *International Journal of Tourism Research*, **2** (6), 345-353.

Thomas, R. (ed.) (2004) *Small Firms in Tourism: International Perspectives*, Oxford: Elsevier.

Tiessen, J.H., Wright, R.W. and Turner, I. (2001) 'The model of e-commerce use by internationalizing SMEs', *Journal of International Management*, **7** (3), 211-233.

Tyebjee, T.T., Bruno, A.V. and McIntyre, S.M. (1983) 'Growing ventures can anticipate marketing stages', *Harvard Business Review*, January–February, 62-66.

Wanhill, S. (2004) 'Government assistance for tourism SMEs: from theory to practice', in R. Thomas (ed.), *Small Firms in Tourism*, Oxford: Elsevier, pp.53-70.

Weidenfeld, A., Williams, A. M. and Butler, R.W. (2010) 'Clustering and compatibility between tourism attractions', *International Journal of Tourism Research* **12**(1), 1-16.

Williams, A.M., Shaw, G. and Greenwood, J., (1989) 'From tourist to tourism entrepreneur, from conception to production', *Environment and Planning A*, **21**, 1639-1653.

Yang, J.-T. (2007) 'Knowledge sharing: investigating appropriate leadership roles and collaborative culture', *Tourism Management*, **28** (2), 530-543.

Yang, J.-T. and Wan, C.-S. (2004) 'Knowledge management in hospitality and tourism', *Annals of Tourism Research*, **31** (4), 1064-1065.

Zschiegner, A.-K. (2008) 'Innovation, knowledge transfer and destination development: a space for leadership', *Regional Studies Association*, Aalborg, Denmark: Working Group on Tourism, November.

8 Tourism distribution: a review and strategic research agenda

Douglas G. Pearce

Tourism distribution has attracted an increasing amount of attention from researchers over the past two decades. Factors accounting for this interest include a growing
awareness that distribution constitutes one of the few remaining areas of competitive advantage; the emergence of new markets, especially in Asia, and a need to understand how best to tap them; and major changes brought about by technological
advances, especially in IT. These same factors are likely to ensure ongoing interest
in the field in coming years while the impact of the global economic recession will
heighten the immediate drive for increased efficiencies in an activity that can account for a quarter or more of a tourism enterprise's operating costs. More generally, a focus on distribution offers tourism researchers a potentially powerful unifying
concept, one that bridges the demand/supply dichotomy of much tourism research
by bringing together markets and destinations, consumers, producers and intermediaries and stressing the linkages among these. This chapter traces the development
of tourism distribution research, outlines its major features, and then proposes a
strategic research agenda advocating a more integrated and focused approach that
might advance research in this field more systematically.

Development

While distribution research on manufacturing and other sectors dates back to the
1950s and 1960s (Ford, 2002), the first tourism-related studies began to appear
intermittently only in the 1970s and 1980s (Kaven, 1974; WTO, 1975; Wahab *et
al.*, 1976; Bitner and Booms, 1982). It is not until the 1990s that more sustained
attention was given to tourism distribution. Three books at the turn of the century
focused specifically on the topic and provide a good insight into the state-of-the-art
at that time. O'Connor (1999) discusses the application and impact of new information technologies including GDSs (global distribution systems) and emerging online mechanisms. The edited volume by Buhalis and Laws (2001) demonstrates the
breadth of interest in the field with chapters dedicated to theory and practice, channel structures, national and regional studies and technological transformations. Alcazar Martínez (2002), in the most significant non-English language contribution,

draws more directly on the broader distribution literature to discuss tourism distribution in more systematic terms before considering issues related to mass tourism in a European context.

As the literature has developed there has been no hotly-contested search for a common definition which often engages researchers in newly emerging fields. Distribution has been variously portrayed as that part of the marketing mix that 'makes the product available' to consumers (Wahab *et al.*, 1976: 96), as the bridge between supply and demand (Alcazar Martínez, 2002). Others draw on Stern and El-Ansary's (1992: 1-2) statement that marketing channels are:

> *sets of interdependent organizations involved in the process of making a product or service available for use or consumption – not only do marketing channels satisfy demand by supplying goods and services at the right place, quantity, quality and price, but they also stimulate demand...Therefore, the channels should be viewed as an orchestrated network that creates value for the user through the generation of form, possession, time and place utilities.*

Approaches

In a recent review incorporating a more detailed list of references than can be included here, Pearce (2009a) identified five major approaches which capture the main thrust of extant research efforts.

1. A structural approach

The most common approach has been to focus on the structure of distribution channels, either of channels linking international markets and destinations (especially in Europe and Asia) or those relating to specific sectors (notably hotels and airlines). A particular focus has been on the ways in which changes in IT have impacted on traditional structures. These structural studies have generally been fairly descriptive accounts and often involve a tier-by-tier discussion of direct and indirect channels in terms of such attributes as channel depth, intermediary characteristics, the degree of integration and amount of channel specialization. Pearce *et al.* (2007) propose a more comprehensive analytical framework, based on comparative research, which links these channel attributes with market and destination characteristics and intervening distance. Scope also exists to go beyond a tier-by-tier analysis and develop a more extensive nodal network approach which emphasizes all actors in the network rather than pair-wise layers of players (Pearce, 2009b).

2. A behavioural approach

Other studies examine the factors that influence the behaviour of the different channel members and the relationships between them, a well-established theme in the broader distribution literature (Frazier, 1999). Research focusing on intermediaries and suppliers commonly takes a buyer–seller perspective, adopting one of two basic models – the adversarial or the cooperative – to investigate respectively constructs such as conflict, control and power or satisfaction, success and trust. Some research on tourists has been set squarely in the context of channel-choice behaviour (Williams and Dossa, 1998; Pearce and Schott, 2005) but many relevant studies are found in related literatures, particularly that on information search and travel planning behaviour, where the explicit links to distribution are only now being made.

3. A functional approach

Although functions are seen in the broader distribution literature as 'the basic building blocks of any distribution channel' (Frazier, 1999: 235) only a limited amount of work has been done with regard to the functional aspects of tourism distribution, mainly with regard to the role of intermediaries. The functions of tourism distribution have been presented in terms of information provision and facilitating the search process of buyers and sellers, sorting, bundling components into travel packages, extending points of sale and fostering the advance purchase of products, and minimizing costs by making transactions routine. Pearce (2008) synthesizes many of these elements in a needs–functions model which emphasizes tourist needs, expressed with regard to time, place, form and possession utilities and the functions required to meet those needs: information provision, sorting, bundling, booking and purchase. The model recognizes the spatial and temporal complexity of tourism distribution by acknowledging needs and functions occur in the market ahead of travel, at the destination or en route between the two.

4. An evaluative approach

As the range of channels available to tourism suppliers has increased and the significance of distribution costs has been underlined, practitioners and researchers have recognized the need to evaluate channel performance, particularly where multi-channel research is concerned (O'Connor and Frew, 2004; Green, 2005; Pearce and Taniguchi, 2008). Evaluative research is technically challenging, relatively few studies have yet been done but fruitful research links are now being made between distribution and revenue management (Vinod, 2009a).

5. A strategic approach

Strategic research has largely centred on examining strategic issues and implications facing larger tourism enterprises, particularly the impact of new technologies (O'Connor, 1999; Alamdari and Mason, 2006). There has been little research on the way in which these strategies have been or might be developed (Dale, 2003; Green, 2005; Pearce, 2009c).

Characteristics

The sense of structure that reviewing the major approaches in this way brings to the literature should not be overstated. Research on tourism distribution remains fragmented and considerable scope exists to strengthen methodological approaches, develop underlying concepts and enhance the practical application of results. One way forward is to identify and address the recurring features which run across these approaches.

Variable coverage

Whatever the theme, coverage of the tourism sector has been very variable. Research has concentrated on the hotel and airline industries with limited attention to other forms of accommodation and modes of transport. Few studies have been carried out on attractions (Williams and Dossa, 1998; Yamamoto and Gill, 2002; Schott, 2007). Much of the initial work has been and continues to be associated with mass, packaged tourism, especially in Europe (Chaintron, 1995) and out of Asia. Distribution in developing markets and destinations remains neglected (Sharda and Pearce, 2006). However, markets and destinations in Asia, Africa and Latin America offer researchers invaluable opportunities to study processes as they evolve rather than after the basic structures have been well established, as was the case in Europe. The distribution of independent travel has only recently attracted interest and domestic travel remains the poor cousin of international tourism. Much work is now being done on e-distribution; some of this considers links with other channels but often information technology is dealt with in isolation in an essentially self-contained literature on e-commerce (O'Connor and Murphy, 2004; Buhalis and Law, 2008). Moreover, within that, O'Connor and Murphy (2004: 481) observe 'researchers are currently focusing on a limited... range of issues and ignoring important areas'.

While some commonalities do exist within and across sectors, especially with regard to the distribution of packaged travel, sector and segment differences are found (Pearce, 2008). The work on independent travellers and on sectors other than hotels and airlines emphasizes a greater diversity of structures, issues and strategies beyond those associated with the more conventional supplier–wholesaler–travel agent–customer system or a basic direct/indirect – online/offline matrix classification of channels. Independent travellers, for example, favour choice, flexibility and spontaneity, arrange the majority of their travel independently of market-based intermediaries and make a series of bookings and purchases, often from the suppliers at the destination or en route to it (Pearce and Schott, 2005). Hotel chains and airlines make up some of the larger enterprises and have often been quicker to adopt new technologies than smaller accommodation units or surface transport providers who may still rely heavily on more informal channels and 'at destination' distribution, or use intermediaries such as information offices or other providers. This diversity highlights the need to broaden the scope of the research being done and underlines the value of undertaking more comparative studies.

Limited linkages

Fragmentation is also evident in the limited linkages that have been made on all levels: within approaches, across approaches, and to other literatures and functions. For instance, although the structural studies have clearly demonstrated the multi-tiered nature of many distribution systems and the role of indirect distribution, most of the behavioural studies still concentrate on relationships between sets of channel members, such as hotels and tour operators, wholesalers and inbound operators or travel agencies and customers. This is understandable given the resources needed to investigate any one set of relationships but it is also limiting if it is recognized that any pair of relationships may be influenced by other channel members: inbound operators may play an intermediate role between suppliers and wholesalers; customers of a travel agent may have their choices restricted by the agent's arrangements with a wholesaler. One way forward here is to adopt a 'whole systems' approach which would enable an integrated analysis of the behaviour of all channel members (Pearce, 2008). Likewise, more links are needed across the approaches, for example, by investigating the extent to which certain channel structures perform better than others or by assessing the way in which the behaviour of different channel members influences the setting or achievement of strategic objectives.

Relatively few connections are also being made between distribution research on tourism and that on other sectors. Surprisingly few tourism researchers draw on the wider distribution literature and, conversely, little or no reference to tourism is found in the latter (Frazier, 1999; Ford, 2002). While some of this lack of interaction might be attributed to differences between distributing manufactured products (until recently the main focus of distribution studies) and tourism products and services, tourism researchers have been slow to capitalise on the well developed body of methods and theories found elsewhere and their approaches have arguably been less robust and sophisticated as a result. The quantitative proposition testing approach which typifies much distribution research, for example, has few parallels in the tourism sector (Campo and Yagüe, 2007). Likewise, much tourism distribution research is not under-pinned by a strong theoretical basis as only occasionally is reference made to mainstream disciplinary writers such as Stern and El-Ansary (1992) in applying an economics transactions perspective (Ujma, 2001; Wynne *et al.*, 2001; Alcazar Martínez, 2002) or employing the concept of production systems (Yamamoto and Gill, 2002). More recent work on distribution in the service sector also offers useful theoretical insights for tourism (Schoenbachler and Gordon, 2002).

This writer took some time to move beyond the tourism literature to mainstream distribution material but once there found immense value in referring to related issues and contextualizing his work more widely. Better understanding of the distribution of international tourism in India was obtained by reviewing the literature on distribution in emerging markets (Sharda and Pearce, 2006), the development of a tourism distribution strategy was shaped by reference to the more established field of distribution strategy formulation (Pearce 2009c) and the elaboration of the needs–functions model benefited from recourse to the basic principles of distribution

(Pearce, 2008). This should not be a one-way exchange for the results of tourism research might also profitably be fed back into the general literature. Multi-channel distribution, for example, is common in tourism (Kang *et al.*, 2007), but has only recently attracted attention in other sectors (Frazier, 1999).

Despite distribution being acknowledged as one of the four 'Ps' (place), research in this field also remains largely divorced from other aspects of tourism marketing with relatively few explicit links being made to promotion, pricing and products (Woodward, 2000; Miller, 2004; Tso and Law, 2004; Campo and Yagüe, 2007; Vinod, 2009b; Zaoui and Rao, 2009). These elements are all interrelated and strengthening these links is vital if distribution research is to contribute fully to the marketing of tourism products. An analysis of supplier selection in the New Zealand inbound tourism industry found intermediaries put as much or more emphasis on the product as on supplier attributes and questions of pricing (Pearce, 2007). Again, these linkages are not uni-directional; taking a distribution channels perspective proved a useful framework for examining the perceptions and images of Samoa held by various groups of New Zealanders (tourists, travel agents, wholesalers, airline representatives) (Pearce, 2002).

The lack of a clear sense of direction

The fragmentation outlined in the preceding sections is typical of an emerging field where much of the research is being undertaken by researchers from diverse backgrounds who venture into the area, write an article or two and then move on. Few researchers have yet to make sustained contributions as Buhalis (1998; 2004; Buhalis and Law, 2008) and O'Connor (1999; O'Connor and Frew, 2004; O'Connor and Murphy, 2004) have done with information technology and e-distribution. The integrated five-year project on distribution channels for New Zealand tourism has enabled the synthesis of related studies into the needs–functions model (Pearce, 2008) and the elaboration of a tourism distribution strategy process (Pearce, 2009c) but such a concerted approach is uncommon. Despite a growing number of studies there is no real cumulative body of work based on a clear sense of direction, well-defined research problems and goals, common approaches and unifying theory. There has been no central question or set of questions driving and guiding this research and many papers have been framed narrowly in terms of distribution channels. More direction might be found by focusing on the process of tourism distribution per se. In this way sharper research designs might be formulated in terms of such questions as what are the goals of tourism distribution, how might these goals be reached more effectively, what are the key factors we need to understand better about bridging supply and demand, how can distribution be improved to meet changing consumer preferences, adapt to a new economic climate or respond to technological advances? This approach might be developed by advancing and pursuing a research agenda that systematically draws on the steps of a strategy design process for tourism (Figure 8.1). It is an approach that provides both structure and focus and a means to integrate future research in this field, particularly applied research.

A strategic research agenda

Figure 8.1 depicts a strategy design process based on a review of the wider literature on distribution strategies and channel design together with the key findings resulting from the New Zealand project (Pearce, 2009c). The process outlined in Figure 8.1 stresses the need to be customer-focused, to take account of the distribution needs of tourists as well as the business's own requirements. It involves taking a series of basic steps, each of which requires certain information to provide a basis for decision-making. While existing research provides a solid foundation in some areas, much more specific data are needed in many cases. These steps can thus be used to develop relevant questions and frame a research agenda. Issues arising at each stage will now be outlined and ways of tackling these will be suggested and illustrated. It should be noted, however, that Figure 8.1 has been developed to assist suppliers to formulate a distribution strategy. The research agenda outlined reflects this emphasis but also acknowledges the role of other channel members. A similar stepwise approach could be taken to broaden the research agenda and take account more fully of the distribution needs of wholesalers, travel agents, inbound operators and other intermediaries as well as those of such channel members as national and regional tourism organizations.

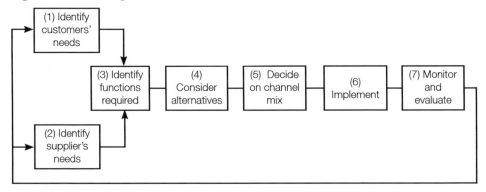

Figure 8.1: A distribution strategy design process for tourism.
Source: Pearce (2009c) reproduced with permission

1. Identify customer needs and selection preferences

To travel, tourists need to acquire information, have a range of products and services available, an assortment of these from which to choose; and mechanisms to book and pay. As the needs–functions model demonstrates, these needs may be fulfilled in different ways at various times and places (Pearce, 2008). Tourist needs can also be expressed in terms of such factors as ease, flexibility and trust. Further research into understanding distribution from the customer's perspective will help providers and intermediaries cater to them more effectively as technologies and consumer preferences evolve. In particular, scope exists to explore how needs and behaviour vary from one segment to another, for example: inbound/outbound/domestic; leisure/business/VFR; independent/packaged/customized... Framing studies of tourist behaviour in this way may also help bridge the gap to much of the existing travel decision-making literature which has only recently started to converge with distribution studies.

2. Identify suppliers' distribution needs

Suppliers' needs will vary by sector and business but are generally influenced by three broad sets of interrelated factors: market coverage, product characteristics and business characteristics. Recent studies have tackled diverse aspects of these issues and indicate directions future research might take. Kang *et al.* (2007), for example, review issues of multi-channel distribution strategies and address questions of hotel profitability and survivability using perceptual maps. Cho (2005) provides a very useful product/service process matrix for e-commerce by which the distribution requirements of particular products can be identified in terms of the degree of standardization and product volume, online substitution and the need for online/offline interaction and customization.

3. Identify the functions to be performed to meet the distribution needs of the customers and suppliers

As the basic building blocks of distribution, functions must be a central concern of any distribution strategy if the needs of both customers and suppliers are to be met. Considerable work has already been done on information search and provision, and to a lesser extent booking and purchase. Sorting and bundling, two other key functions, are under-researched yet play a crucial role in determining customer choice and the ease with which travel arrangements can be made and a supplier's product accessed. Questions here include who does the sorting and bundling and how are they done, what are the criteria for selection, and what are the consequences of the assortment for consumers and suppliers? Moreover, the ways in which all these and other functions are shared in any distribution system warrants careful analysis. Figure 8.2 provides a schematic representation of the multiple functions involved in the distribution of an all-inclusive circuit package tour to international tourists. Here bundling is central to the whole process. Figure 8.2 also depicts the efficiencies that distribution channels bring as demand is progressively concentrated throughout the market and then dispersed at the destination while product is progressively concentrated and made available for sale to individual consumers. Through the incorporation of functions, structural diagrams such as this provide greater understanding and more refined analytical frameworks than those limited to unlabelled unidirectional arrows.

4. Consider the alternative ways by which these functions might be performed

The different functions may be performed in different ways, directly or indirectly, offline or online, with various options available in each of these categories. Considering distribution in the light of functions rather than channels opens up a greater range of choice and draws attention to determining how, when and where which functions might be performed to suit particular markets, sectors and travel products. Attention has been directed at the way in which online functions have evolved from information provision, through booking and purchase transactions to a limited amount of bundling and dynamic packaging (Buhalis and Law, 2008; Zaoui and Rao, 2009). How online systems evolve to handle these latter functions in coming years will be an ongoing focus of enquiry but the diverse forms of offline delivery should not be neglected. Varying revenue and cost structures are associated with different functions and with how they are carried out (Ng, 2007; Pearce and Taniguchi, 2008; Vinod, 2009b); these are key issues which again warrant further investigation.

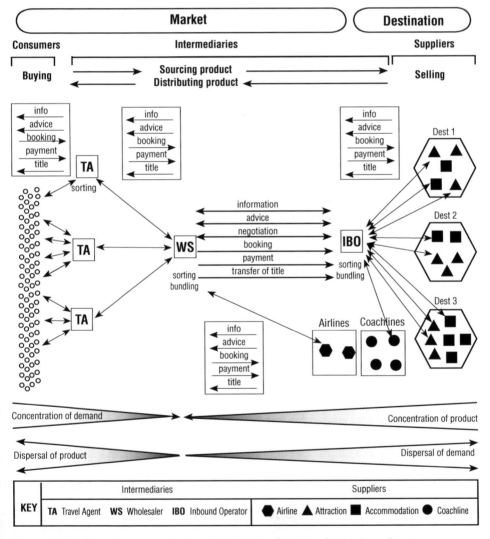

Figure 8.2: Schematic representation of distribution functions for packaged tours. Source: Pearce (2008) reproduced with permission

5. Decide on the distribution mix

Given the range of channels now available and the need of many suppliers to adopt a multi-channel strategy to satisfy theirs and their customers' needs, measuring and deciding on the right distribution mix can be very challenging. Even quantifying existing channel mixes is rarely done (Bote Gómez and Álvarez Cuervo, 2001). Hence, considerable scope exists for decision-support research to assist with three levels of decision-making: determining channel mix, channel width and channel partner selection. In particular, invaluable contributions could be made from the fields of revenue management and operations research where published work on tourism distribution has only recently started to appear (Vinod, 2009a). Huang *et al.* (2009) use the analytic hierarchy process to examine which distribution mix can maximize the revenues of wholesaler travel agencies. Complementary research is also required dealing with the needs of customers; how they are best served by different distribution mixes should be taken into account and researched further (Brunger and Perelli, 2009).

6. Implementation (and management)

Studies on the content of distribution strategies need to be complemented by research into how such strategies are designed and what factors lead to their successful implementation. This includes research into the preparedness of suppliers to enter new markets or adopt new distribution channels (Dabas and Manaktola, 2007). The more established work on buyer–seller relationships might also be cast in this light and extended further, for example by taking a network approach (Dale, 2003; Pearce, 2009b). The ongoing management of distribution and associated relationships constitutes a further avenue for research. In their extensive review in the broader context of supply chain management, Zhang *et al.* (2009) identify the following key management issues: demand, two-party-relationships, supply, inventory, tourism supply chain (TSC) coordination and information technology. They also suggest opportunities for future investigation including TSC planning and forecasting, coordination, dynamics and design (see Chapter 9).

7. Monitor and evaluate

Regular monitoring and evaluation is needed to ensure distribution strategies are meeting customers' needs and business requirements – the feedback loop in Figure 8.1. Consideration of strategies in terms of the delivery of particular functions or performance of different channels will assist decisions about which of these are to be expanded, reduced, added, abandoned or improved. Research needs to move beyond describing channel structures to evaluating their performance. A similar range of approaches to those discussed under Steps 4 and 5 will be useful here. Longitudinal studies are also needed to track the impact of changes in distribution strategies over time. In addition, attention must be directed at environmental factors to identify emerging opportunities or threats.

Conclusions

As the bridge between supply and demand, issues of tourism distribution will remain important or even become more significant as competition increases. While a range of interesting studies are being undertaken, research to date has been very fragmented and more concerted effort is needed to address the issues raised. The strategic research agenda outlined has been offered as one way to provide a greater sense of direction and build a more focused and cumulative body of knowledge in this field. At the same time, as the review of recurring themes has revealed, research on tourism distribution needs to be integrated more closely with the wider literature on distribution and links with other aspects of marketing need strengthening. If a more cohesive approach to tourism distribution can be developed then research in this field can also realize its potential to act as a unifying focus for tourism studies more generally given the diversity of channel members involved and the bridging role that distribution plays.

References

Alcázar Martínez, B. del (2002) *Los Canales de Distribución en el Sector Turístico*, Madrid: ESIC Editorial.

Alamdari, F. and Mason, K. (2006) 'The future of airline distribution', *Journal of Transport Management*, **12**, 122-134.

Bitner, M.J. and Booms, B.H. (1982) 'Trends in travel and tourism marketing: the changing structure of distribution channels', *Journal of Travel Research*, **20** (4), 39-44.

Bote Gómez, V. and Álvarez Cuervo R. (2001) 'Promoción y Comercialización del Turismo Cultural de la Ciudad de Sevilla: Diagnóstico y Orientaciones Estratégicas', in *Documentos de Trabajo Serie A No 20018*, Escuela Universitaria de Turismo, Universidad de Alcalá.

Brunger, W.G. and Perelli, S. (2009) 'The impact of the internet on airline fares: customer perspectives on the transition', *Journal of Pricing and Revenue Management*, **8** (2/3), 187-199.

Buhalis, D. (1998) 'Strategic use of information technologies in the tourism industry', *Tourism Management*, **19** (5), 409-421.

Buhalis, D. (2004) 'eAirlines: strategic and tactical use of ICTs in the airline industry', *Information and Management*, **41** (7), 805-825.

Buhalis, D. and Laws, E. (2001) *Tourism Distribution Channels: Practices, Issues and Transformations*, London: Continuum.

Buhalis, D. and Law, R. (2008) 'Progress in information technology and tourism management: 20 years on and 10 years after the internet – the state of eTourism research', *Tourism Management*, **29** (4), 609-623.

Campo, S. and Yagüe, Y.M. (2007) 'The formation of tourist's loyalty to the tourism distribution channel: how does it affect price discounts?', *International Journal of Tourism Research*, **9** (6), 453-464.

Chaintron, B. (1995). 'Industrie touristique: le choc des modèles anglais et français,' *Cahier Espaces*, **44**, 31-36.

Cho, S-E. (2005) 'Developing new frameworks for operations strategy and service system design in electronic service', *International Journal of Service Industry Management*, **16** (3/4), 294-314.

Dabas, S. and Manaktola, K. (2007) 'Managing reservations through online distribution channels', *International Journal of Contemporary Hospitality Management*, **19** (5), 388-396.

Dale, C. (2003) 'The competitive networks of tourism e-mediaries: new strategies, new advantages', *Journal of Vacation Marketing*, **9** (2), 109-118.

Ford, D. (2002) 'Distribution, internationalisation and networks. Solving old problems, learning new things and forgetting most of them', *International Marketing Review*, **19** (3), 225-235.

Frazier, G.L. (1999) 'Organizing and managing channels of distribution', *Journal of the Academy of Marketing Science*, **27** (2), 226-240.

Green, C.E. (2005) *De-Mystifying Distribution: Building a Distribution Strategy one Channel at a Time*, McLean, VA: HSMAI Foundation.

Huang, L., Chen, K.-H. and Wu, Y.-W. (2009) 'What kind of marketing distribution mix can maximize revenues: the wholesaler travel agencies' perspective?', *Tourism Management*, **30** (5), 733-739.

Kaven, W.H. (1974) 'Distribution channels of the hotel industry', *Cornell Hotel and Restaurant Administration Quarterly*, **14**, 21-23.

Kang, B., Brewer, K.P. and Baloglu, S. (2007) 'Profitability and survivability of hotel distribution channels: an industry perspective', *Journal of Travel and Tourism Marketing*, **22** (1), 37-50.

Miller, B. (2004) 'Building e-loyalty of lodging brands: avoiding brand erosion', *Journal of Travel and Tourism Marketing*, **17** (2/3), 133-142.

Ng, I.C.L. (2007) 'Establishing a service channel: a transaction cost analysis of a channel contract between a cruise line and a tour operator', *Journal of Services Marketing*, **21** (1), 4-14.

O'Connor, P. (1999) *Electronic Information Distribution in Tourism and Hospitality*, Wallingford: CABI Publishing.

O'Connor, P. and Frew, A.J. (2004) 'An evaluation methodology for hotel electronic channels of distribution', *Hospitality Management*, **23** (2), 179-199.

O'Connor, P. and Murphy, J. (2004) 'Research on information technology in the hospitality industry', *Hospitality Management*, **23** (5), 473-484.

Pearce, D.G. (2002) 'New Zealand holiday travel to Samoa: a distribution channels approach', *Journal of Travel Research*, **l41** (2), 197-205.

Pearce, D.G. (2007) 'Supplier selection in the New Zealand inbound tourism industry', *Journal of Travel and Tourism Marketing*, **23** (1), 57-69.

Pearce, D.G. (2008), 'A needs–functions model of tourism distribution', *Annals of Tourism Research*, **35** (1), 148-168.

Pearce, D.G. (2009a). 'Tourism distribution: from structure to strategy', in J. Atel-jevic and S. Page (eds), *Progress in Tourism and Entrepreneurship: Global Perspective*, Oxford: Elsevier, pp. 313-334.

Pearce, D.G. (2009b) 'Beyond tiers: a network approach to tourism distribution', *Tourism Analysis*, **13** (5/6), 517-530.

Pearce, D. G. (2009c) 'Channel design for effective tourism distribution strategies', *Journal of Travel and Tourism Marketing*, **26** (5/6), 507-521.

Pearce, D.G. and Schott, C., (2005) 'Tourism distribution channels: the visitors' perspective', *Journal of Travel Research*, **44** (1), 50-63.

Pearce, D.G., Tan, R. and Schott, C., (2007) 'Distribution channels in international markets: a comparative analysis of the distribution of New Zealand tourism in Australia, Great Britain and the USA', *Current Issues in Tourism*, **10** (1), 33-60.

Pearce, D.G. and Taniguchi, M. (2008) 'Channel performance in multi-channel tourism distribution systems', *Journal of Travel Research*, **46**, 256-267.

Schoenbachler, D. D. and Gordon, G. L. (2002), 'Multi-channel shopping: understanding what drives channel choice', *Journal of Consumer Marketing*, **19** (1), 42–53.

Schott, C. (2007) 'Selling adventure tourism: a distribution channels perspective', *International Journal of Tourism Research*, **9** (4), 257-274.

Sharda, S. and Pearce, D.G. (2006) 'Tourism distribution in emerging markets: the case of Indian travel to New Zealand', *Asia Pacific Journal of Tourism Research*, **11** (4), 339-353.

Stern, L.W. and El-Ansary, A.I. (1992) *Marketing Channels*, 4th edn, Englewood Cliffs, NJ: Prentice Hall.

Tso, A. and Law, R. (2004) 'Analysing the online pricing practices of hotels in Hong Kong', *Hospitality Management*, **24** (2), 301-307.

Ujma, D. (2001) 'Distribution channels for tourism: theory and issues', in D. Buhalis and E. Laws (eds), *Tourism Distribution Channels: Practices, Issues and Transformations*, London: Continuum, pp. 33-72.

Vinod, B. (ed.) (2009a) 'Special Issue: distribution and revenue management', *Journal of Pricing and Revenue Management*, **8** (2/3).

Vinod, B. (2009b) 'Distribution and revenue management', *Journal of Pricing and Revenue Management*, **8** (2/3), 117-133.

Wahab, S., Crampon, L.J. and Rothfield, L.M. (1976) *Tourism Marketing*, London: Tourism International Press.

Williams, P.W. and Dossa, K.B. (1998) 'Ski channel users: a discriminating perspective', *Journal of Travel and Tourism Marketing*, 7 (2), 1-29.

Woodward, T. (2000) 'Using brand awareness and brand image in tourism channels of distribution', *Journal of Vacation Marketing*, **6** (2), 119-130.

WTO (1975) *Distribution Channels*, Madrid: World Tourism Organization.

Wynne, C., Berthon, P., Pitt, L., Ewing, M. and Napoli, J. (2001) 'The impact of the internet on the distribution value chain: the case of the South African tourism industry', *International Marketing Review*, **18** (4), 420-431.

Yamamoto, D. and Gill, A. (2002) 'Issues of globalisation and reflexivity in the Japanese tourism production system: the case of Whistler, British Columbia', *Professional Geographer*, **54** (1), 83-93.

Zaoui, F. and Rao, B.J. (2009) 'Dynamic pricing of opaque airline tickets', *Journal of Pricing and Revenue Management*, **8** (2/3), 148-154.

Zhang, X., Song, H. and Huang, G.Q. (2009) 'Tourism supply chain management', *Tourism Management*, **30** (3), 345-358.

9 Tourism supply chain forecasting: a collaborative approach

Haiyan Song, Stephen F. Witt and Xinyan Zhang

Introduction

Since demand plays a key role in determining the profitability of tourism businesses, estimates of the future demand for tourism constitute a very important element in all tourism planning activities. As a result, tourism demand forecasting has attracted much attention in both the academic literature and from tourism practitioners (Song and Turner, 2006). Tourism products are often configured from a variety of service providers such as accommodation, transportation and attractions, which form tourism supply chains (TSCs). The fragmented nature of the tourism industry implies that individual firms often rely on cooperating with other private or public organizations, which creates a need for collaboration in tourism demand forecasting.

Unlike traditional forecasting methods, collaborative forecasting is an approach that breaks down the units of analysis and involves reliance on supply chain partners to provide specific and timely information. It is based on cooperation and information sharing between the links in the chain. Accordingly, collaborative forecasting for a TSC requires a variety of people from various echelons of the chain to work together.

This chapter first examines the current situation of tourism demand forecasting and then discusses the potential benefits as well as challenges of collaborative forecasting for the tourism industry. After that, practical solutions for setting up collaborative forecasting in tourism supply chains are put forward. The forecasting methodology and the design of a collaborative TSC forecasting system are described in detail. In order to facilitate the collaborative forecasting process and information sharing, the system is designed as a web-based system and can be established using ASP. NET technology. It should be noted that the discussion in this chapter only relates to a TSC that deals exclusively with package holidays and does not consider supply chains for independent travel.

Tourism demand forecasting: current status

The past two decades have witnessed great advances in tourism demand forecasting research in terms of the diversity of research focus, depth of theoretical foundation, and advances in forecasting methods. Numerous researchers have been involved in the area of tourism demand forecasting and a wide variety of techniques has been used. Many advanced quantitative tourism demand forecasting models have been developed in the academic literature. This section aims to provide a brief overview of the recent developments in tourism demand forecasting approaches.

Tourism demand forecasts are traditionally generated by either quantitative or qualitative approaches. According to a comprehensive review by Li *et al.* (2005), 420 studies on the topic of tourism demand forecasting were published during the period 1960–2002. Most attention was directed at the development of advanced statistical forecasting methods including both time-series and econometric approaches. Time-series methods use past patterns in data to extrapolate future values and whilst time-series approaches are useful tools for tourism demand forecasting, a major limitation of these methods is that they cannot be used for policy evaluation purposes. By contrast, econometric models, which estimate the quantitative relationship between tourism demand and its determinants, can be used for policy evaluation. The large body of literature that has been published on tourism demand forecasting using modern econometric techniques is reviewed by Li *et al.* (2005).

In a more recent survey, Song and Li (2008) review 121 studies on tourism demand modelling and forecasting published since 2000. In this review, the latest developments in quantitative forecasting approaches are summarized in three categories: time-series models; the econometric approach; and other emerging artificial intelligence (AI) methods such as artificial neural networks, rough set approaches, fuzzy time-series methods, genetic algorithms, and support vector machines. The main advantages of AI techniques is that they do not require any preliminary or additional information about data such as distribution or probability, but their limitations include lack of a theoretical underpinning and being unable to interpret tourism demand from the economic perspective.

Collaborative supply chain forecasting, an approach facilitated by supply chain management (SCM) concepts, has become popular in the non-tourism-related SCM literature (Småros, 2003; Li, 2007). The value of collaborative forecasting lies in the broad exchange of information to improve forecasting accuracy when supply chain members collaborate through joint knowledge of sales promotions, pricing strategies, marketing, and production information. Unlike traditional forecasting, collaborative forecasting is an approach that breaks down the 'island of analysis' and involves supply chain partners in providing specific and timely information (Helms *et al.*, 2000). It is based on cooperation and the sharing of information between the links in the chain. However, recent research has mainly focused on conceptual research (Mentzer and Kahn, 1997; Fosnaught, 1999; Helms *et al.*, 2000; Wilson, 2001; Småros, 2003) with scant attention being paid to empirically testing the conceptual frameworks developed. Little academic research can be found on how forecasting collaboration should be set up in practice, what methods there are and how suitable different alternatives are in different situations (Småros, 2003). In addition, although there is a wide body of literature concerning collaborative forecasting within supply chains for physical goods, it has not yet been considered in the tourism literature with the exception of the study by Song *et al.* (2008).

Collaborative tourism supply chain forecasting

The lack of attention paid to collaborative forecasting in the tourism literature is partly due to the lag of development and employment of supply chain management (SCM) strategies in the tourism industry. This section first focuses on the definition of tourism supply chains based on a brief introduction to the concept of SCM, and then discusses the benefits and challenges of collaborative tourism supply chain forecasting.

Supply chain management

Fierce global competition in the 21st century has resulted in a focus on supply chains rather than individual companies. From the macro perspective, a supply chain is a network of enterprises that are engaged in different functions, ranging from the supply of raw materials through the production and delivery of end-products to target customers. From the micro perspective of a firm, a supply chain is a network of nodes that perform functions such as the procurement of raw materials, fabrication of parts, assembly and subassembly of components, final assembly of end products, and delivery of finished products to regional distribution centres/customers. A supply chain is characterized by a forward flow of goods and a backward flow of information.

A supply chain is a complex system. It normally comprises seven main business processes: customer relationship management, customer service management, demand management, order fulfilment, manufacturing flow management, procurement, product development, and commercialization (Cooper *et al.*, 1997). Since Houlihan (1985) first coined the term 'supply chain management', the concept has been used extensively in the manufacture of products to improve efficiency across the value chain, including the efficiency of logistics and planning activities and material and information control, both internally, within companies, and externally, between companies (Christopher, 1992; Cooper *et al.*, 1997; Fisher, 1997). However, despite the popularity of the concept both in academia and practice, there is no commonly accepted definition of SCM. The most popular definition is that given by Simchi-Levi *et al.* (2000: 1), who define it as:

a set of approaches utilized to efficiently integrate suppliers, manufacturers, warehouses, and stores, so that merchandise is produced and distributed at the right quantities, to the right locations, and in the right time, in order to minimize system-wide costs while satisfying service level requirements.

The key SCM concerns are recognition of the interdependency of members in the supply chain and the generation of strategies that support the efficient integration of the various links. In other words, SCM takes a systems approach, viewing the supply chain as a whole (Simchi-Levi *et al.*, 2000) and emphasizing the need for the integration of the various links of the chain (Cooper *et al.*, 1997; Lambert *et al.*, 1998).

Tourism supply chain

Much of the SCM literature focuses on the manufacturing industry, with little attention paid to the service sector. From the perspective of the tourism industry, this lack of research attention is somewhat surprising. As early as 1975, the World Tourism Organization (WTO, which was changed to UNWTO in December 2005) published a report on distribution channels in the tourism industry (WTO, 1975). A distribution channel is essentially one type of supply chain, and can be narrowly defined as a supply chain that involves mainly the distribution and marketing activities in the chain (see Chapter 8).

The attention paid by the academic community and industrial sectors to tourism supply chains (TSCs) has not kept pace with the rapid development of the tourism industry in recent decades. Nevertheless, several studies have appeared on these supply chains, including those of the WTO (1994), Sinclair and Stabler (1997), Buhalis and Laws (2001), and Page (2003). Sinclair and Stabler (1997) emphasize the importance of the supply side of the tourism industry. *Tourism Distribution Channels: Practices, Issues and Transformations*, a key text edited by Buhalis and Laws (2001), consists of 23 chapters written by various contributors, and many of these chapters are related to distribution networks in the tourism industry. Page (2003) points out that the provision of tourism products and services involves a wide range of interrelated tourism suppliers, and plots a structure of a tourism supply chain. Descriptive studies of tourism supply chains include those of Scavarda *et al.* (2001), Tapper and Font (2004), Alford (2005), and Yilmaz and Bititci (2006). Other notable studies include Yang *et al.* (2008, 2009).

Although studies of TSCs are limited, some authors have alluded to or touched on the concept or its equivalents, such as tourism value or tourism industry chains. Kaukal *et al.* (2000) note that a typical tourism value chain consists of four components, the tourism supplier, tour operator, travel agent and customer, which are in a single linked chain. Alford (2005) gives a visual presentation of a tourism supply chain produced by the Business and Cost Analysis Working Group to analyse pressure points at which costs can be stripped out. Yilmaz and Bititci (2006) develop a tourism value chain model to manage the tourism product as an end-to-end seamless entity. In their report, Tapper and Font (2004) define a TSC as a chain that 'comprises the suppliers of all the goods and services that go into the delivery of tourism products to consumers'. That is, every supply chain varies according to the type of products supplied. Thus, identifying the features of the tourism industry and its products is of great importance in describing a TSC. For instance, tourism products are normally based in a specific territory and provided to tourists from a specific source market, so they often vary according to destination and source market. Based on the existing definitions of TSCs in the literature and taking into consideration the characteristics of the tourism industry, Zhang *et al.* (2009) advance the definition of a TSC as:

> *a network of tourism organizations engaged in different activities ranging from the supply of different components of tourism products/services such as flights and accommodation to the distribution and marketing of the final tourism product at a specific tourism destination, and involves a wide range of participants in both the private and public sectors.*

A general TSC network within a destination is shown in Figure 9.1. TSC members can be grouped into different layers or echelons according to their roles played in the supply chain. The downstream end includes tourists from the target market. Travel agents are the retail branches of tourism products dealing with tourists and tour operators. Travel agents and tour operators can be the same or separate business entities. Tour operators have enormous influence over all the activities involved in the TSC. They buy individual travel services (such as transport and accommodation) from their suppliers (such as carriers and hotels) and assemble them into holiday packages, which are sold to the public directly or through travel agents (Ujma, 2001). On the one hand, they negotiate with suppliers of package components for favourable contracts and adopt appropriate strategies to promote these tour components. On the other hand, tour operators provide professional advice to tourists about local products and services. In addition, tour operators can oversee the entire holiday experience so that they normally have first-hand knowledge of the behaviour of tourists during their holiday in the destinations. They also can assess the satisfaction of their clients with the services provided after the trips. The first tier of the upstream end of a TSC involves direct suppliers that directly supply tourism services to intermediaries. Typical direct suppliers include theme parks, shopping centres, hotels, bars and restaurants, handicraft shops, and transportation operators. A more complex TSC may also include second-tier suppliers that supply services or products to first-tier suppliers. These second-tier suppliers, which are located toward the upstream end, include attraction equipment manufacturers, food and drink manufacturers, and handcraft makers. Services such as cleaning and waste disposal and water and energy supply also belong to this layer. It is noteworthy that non-business entities are also involved in the TSC, one of which is the natural environment or scenery. Another typical player in the TSC is the local government or business association that facilitates public and private sector collaboration through policy intervention.

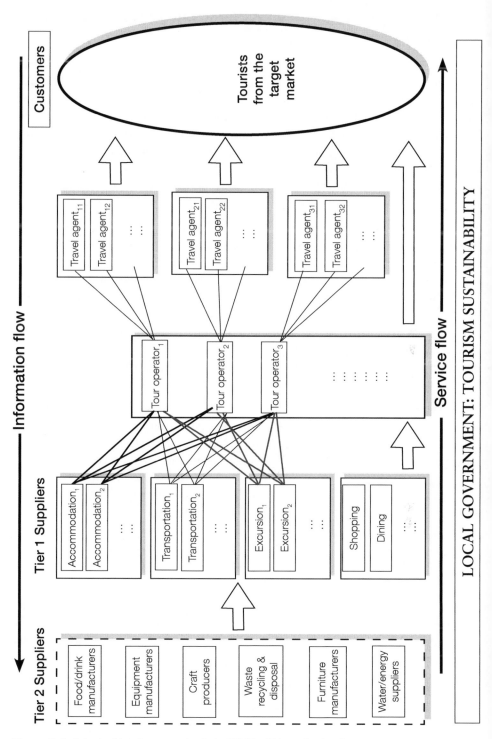

Figure 9.1: A typical tourism supply chain (TSC) within a destination.
Adapted from Zhang *et al.* (2009)

Benefits and challenges of collaborative tourism supply chain forecasting

Tourism is one of the fastest growing service industries that contributes significantly to the growth of many national, regional, and local economies. The World Travel and Tourism Council (WTTC, 2008) estimated that total world tourism receipts would reach US$5890 billion in 2008, accounting for 9.9 per cent of world gross domestic product (GDP), and that the industry would generate 238.3 million jobs or 8.4 per cent of total employment. By 2018, the economic contribution of tourism is forecast to account for 10.5 per cent of global GDP, and generate 297 million jobs (WTTC, 2008). Meanwhile, the tourism industry also faces higher demand uncertainty and more complex dynamics than its counterparts.

The WTO (1992) stated that tourism 'compromises the activities of persons travelling to and staying in places outside their usual environment for not more than one consecutive year for leisure, business and other purpose'. This definition indicates the sheer number of private and public sector enterprises involved in supplying services for tourism products. More specifically, Middleton (1989) and Middleton and Clarke (2001) conceptualize tourism products as a bundle of different components which include transport, accommodation, attractions and other facilities such as catering and entertainments. These tourism products may be purchased from a tour operator (package holiday or inclusive tour) or the tourists themselves may assemble the components (independent holiday).

As the tourism product is normally produced by a wide range of tourism businesses, the impacts of the economic conditions in the destination and the source markets tend to be far-reaching as a result of the multiplier effect. Therefore, the tourism industry is very vulnerable to the influence of economic conditions. Since travel is a luxury product, people tend to cut back on holidays when economic conditions are bad. Such unpredictable economic shocks as the current global financial turmoil and economic recession can cause significant demand uncertainty in tourism. In addition, many other factors also contribute to market uncertainty in terms of the demand for tourism products. For example, effective advertising can increase the number of tourist arrivals, whereas negative word-of-mouth publicity can lead to a fall in demand.

The most often used method of dealing with uncertainty is by building inventory. However, tourism services cannot be stored for future use, which constitutes one of the unique features of services, referred to as 'perishability' (Lovelock, 1980). Meanwhile, unlike the goods manufacturing industry, tourism service providers are normally unable to increase supply rapidly in accordance with any increase in demand. Therefore, uncertainty about levels of demand can precipitate losses for tourism businesses due to insufficient capacity to meet demand or excess capacity as a result of over-investment. Given that capacity is a fixed component in the short term, the only viable option for managers is to follow strategies that assist them to get more accurate predictions in order to match supply and demand more closely.

As mentioned in the previous section, most studies on tourism demand forecasting have been based on statistical methods and rely on the availability and quality of historical data. Current knowledge about special events or information about marketing activities of TSC partners is difficult to include in statistical models. Two benefits that can be expected from collaborative TSC forecasting are a reduced reliance on historical records and enhanced information sharing among TSC partners. The focus of collaborative TSC forecasting is, therefore, not merely on the improvement of forecast accuracy but also on breaking down functional separation and smoothing the information flow along the TSC to benefit the entire TSC.

However, achieving collaborative TSC forecasting is not an easy task. It requires a variety of participants from various echelons of the chain to work together. The first challenge is to establish a trusting relationship among TSC partners striving to help each other. Second, the design of the forecasting process and the steps for effective implementation of the process constitute a challenging task. The third challenge comprises the technical aspects, such as the establishment of forecasting support systems to facilitate the forecasting process and information sharing among the players within a TSC. While the first challenge is by itself a complex problem which needs to be discussed in a separate article, this chapter will endeavour to propose solutions for the latter two problems.

Forecasting methodology and process design

As stated above, collaborative forecasting needs a variety of personalities from various echelons of the chain to work together. In order to facilitate this need to share information during the forecasting process, web-based technologies are used. The detailed design of a web-based collaborative forecasting system, which is shown in Figure 9.2, will be discussed later.

Although there have been many web-based applications developed for various design and decision making purposes, research on web-based forecasting systems is rare. It is beyond dispute that web-based technologies can benefit TSC collaborative forecasting, as not only do they facilitate information sharing and communication but also they bring considerable convenience to practitioners who are engaged in collaborative forecasting at different locations. The system has the following advantages: *ease of use, easy to update, cheap to run*, and *platform independence*.

Forecasting process design

Two key points need to be considered for the process design. First, the forecasting process will be improved if the advanced tourism demand forecasting methods developed in the tourism literature are used. The second point concerns how to set up and generate collaborative forecasts by combining the inputs of various TSC members. Taking into consideration these two points, we propose a general collaborative tourism supply chain forecasting process as follows.

Specifically, the collaborative forecasting process begins with the baseline statistical forecasts generated by modern econometric/time series techniques embedded in the web-based forecasting system. Then, a variety of TSC members are invited to the collaborative forecasting system on a regular basis to bring their relevant knowledge by making forecasts based on their individual views about the baseline forecasts. After that, the system generates collaborative forecasts by combining both the baseline forecasts and the adjusted forecasts generated by the TSC members.

The problems that need to be tackled include what forecasting techniques to use for the creation of the baseline forecasts and how to bring together the various pieces of information given by the collaborative forecasting members. The following two sub-sections propose practical solutions for these problems.

Creation of the baseline forecasts

As indicated earlier, most studies on tourism demand forecasting have been based on econometric and/or time-series techniques. The most significant difference between these two approaches is that time-series methods cannot be used for policy evaluation purposes whilst with econometric models, the estimated parameters of the models can be used for policy evaluation. The established quantitative relationships between tourism demand and its determinants within econometric models enables 'what-if' scenario analyses on tourism demand forecasts, which can be very useful for judgmental inputs during collaborative forecasting. Therefore, econometric approaches are chosen to generate the baseline statistical forecasts.

Standard economic theory suggests that the most important factors that influence the demand for tourism are the own price of tourism product, the prices of substitute tourism products, tourists' incomes, tourism marketing expenditure, travel costs from origin countries/regions to the destination and one-off socio-economic events (Song et al., 2008). The forecasting model is constructed by taking all the possible economic factors into consideration and the model may be written as:

(9.1) $$Q_i = f(P_i, P_{is}, X_i, M_i, C_i, dummies, \varepsilon_i)$$

where Q_i is the quantity of the tourism product demanded in the destination by tourists from country/region i; P_i is the cost of living for tourists in the destination relative to the cost of living in the home country i; P_{is} is the cost of living for tourists from origin i in substitute destinations relative to the cost of living in the destination; X_i is the level of income in origin country/region i; M_i is the tourism marketing expenditure of the destination in country i; C_i is the average travelling cost from country i to the destination. *dummies* are the one-off socio-economic events, and ε_i is the disturbance term that captures all other factors which may influence the quantity of the tourism product demanded in the destination by tourists from origin country/region i (see, for example, Song and Witt, 2000).

Equation (9.1) is a theoretical model of tourism demand, which is simply a statement that indicates that there is a relationship between the variables under consideration. In practice, we need to specify the mathematical form of the tourism demand function.

Achieving collaborative forecasting through the Delphi approach

Producing collaborative forecasts by integrating opinions of a forecasting group involves qualitative forecasting techniques. The number of published studies on qualitative forecasting in tourism is limited and the Delphi method of forecasting is the qualitative forecasting method that has attracted the most attention in the tourism literature (Witt and Witt, 1995). The Delphi technique is a means of forecasting by using individual opinion and group consensus. There are several important features of the Delphi method: anonymity, iteration, controlled feedback, and the statistical aggregation of group responses (Rowe and Wright, 1999).

In the Delphi type of approach, the baseline forecasts are circulated through the forecasting group and changes are suggested by members. The primary advantage of the Delphi method is that it allows contributions from various group members who may be geographically dispersed. Most important, the Delphi approach is more accurate than traditional group meetings (Rowe and Wright, 1999).

The detailed Delphi process is designed as follows. It is initiated by the administrator regularly and there are at least two rounds per Delphi survey. In the first round, the collaborative forecasting system presents baseline forecasts produced by the econometric models and members are encouraged to give their own estimates of the future demand. The supporting reasoning for changes needs to be made clear. After the forecast has cycled through the entire team, the administrator generates the revised forecasts by averaging the group's inputs. The reasons for adjustments provided by the experts are also summarized anonymously for the group's information in the next round of adjustment. In the second round, the system provides the revised forecasts and comments obtained in the first round, and members are asked whether they agree with these revised forecasts or not. If they all agree, the Delphi process ends; if they do not agree, they give their own forecasts and reasons and the administrator then averages these forecasts again to arrive at the average forecasts based on the second round adjustments. If there is still variation in the forecasts in the second round, the same process may continue for a third round, etc.

Designing a web-based collaborative forecasting system

In order to facilitate the forecasting process described above, a web-based collaborative forecasting system has been designed. The preliminary design of the software architecture for the system is presented in Figure 9.2.

As is the case for many web applications, the system is built on three-tier architecture. The first/client tier contains the user interface in the form of a 'thin client' web browser (typically Microsoft Internet Explorer). Various TSC forecasting group members can simultaneously access the web-based system independently through this tier. The forecasters and their machines are not actually a part of the web-based system initially. They become a part of the system only when they visit the web server and interact with the system directly for data inputting, forecasting, analysing, decision making, etc.

In the second tier, the system has the core of the architecture called the system engine. This tier is the centre of the system. It provides the procedures used by the forecasting group members and controls the information communication between various tiers. Specifically, the system engine contains a collection of software procedures written in ASP.NET and hosted on a Microsoft IIS (Internet Information Server) web server. The communication between the user interface and the engine is accomplished through HTTP. Procedures residing in the system engine constitute five main components: security management, user interfaces, forecasting models, scenario analysis, and forecast adjusting tools.

The security management component is responsible for authentication and permission regarding the level of service for the users, the entrance of a user to the system, and the customization of the application environment. It supports the following basic types of users: administrator, forecasting group members and experts. User interfaces of the system are provided in the application tier in the format of web pages. They are responsible for the interaction between the system and its users, especially acting on the users' preferences and commands and controlling the input/output data and the form of display. In this component, OWCs (Office Web Components) are used to display data graphically (the same as in MS Office).

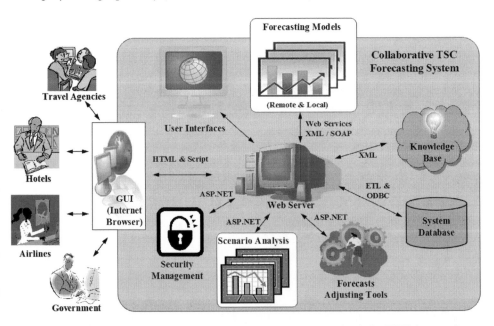

Figure 9.2: System architecture of the collaborative tourism supply chain (TSC) forecasting system.

The forecasting models component is responsible for generating the baseline forecasts and forecasts needed by the forecasting group members to support their decisions. The component is designed to be modular (all models can be plugged and unplugged and re-plugged without affecting other parts of the system) and flexible (prediction capabilities of models are monitored over time to detect deterioration and maintained accordingly). In order to accomplish these goals, we use 'web services' to design and implement every forecasting model as a distributed software component. A web service is a middleware system which can be developed in any kind of programming language and can be accessed by different kinds of software applications located in both near and remote locations. These systems access web services via ubiquitous web protocols and data formats such as HTTP (Hypertext Transfer Protocol), XML (eXtensible Markup Language), and SOAP (Simple Object Access Protocol), without worrying about how each web service is internally implemented. Web services can be accessed by a software application written in any language, using any component model, running on any operating system. The system server will use XML and SOAP to communicate with the models located in near and remote locations. These forecasting models can be developed using Visual Basic.NET and C++ programming languages.

Scenario analysis is another key component of the forecasting system. Generally speaking, scenarios are plausible predictions that are produced by integrating the statistical forecasting models and different user requests. Scenario analysis is an important and systematic way of examining the impacts of the alternative values of the influencing factors on future demand. The scenario analysis component in the system will allow the members to create their own scenarios by manipulating the values of the determinant variables of tourism demand in the forecasting models on the basis of their knowledge. In addition to the scenario analysis component, the system also provides other ways for the members to bring their pieces of information to the system or make their adjustments through forecast adjusting tools within the system. These two components will be developed using ASP.NET and hosted on the web server.

The third/data tier is the system database where the forecasts related data are stored. It is a local or remote computer running the relational database management system (RDBMS) such as SQL server and Oracle. The server retrieves data from the database by open database connectivity (ODBC) and extract–transport–load (ETL) procedures. The knowledge base is a collection of information and knowledge that members have accumulated from previous collaborative forecasting exercises using the system. It also contains the criteria that monitor the accuracy of the individual forecasting models and determine the adaptability of the models. This knowledge base can serve as a forecasting support module or a system expert in the collaborative forecasting process.

Concluding remarks

Tourism supply chain management (TSCM) is increasingly developing into one of the most critical factors that is affecting the development of the tourism industry, and is attracting increasing attention from both the academic and practitioner communities. Forecasting tourism demand is particularly important for policymakers and practitioners involved in TSCM. The success of many businesses depends largely on the level of tourism demand, and market failure quite often results from tourism firms failing to meet market demand. However, there is no standard forecasting method available for TSCs even though significant progress has been made in developing advanced tourism demand forecasting methods.

Recognizing the important role of tourism supply chains and tourism demand forecasting, this study is the first attempt to identify and develop collaborative forecasting involving multiple stakeholders. Unlike the traditional stand-alone tourism demand forecasting process in which individual tourism firms produce demand predictions based on their own or publicly available information, collaborative forecasting breaks down the barriers of information sharing between firms and involves supply chain partners in providing specific and timely information on future demand for their respective products/services.

After exploring the current situation regarding tourism demand forecasting, this chapter has discussed the benefits and challenges of collaborative TSC forecasting, and has proposed practical solutions for setting up collaborative forecasting in tourism supply chains. In order to facilitate the collaborative forecasting process, a collaborative forecasting system has been designed and put forward to enhance knowledge sharing and take advantage of the modern tourism demand forecasting methods that have been developed. The establishment of such a system will improve the performance and coordination of different tourism service providers within a TSC. Information sharing among TSC members is the key to success in collaborative forecasting. However, this can be very difficult in practice due to conflicts of business objectives among TSC members.

Acknowledgement

The authors would like to acknowledge the financial support of the Hong Kong Polytechnic University (Grant No: 1-ZV78).

References

Alford, P. (2005) 'A framework for mapping and evaluating business process costs in the tourism industry supply chain', in A. Frew (ed.), *Information and Communication Technologies in Tourism 2005*, Vienna: Springer Verlag, pp. 125-136.

Buhalis, D. and Laws, E. (2001) *Tourism Distribution Channels: Practices, Issues and Transformations*, London: Continuum International Publishing Group.

Christopher, M. (1992) *Logistics and Supply Chain Management*, London: Pitman.

Cooper, M. C., Lambert, D. M. and Pagh, J. D. (1997) 'Supply chain management: more than a new name for logistics', *International Journal of Logistics Management*, **8**, 1-13.

Fisher, M. L. (1997) 'What is the right supply chain for your product?', *Harvard Business Review*, **75**, 105-116.

Fosnaught, K. (1999) 'The strategic power of consensus forecasting: setting your organization up to win', *Journal of Business Forecasting Methods and Systems*, **18** (3), 3-7.

Helms, M.M., Ettkin, L.P. and Chapman, S. (2000) 'Supply chain forecasting – collaborative forecasting supports supply chain management', *Business Process Management Journal*, **6** (5), 392-407.

Houlihan, J. B. (1985) 'International supply chain management', *International Journal of Physical Distribution and Materials Management*, **15**, 22-38.

Kaukal, M., Höpken, W. and Werthner, H. (2000) 'An approach to enable interoperability in electronic tourism markets', *Proceedings of the 8th European Conference on Information System* (ECIS 2000), pp. 1104-1111.

Lambert, D., Stock, J. and Ellram, L. (1998) *Fundamentals of Logistics Management*, Boston, MA: Irwin/McGraw-Hill.

Li, G., Song, H. and Witt, S.F. (2005) 'Recent developments in econometric modelling and forecasting', *Journal of Travel Research*, **44**, 82-99.

Li, L. (2007) *Supply Chain Management: Concepts, Techniques and Practices Enhancing Value through Collaboration*, Singapore: World Scientific.

Lovelock, H.C. (1980) 'Why marketing management needs to be different for services', in J.H. Donnelly and W.R. George (eds), *Marketing of Services*, Chicago: American Marketing Association, pp 5-9.

Mentzer, J. and Kahn, K.B. (1997) 'State of sales forecasting systems in corporate America', *Journal of Business Forecasting*, **16**, 6-13.

Middleton, V.T.C. (1989) 'Tourist product', in S.F.Witt. and L. Moutinho (eds), *Tourism Marketing and Management Handbook*, Hemel Hempstead: Prentice-Hall, pp. 573-576.

Middleton, V.T.C. and Clarke, J. (2001) *Marketing in Travel and Tourism*, Oxford, Boston: Elsevier.

Page, S.J. (2003) *Tourism Management: Managing for Change*, Oxford: Butterworth-Heinemann.

Rowe, G. and Wright, G. (1999) 'The Delphi Technique as a forecasting tool: issues and analysis', *International Journal of Forecasting*, **15**, 351-381.

Scavarda, A.J., Lustosa, L.J. and Scavarda, L.F. (2001) 'The tourism industry chain', *Proceedings of the Twelfth Annual Conference of the Operations Management Society* (POM 2001), 30 March–2 April, Orlando, FL.

Simchi-Levi, D., Kaminsky, P. and Simchi-Levi, E. (2000) *Designing and Managing the Supply Chain*, Boston, MA: Irwin McGraw-Hill.

Sinclair, M.T. and Stabler, M. (1997) *The Economics of Tourism*, London: Routledge.

Småros, J. (2003) 'Collaborative forecasting: a selection of practical approaches', *International Journal of Logistics: Research and Applications*, **6** (4), 245-258.

Song, H. and Li, G. (2008) 'Tourism demand modelling and forecasting – a review of recent research', *Tourism Management*, **29** (2): 203-220.

Song, H. and Turner, L. (2006) 'Tourism demand forecasting', in L. Dwyer and P. Forsyth (eds), *International Handbook on the Economics of Tourism*, Cheltenham: Edward Elgar, pp. 89-114.

Song, H. and Witt, S.F. (2000) *Tourism Demand Modelling and Forecasting: Modern Econometric Approaches*, Oxford: Pergamon.

Song, H., Zhang, X. and Witt, S.F. (2008) 'Collaborative forecasting for tourism supply chain via the Internet', paper presented at the 18th International Symposium on Forecasting, 22–25 June, Nice, France.

Tapper, R. and Font, X. (2004) *Tourism Supply Chains: Report of a Desk Research Project for the Travel Foundation*, Leeds Metropolitan University: Environment Business and Development Group, available from http://www.lmu.ac.uk/lsif/the/ Tourism-Supply-Chains.pdf. (accessed on 11 September 2006)

Ujma, D. (2001) 'Distribution channels for tourism: theory and issues', in Buhalis, D. and Laws, E. (eds), *Tourism Distribution Channels: Practices, Issues and Transformations*, London: Continuum International Publishing Group, pp. 33-52.

Wilson, N. (2001) 'Game plan for a successful collaborative forecasting process', *Journal of Business Forecasting Methods and Systems*, **20** (1), 3-6.

Witt, S.F. and Witt, C.A. (1995) 'Forecasting tourism demand: a review of empirical research', *International Journal of Forecasting*, **11**, 447-475.

WTO (1975) *Distribution Channels*, Madrid, Spain: World Tourism Organization.

WTO (1992) *Guidelines: Development of National Parks and Protected Areas for Tourism*, Madrid: World Tourism Organization.

WTO (1994) *Global Distribution Systems in the Tourism Industry*, Madrid: World Tourism Organization.

WTTC (2008) *Progress and Priorities 2008/09*, Washington, DC: World Travel and Tourism Council.

Yang, S., Huang, G.Q., Song, H. and Liang, L. (2008) 'A game-theoretic approach to choice of profit and revenue maximization strategies in tourism supply chains for package holidays', *Journal of China Tourism Research*, **4** (1), 45-60.

Yang, S., Huang, G.Q., Song, H. and Liang, L. (2009) 'Game-theoretic approach to competition dynamics in tourism supply chains', *Journal of Travel Research*, **47**, 425-439.

Yilmaz, Y. and Bititci, U.S. (2006) 'Performance measurement in tourism: a value chain model', *International Journal of Contemporary Hospitality Management*, **18** (4), 341-349.

Zhang, X., Song, H. and Huang, G.Q. (2009) 'Tourism supply chain management: a new research agenda', *Tourism Management*, **30** (2), 345-358.

10 Understanding the value of tourism: a conceptual divergence

Richard R. Perdue, Timothy J. Tyrrell, and Muzaffer Uysal

Introduction

Across a variety of disciplines, the value of tourism as a measure of management and development success is a core construct of tourism research. Much of the existing tourism scholarly literature focuses on various attempts to measure and understand the value of tourism and its contributions to tourism development, tourism promotion, the tourism experience, various tourist segments, and special events/mega-events. Great disparity exists in the meaning of the term 'value' across these different literatures.

Moreover, over the past two decades, two key structural changes in tourism development and management have impacted the conceptual foundations of the 'value of tourism'. First, the time perspective of both tourism policy and tourism research has shifted significantly over the past decade, becoming increasingly concerned with the future. Two major examples reflect this shift. The framework for tourism planning and development has largely shifted to 'sustainable tourism' (McCool, 2009). One of the key provisions of sustainability is the protection of resources, services, and facilities for 'future generations' (Saarinen, 2006). Also, the tourism services and consumer research literature has largely shifted to concepts of 'relationship management' (Sheth and Parvatiyar, 1995) and 'customer centricity'. The key provision of relationship management is to shift tourism services management away from the individual transaction toward creation and management of relationships with consumers (Berger *et al.*, 2006). Second, another key provision of sustainable tourism is the growing importance of understanding tourism destination 'stakeholders', defined as the key constituent groups that affect and are affected by the destination's tourism planning and development decisions (Perdue, 2004). While several streams of stakeholder theory exist, the basic premise across these theories is the importance of identifying stakeholder groups and understanding their key concerns (Jones and Wicks, 1999). A key part of determining those concerns is better understanding how each stakeholder group determines and perceives the value of tourism.

Thus, the purpose of this chapter is to examine the conceptual foundations for measuring the value of tourism, specifically focusing on the evolving differences in these conceptual foundations across time and key stakeholder groups. The chapter's focus is not to propose or suggest any movement toward a common conceptual definition or operationalization of the value of tourism. In fact, the chapter demonstrates how the conceptual foundations of the value of tourism have diverged. For the purpose of this chapter, we are broadly defining the 'value of tourism' as the 'relative worth or contribution of tourism to a business, community or society'.

Philosophy of value

The fundamental question of the ontology of value is: 'Are things valuable because we value them or do we value them because they are valuable?' (Frondizi, 1971). If the answer to this question is the former then we can relate values uniquely to personal human preferences. If the answer is the latter, we must assume that values may then depend on preferences of other people, other living things or even non-living things.

Philosophical discussions about value suggest two alternative bases for determining value: an anthropocentric basis and a naturocentric basis (Vilkka, 1997: 87). While it is an intriguing notion that other living things might have equal right to the determination of value, it seems impossible to believe that humans could identify those things much less measure their value without imposing human values. The questions of intrinsic value and rights of other living things are interesting, but for this chapter we focus on the value of tourism from a purely human, anthropocentric perspective.

Importantly, we must recognize that a basic tenant of the anthropocentric perspective is that it conceptually gives humans the right to alter nature for utilitarian reasons. This tenant of human utilitarian interaction with nature has, in some cases, led to the reduction/destruction of natural resources. The anthropocentric value of 'things' naturally implies that we, as humans, have the right to alter and change the environment to meet and fit our needs and consumption levels. At some level, this impacts the concept of 'sustainability', leading to an important, future philosophical discussion of 'value'.

Value as a measure of success

Importantly, for the purposes of this chapter, we have taken the position that understanding the 'value of tourism' by itself is relatively unimportant. Rather, we measure the value of tourism as a means of measuring development, marketing and management success. In the private sector, shareholder value is considered the key measure of business success (Kaplan and Norton, 1992). In the governmental and NGO sector, the primary focus is on improving quality of life. In both sectors, 'value measures' are used as a means to either evaluate existing programmes and services or to compare and argue for alternative programme investments. For the individual tourist or resident, the 'value of tourism' equates to satisfaction or happiness. It measures the success of holiday planning and execution or the benefits generated by the tourism industry for the individual community resident.

Value measure dimensions

Two key conceptual dimensions of the 'value of tourism' are proposed for this chapter. First, measures of value can range from 'exchange values' to 'use values'. Exchange values (also referred to as the 'income concept', or 'value added' approach) are defined by the marketplace and measure the relative worth of something in terms of other things, especially in terms of money. The use of satellite accounting to measure the economic value of goods and services marketed to tourists falls squarely under this definition.

Use value (also referred to as the 'gains from trade') measures the benefits associated with the individual consumer's subjective appreciation (use) of goods and services, whether or not they are provided through a formal market. Thus, the use value of a thing is the subjective, perceived benefit received by an individual or a community from the 'use' of that thing (Smith, 1995). Since a good or service may have both use value and exchange value, or one or the other this is not a true continuum of value measurements. However, the exchange–use value is an effective means of examining how values of tourism which clearly differ by stakeholders have changed over time. We might call it the *universality of value*.

Markets have evolved to support the transfer of goods and services on the basis of exchange values. Importantly, goods and services exist which have very little exchange value, but high use value, e.g. family holiday photographs or personal recreational achievements (in golf, a hole in one). In many cases, exchange markets have evolved to provide goods and services which complement the use value of other goods – e.g. photography guides, technology, and services to enhance the quality of personal photographs. Many publicly provided tourism services offer both exchange and use values. Tourism information centres, attractions, and public safety services provide considerable use value to those who are served. At the same time, these services may be a charge on the community and are supported by private sector investment. Therefore, many people have similar values (exchange values) for the services provided.

Second, measures of the value of tourism also range on a 'measurability' dimension reflecting a continuum of concrete to abstract measures. Prototypically, economists measure value as the relative worth of something in terms of other 'real or actual' things, especially in terms of money. A central focus of much of the economic research in tourism is to create and validate concrete, monetary measures of the value of tourism to individuals, to businesses or to society. Similarly, in the private tourism sector, accountants and financial managers focus much of their work on creating concrete, financial measures of business success. By comparison, sociology and psychology researchers more commonly focus on abstract value measures which tend to reflect qualities or states of being, rather than specific objects or instances. From these perspectives, the value of tourism is related to its contribution to the ideals, convictions or beliefs of a society or individual. Particularly for governments and NGOs, tourism developers focus heavily on improving the quality of life for community residents. Similarly, psychologists emphasize satisfaction and self-actualization as measures of personal success/value (Pearce, 2009). Thus, if we broaden the definition of 'value' to emphasize its contributions to society and/or individual well-being, values can be organized on a concrete to abstract dimension that reflects the degree to which the value can be objectively and uniquely measured.

Importantly, there is an obvious correlation between these two dimensions of value measures: exchange values are usually measured by concrete measures (money) and purely use values can be very abstract and are hard to measure. While it would be reasonable to expect movement along the intersect of the two types of measures, substantive deviations from that intersect line represent basic conceptual shifts in the measurement and universality of the 'value' of tourism.

Tourism industry stakeholders

For this chapter, we decided to focus on three key stakeholder groups in tourism development and management: tourism businesses, destination marketing/management organizations, and community economic development authorities. For each of these stakeholder groups, we reviewed existing studies and reflected on our experiences over the past 30 years. The following reflects our observations of changes in the measurement of the 'value of tourism' over this time frame for each of these stakeholders.

Tourism businesses

Most private sector research examining the value of tourism has derived from the marketing and consumer psychology literature. As reflected by Kotler *et al.* (1998), measures of success in tourism marketing have evolved from focusing on current sales volume to a growing emphasis on long-term customer equity. Specifically, up until the mid-1980s, sales volume was the primary measure of private sector tourism marketing success (Cooper and Nakanishi, 1988; Powell and Allgaier, 1998). Building from Oliver's (1980) recommendation that a firm's success and marketing effectiveness should be evaluated from the customer perspective, customer satisfaction became a more important measure of success. Beginning in the late 1990s, marketing theory largely shifted from focusing on the value of business transactions to increasingly emphasize the value of customer relationships. Long-term customer relationship value became an integral component of a firm's long-term net worth (Berger *et al.*, 2002). Initially, this shift was characterized by increasing research on customer loyalty and repeat visitation/ intentions to return. Given the abstract relationship between loyalty and economic success, this research has continued to evolve with growing emphasis on operationalizing customer equity, defined as 'the total of the discounted lifetime values summed over all of a firm's customers' (Blattberg and Deighton, 1996). As stated by Rust *et al.* (2000), 'the long-term value of the company is largely determined by the value of the company's customer relationships, which is called customer equity' (p. 4). Increasingly, the focus of this work has been to create a more concrete measure of the long-term value of a company's customers. Rust *et al.* (2000) calculate customer equity as:

$$\text{Customer equity} = \sum_{t=0}^{T}[(1+d)^{-t}F_{it}S_{it}\pi_{it}]$$

Note: T: the length of the planning horizon
t: time period
F_{it}: expected frequency of the customer's purchases/visit per time period
π_{it}: the customer's average spending/contribution per visit
S_{it}: the probability of return
d: the company's discount rate.

When examined across the concrete/abstract dimension of value as discussed earlier, the value of tourism, as measured by private sector and tourism marketing organizations has evolved over the past three decades from a very concretely measured 'sales' basis, to a much more abstract concept of 'customer satisfaction' and 'customer loyalty' and now back to a more concrete measure of 'customer equity'. Similarly, across the exchange/use dimension of value measures, tourism businesses have evolved from emphasizing exchange (sales volume) to a greater emphasis on use (satisfaction and loyalty) and long-term values (customer equity).

Destination marketing management organizations

Destination marketing organizations (DMOs) are mostly non-profit organizations initially created to represent tourism accommodations for the purpose of generating tourist visitation to the area (Gretzel *et al.*, 2006), almost exclusively through promotional strategies and campaigns. Success was defined as 'putting heads in beds' with either tourist visitation or area tourist revenues as the primary value measures. Particularly as reflected by collective works of the U.S. Travel and Tourism Administration's Task Force on Accountability Research in the early 1990s, substantial research was focused on determining the 'return on investment' from DMO promotional efforts, with particular emphasis on inquiry-conversion research methodologies (Toepper and Burke, 1992; Perdue and Pitegoff, 1990). Beginning in the late 1990s/early 2000s, the term 'destination marketing organization' has been largely replaced with 'destination management organization', implying a shift both in responsibilities and in the appropriate measures of success. Initially this was operationalized by demonstrating DMO contribution to resident quality of life. More recently, DMOs are increasingly being asked to demonstrate their contributions to the 'quality and sustainability' of the area's tourism industry. Collectively, on the concrete/abstract measurement scale, this implies a movement from concrete to very abstract and, at least in the sense of being more focused on tourism industry contributions, somewhat back towards a more concrete measure. On the exchange to use dimension, DMOs have moved strongly from an exchange basis of measuring the value of tourism toward a much more use-based measure.

Community economic development authorities

Most governmental entities have agencies which focus on the economic development of the community/region/state/country. The premise of these agencies is that by contributing to economic development, the agency contributes to constituent economic well-being and tax revenues. Historically, economic development authorities have focused on generating jobs (not necessarily for locals) and increasing the tax base. Manufacturing industries received by far the most attention, but, particularly in the last two decades, tourism and hospitality businesses have also been targeted. Moreover, these agencies have often been the direct driving force behind the development of many tourism and hospitality facilities, most notably conference centres, airports, cruise ports, and sports stadia. While property tax waivers have been the most common tool used as incentive for such development, favourable financing, infrastructure and superstructure development, and even direct land grants are also commonly used. These authorities have historically measured success in the forms of tourist expenditures and the consequent job generation and tax revenues. More recently, growing concerns exist questioning the relationships between tourist expenditures and job creation, whether or not the jobs thus generated actually benefit the local residents and the overall contribution to resident quality of life. Consequently, the value of tourism to economic development authorities has largely shifted to understanding the contributions of tourism development to local resident quality of life. Initially, this was operationalized through tracking of several objective measures of resident quality of life, e.g. value added GDP contributions of wages, profits and tax generation. More recently, there is a growing shift to more subjective measures of resident quality of life, particularly environmental quality, natural resource access, and the social and cultural impacts of tourism development. Triple bottom line and happiness measures have been suggested as embracing quality of community life goals. Thus, on the exchange–use dimension of value measurement, there has been a sustained move toward more 'use based' measures of the value of tourism development. On the concrete–abstract dimension, the shift has been from very concrete measures of job creation, to somewhat more abstract 'objective quality of life' measures, to very abstract 'subjective quality of life' measures.

A divergence of measurement

This chapter was motivated by an interest in examining the value of tourism as a measurement of tourism management and development success. Clearly, such measures have been a core construct of tourism research. Building on sustainability theory, three key tourism stakeholders were identified – tourism businesses, destination management organizations, and community economic development authorities. The 'value of tourism' was defined as the measures of success used by these stakeholders. The evolution of these measures was then examined historically on two value dimensions – concrete to abstract and exchange to use. Figure 10.1 reflects the results of this examination with the concrete/abstract and exchange/use dimensions reflected as the graph axes. The time dimension is reflected by the use of T1 and T3 to reflect historical and current perspectives, respectfully. Most importantly, the resulting graph demonstrates a divergence in the types of measures being used. While all three stakeholders initially tended to focus on relatively concrete exchange based measures of value; the historical trends for the different stakeholders have diverged pretty dramatically. All have moved toward more abstract measures of value; while tourism businesses have continued to use relatively concrete measures of success, the move from sales volume to customer equity certainly reflects both a more abstract measure and one that is more use based. Still customer equity is far less abstract than customer satisfaction and loyalty.

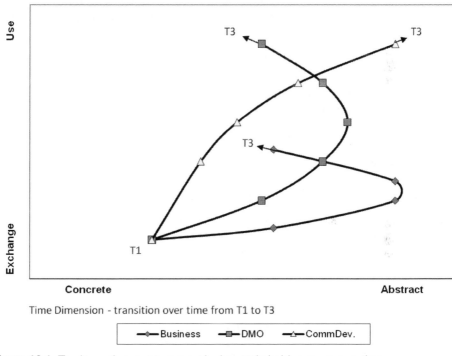

Figure 10.1: Tourism value measurement by key stakeholder group over time

For both destination management organizations and economic development authorities, the move is more dramatic. Both have moved from exchange measures (e.g. inquiry conversion and jobs, respectively) to more use-based measures (tourism sustainability and quality of life, respectively). Destination marketing organizations moved from concrete to very abstract (enquiry conversion to quality of life) to less abstract (tourism sustainability). Economic development authorities moved in the opposite direction, i.e. from concrete to somewhat abstract (jobs to objective quality of life measures) to very abstract (quality of life) measures. Such a divergence of measurement has profound implications for tourism management and development as it is very likely that a given tourism management action will have different results depending upon the measure of value being used.

Conclusions

Theoretically, different tourism stakeholders converge on one common goal, to create and build value for their constituencies. Creating value transcends the boundaries of specific management and development goals. Given the observed divergence in measurement, it is obvious that tourism stakeholders must work together, establish community dialogues and identify mutually beneficial strategies. Clearly a 'balanced scorecard' methodology is needed to determine the contributions of tourism development and management (Smith, 2007). While the value of tourism is ultimately measured within the realm of stakeholder domains, measurement differences need to be understood in order for collaboration and common purpose to be successful.

From the perspective of needed research, it is important that in the future, researchers create a viable 'tourism values scorecard' and conduct the necessary research to begin to understand how management strategies and tactics by various tourism stakeholders contribute to changes in that scorecard. It is extremely important that measures of success be created that allow for comparison of investments in tourism versus other activities/industries, in marketing versus other functional areas of business, and across marketing strategies. Regardless of the stakeholder environment (e.g. business, DMOs, and economic development authorities), the ability to effectively measure return on investment is becoming increasingly important.

More broadly, the value of tourism has historically been measured on the basis of its potential to generate economic benefits with marginal understanding or concern for social and environmental consequences. The examination of benefits measured on the basis of quality of life, social well-being, sustainability, cultural and environmental protection and preservation has just started making its way into the question of tourism valuation and values. This shift implies a growing emphasis on understanding how the spill-over effects of objective measures of tourism value eventually affect the well-being of individuals, communities, and society in general. As we move toward a balanced scorecard of value measures, we will be able to capture important aspects of society that are not sufficiently reflected in purely economic terms.

Importantly, the nature of value of tourism is founded on the spatial characteristics of the setting in which tourism production and consumption activities take place. For such research, tourism-settings are defined to include places and environments where the activities of tourists and the tourism industry are important and tourists have the opportunity to gaze (Urry, 2002) and engage in utilitarian and nonutilitarian consumption of goods and services. These include activities such as the planning and implementation of tourism development, the promotion of tourism, as well as the experiences of tourists and residents impacted by tourism related activities and events. This description of the setting is the fully functioning tourism system. So, the nature of the tourism-setting in which tourism activities take place plays a significant role in the economic valuation and perceived benefits of both market and non-market goods and services. This suggests that the nature of tourism consumption is strongly influenced by settings and its attributes are conducive to creating the desired outcomes of non-market value to consumers. Thus, tourism value cannot be examined without consideration of the collective effects of both tangible and intangible benefits, further supporting the importance of both the economic value of marketed goods and services and the perceived intangible and expressive value of non-market goods and services. It is important to recognize that the tourism setting serves dual roles; a place for residents to live in and a place for visitors to create value. Tourism contributes to both the well-being of residents through enhanced and added amenities and to the quality of holiday experiences through aesthetic and appreciative consumption.

Perhaps most important, it is traditional to measure tourism value in terms of growth. An alternative paradigm is balance. As we move from measuring tourism on the basis of exchange values (income) toward use based measures (e.g. quality of life), then balance (of social, environmental and economic impacts) is the critical measure of success. As long as we continue to focus on the outcome of tourism activities as measured by GNP, wages, expenditures, and profits we would mostly emphasize the economic welfare of businesses, employment, tourists, and residents. The non-economic value of tourism to tourists, communities, and residents can only be understood if we examine benefits and values by focusing on 'through-tourism' activities and use or perceived value of goods and services. Through tourism activities we reduce poverty, enhance amenities, and create a better, more balanced community to live in, improve quality-of-life of residents and tourists' experiences.

References

Berger, P.D., Bolton, R.N., Bowman, D., Briggs, E., Kumar, V., Parasuraman, A. and Terry, D. (2002) 'Marketing actions and the value of customer assets: a framework for customer asset management', *Journal of Service Research*, 5 (1), 39–54.

Berger, P.P, Eechambadi, N., Leman, G.M., Rizley, D.R. and Vankateson, R. (2006) 'From customer lifetime value to shareholder value: theory, empirical evidence and issues for future research', *Journal of Services Research*, 9 (2), 156-167.

Blattberg, R.C. and Deighton, J. (1996) 'Manage marketing by the customer equity test', *Harvard Business Review*, 74 (4),136-145.

Cooper, L.G. and Nakanishi, M. (1988) *Market-share Analysis: Evaluating Competitive Marketing Effectiveness*, Boston, MA: Kluwer Academic Publishers.

Frondizi, Risieri (1971) *What is Value?*, LaSalle, IL: Open Court.

Gretzel, U., Fesenmaier, D.R., Formica, S. and O'Leary, J. (2006) 'Searching for the future: challenges faced by destination marketing organizations', *Journal of Travel Research*, **45** (2), 116-126.

Jones, T.M. and Wicks, A.C. (1999) 'Convergent stakeholder theory', *Academy of Management Review*, **24**, 206-225.

Kaplan, R.S. and Norton, D.P. (1992) 'The balanced scorecard: measures that drive performance', *Harvard Business Review*, **70** (1), 71-79.

Kotler, P., Bowen, J. and Makens, J. (1998) *Marketing for Hospitality and Tourism*, 2nd edn, Upper Saddle River, NJ: Prentice Hall.

McCool, S.F. (2009) 'Constructing partnerships for protected area tourism planning in an era of change and messiness', *Journal of Sustainable Tourism*, **17** (2), 133–148.

Oliver, R.L. (1980) 'A cognitive model of the antecedents and consequences of satisfaction decisions', *Journal of Marketing Research*, **17**, 460-469.

Pearce, L.P. (2009) 'The relationship between positive psychology and tourist behavior studies', *Tourism Analysis*, **14** (1), 37-48.

Perdue, R.R. (2004) 'Sustainable tourism and stakeholder groups: a case study of Colorado ski resort communities', in G.I. Crouch, R.R. Perdue, M. Uysal and H. Timmermans (eds), *Consumer Psychology of Tourism, Hospitality, and Leisure*, Cambridge, MA: CABI, pp. 253-264.

Perdue, R.R. and Pitegoff, B.E. (1990) 'Methods of accountability research for destination marketing', *Journal of Travel Research*, **28** (4),10-14.

Powell, T. and Allgaier, C. (1998) 'Enhancing sales and marketing effectiveness through competitive intelligence', *Competitive Intelligence Review,*, **9** (4), 29-41.

Rust, R., Zeithaml, V. and Leman, K. (2000) *Driving Customer Equity*, New York: Free Press.

Saarinen, J. (2006) 'Traditions of sustainability in tourism studies', *Annals of Tourism Research*, **33** (4), 1121-1140.

Sheth, J.N. and Parvatiyar, A. (1995) 'The evolution of relationship marketing', *International Business Review*, **4**, 397-418.

Smith, R.F. (2007) *Business Process Management and the Balanced Scorecard: Using Processes as Strategic Drivers*, Hoboken, NJ: John Wiley and Sons.

Smith, S.L.J. (1995) *Tourism Analysis; A Handbook*, 2nd edn, Longman, New York.

Toepper, L.K. and Burke, J.F. (1992) *Accountability Research*, Washington, DC: US Travel and Tourism Administration, Dept. of Commerce.

Urry, J. (2002) *The Tourist Gaze*, 2nd edn, Thousand Oaks, CA: Sage.

Vilkka, L. (1997) *The Intrinsic Value of Nature*, Amsterdam: Rodopi.

Part III

National and regional perspectives

11 Tourism research in Latin America: past and future challenges

Regina Schlüter and Rodolfo Bertoncello

Introduction

During the last 20 years, great changes have taken place in the field of tourism research in Latin America, as evidenced in the scientific journal of tourism research for which we are responsible, *Estudios y Perspectivas en Turismo*. For example, 20 years ago, tourism research was not considered to be relevant, and no support from the national agencies linked to science and technological development like CONICET (Consejo Nacional de Investigaciones Científicas y Técnicas), Argentina, or CNPq (Conselho Nacional de Desenvolvimento Científico e Tecnológico), Brazil, was granted to research projects related to tourism. However, as the activity has evolved over the years, and with tourism figuring on the agenda of a number of leading researchers from multiple different areas of studies, the situation has changed. Many experts have attempted to explain this change in circumstances, arguing that, hitherto, negative prejudices abounded in scientific circles with respect to the 'frivolity' of tourism, an activity 'indulged in' by the favoured few, with high incomes and low-weighted work schedules. This was the philosophy embodied in Veblen's (1992) *Theory of the Leisure Class*, a theory which demoted the area from the echelons of higher studies, rendering tourism unworthy of national sponsorship, on account of its elitist nature. In Argentina, Juan José Sebreli (1984: 148), considered tourism to be a new means of 'subtle' oppression where the 'whip' was replaced by the 'sugar' of luxury leisure time, a useful tool with which dictatorial governments could rule over a specific society. Practical experiences have also been significant in consolidating the importance of subjects linked to open-air activities, such as tourism, which previously had been viewed as a phenomenon unworthy of the attention of social scientists (see Hiernaux Nicolás, 2000).

This chapter aims to address this situation, making reference to *Estudios y Perspectivas en Turismo*, a Latin American academic journal on tourism, published uninterruptedly for the last 20 years. We work on the assumption that the articles published in the journal over the last two decades are representative of the evolution of the Latin American tourism literature. The only other tourism journal in the region with a comparable history is *Turismo em Análise*, a Brazilian rather than Latin American review, published in Portuguese. Articles in *Estudios y Perspectivas en Turismo* reflect both the positive interests of tourism, as well as the negative aspects acknowledged as affecting tourism (considered in the broadest possible sense, that is, not only an economic activity, but a wide-ranging social practice) such as: management, planning, working conditions and the availability of human resources, amongst others.

Tourism caught in a positive and negative net

It is common knowledge that after the Second World War, tourism began to be viewed as an activity that could contribute towards development at an international level, where the various independent concerns and issues of countries could find common solutions.

Working on the basis of the model imported from Spain, the less-developed countries, especially in Latin America, foresaw that tourism in general, and international tourism in particular, could be the way to gain the foreign investment with which to finance their industrial development (which, at the end of the day, was what they considered to be the only true driver of economic development). Tourism was also considered, on a complementary level, to be a possible strategy for regional development, a way to eliminate the marked differences which existed in the Latin American countries, since it was largely the poorer regions, unblemished by development, which offered the largest amount of tourist resources, thereby creating employment in these areas, together with economic growth (Schlüter and Winter, 1993).

Tourism, thus, was seen in Latin America as a development tool (Schlüter, 1992). Various different tourism development plans and projects were proposed in all countries, some of which were carried out with clear economic objectives, and evaluated from a purely economic perspective. Most of these projects focused on the need to justify investment by measuring the hypothetical profits to be made, rather then centring on whether the overall results of the plan had been achieved. The first such strongly promoted developments involved 'integrated tourism centres', whose favoured resource was the 'sun, sand, sea' triad. 'Integrated' meant that even the unexpected was foreseen, taking into account the region's environmental, economic, social and cultural factors. The tourism centres of Cancun (Mexico) and Puerto Plata (Dominican Republic) are the clearest examples of such resorts in Latin America (Schlüter, 1998: 218). Countries not favoured with beaches to attract international tourism developed their cultural resources, a good example being the UNESCO-Peru Cultural and Tourism Plan, known as the COPESCO project. Its aim was to expand agriculture, the base economy of the Cuzco–Puno region, and protect the Inca archaeological sites. International agencies also invested in developing ecotourism in those countries with outstanding natural resources. Although attempts were made in many countries, particularly Brazil, which has the Amazon basin and the

Pantanal as great attractions, Costa Rica is the country that has captured the greatest attention and has become 'the' ecotouristic destination (Schlüter, 1993).

The scarce investment directed towards human resource development, manifestly insufficient to meet the needs of the lesser-developed regions, led to greater interest being paid to the need for professional training and for integral management models for tourism. As a result, tourism studies were gradually integrated into the universities in all countries. As of the 1970s, the first tourism graduates of Argentina finished their studies. The training they had received, however, was of a highly vocational nature, with scarce grounding in academic studies and analysis. This generated a divorce between professional circles and academia which, to a certain extent, is now being redressed (Schlüter, 1985).

This positive valuation of tourism as a development tool, predominant during the 1950s and the 1960s, began to be debated in the 1970s, a time of deep-reaching socio-political change. During this time, studies of the negative economic, environmental, social and cultural aspects of tourism abounded. Tourism was not only studied on a national level but rather, and more so, from the perspective of the complex set of international dependency relationships (core as opposed to peripheral countries) established by the economic activity, and by people outside the academic sphere. Emmanuel de Kadt's work is a classic example of this perspective, questioning tourism's role as 'a passport to development' (de Kadt, 1979).

The difficulties that have been encountered along the way, to wed together the positive and the negative aspects of tourism practice in a basic interpretation of tourism, have produced a dichotomy which has lasted through to the present. Depending upon who is looking at what from which perspective, one of two attitudes is usually adopted (positive or negative) to the exclusion of the other, thus making it difficult to produce valid research or truly useful insights which can be used to orient tourism management and policies.

However, things are changing. It has taken us over five years to re-evaluate and re-appraise standpoints and stereotypes in tourism, but the work is in progress. By considering tourism under the umbrella of the social sciences, as a social activity and practice, there has been a total opening up of perspectives, leading to rich debate and enriching new viewpoints. This coincided in time with the reorganization of the system of scientific production and the re-establishment of constitutional order and stability within many countries in the region which, in turn, led to a greater flow of scientific output and more interest being generated.

The polar positive or negative perspectives of the past have been gradually replaced by multidisciplinary insights into the reality of tourism. Once analysed and dissected, tourism began to be seen as a live and dynamic field of activity rather than as a closed book. This lively and dynamic process has given rise to more tourism experts, more selective and critical processes being applied to research in this field and a greater sphere of academic activity, wider ranging than before.

The consolidation of tourism: human resources and publications

The Organization of American States (OAS), played a leading role in the training of human resources, especially in the public sector, at the level of government, and in academia, through the creation of CICATUR (the Centro Interamericano de Capacitación Turística – or Inter American Tourism Training Centre), with its headquarters in Washington DC, which came into being in the 1970s (Guevara *et al.*, n.d.). This intergovernmental body had three branch offices: one in Barbados, which had no impact in Latin America; another in Buenos Aires, Argentina, targeted mainly at the South American countries; and the third in Mexico City, with influence in the whole of Latin America.

The Mexican CICATUR office had professionals who were specially trained by the OAS at the George Washington University, Washington DC, and whose tasks were not limited to teaching but were also devoted to the preparation of the first study manuals available within the region. That is how Miguel Angel Acerenza (Uruguay), Roberto Boullón (Argentina), Fabio Cárdenas Tabares (Colombia) and Edgar Hernandez Diaz (Mexico) became the founding fathers of Latin American tourism as an academic study (Schlüter, 1991). The Trillas Publishing Company in Mexico (Editorial Trillas) also contributed towards promoting knowledge in the region by publishing their books and those of other specialists in the region, together with Spanish translations of tourism works written by foreign experts such as Alister Mathieson and Geoffrey Wall (1990) and Douglas Pearce (1991). In the 1980s Argentina and Colombia began their editorial work in tourism (Schlüter, 1988) and shortly after the Papirus Publishing Company started to publish books on tourism in Campinas (Brazil) and the first contributions came from specialists such as Margarita Barretto, Mario Beni, Doris Ruschmann, Mirian Rejowsky and Luiz Trigo who according to a recent study, continue to be Brazil's top researchers (Leal, 2006).

Even though the CICATUR made very significant contributions towards framing conceptual and methodological aspects, their input is most faithfully reflected in their grounding of methodologies for tourism planning within the region, such as the *Inventory of Tourism Resources* which, despite its age, is still being used in many countries by official tourism offices. Since the CICATUR's main aim, however, was to train government specialists, their contribution to scientific research (as seen from the perspective of national research agencies) was very limited. The Buenos Aires office of CICATUR closed down in 1981 as did the Mexico office shortly after, thereby producing a highly significant gap in training and integration of specialists in the entire region. Nevertheless, the lucky few who had received grants to study their courses had, by that time, established their own networks, capable of generating alternatives for teamwork in the future.

In April 1989, the Latin American Seminar AMFORT / WAPTT (Asociación Mundial para la Formación Profesional Turística – World Association for Professional

Training in Tourism) was held in Buenos Aires. This represented a magnificent opportunity for a significant group of scholars to come together, many of whom had been previously linked to the CICATUR. At the Second Seminar, held in São Paulo, Brazil, the following year, the various proposals directed at creating integration and networking were further strengthened. Amongst these proposals, one in particular highlighted the need to create a journal, with an editorial board of specialists from the region, designed to reflect and promote the work carried out in tourism in each of the various countries represented, with contributions also by international experts, to give a broader perspective on the world.

That is how, in 1990, the first edition of the *Revista Latinoamericana en Turismo* (Latin American Journal of Tourism) was published in Buenos Aires. Its long-term aim was to reach a quality standard similar to that of *Annals of Tourism Research*, focusing on research and practice within the field of tourism. Even though it took some time to consolidate, it aroused general interest among the specialists in the region whilst attracting others from other parts of the world. This latter event made it necessary to expand upon the initial definition of a regional journal to offer greater geographical coverage, allowing for interaction and comparison with research in other parts of the world. As a result, the journal changed its name and became known as *Estudios y Perspectivas en Turismo* (Studies and Perspectives in Tourism). The journal actively accompanied the steady development of the field of tourism studies, bolstering it intellectually.

The consolidation of tourism research

The transition from the working methodology of CICATUR-OAS, to a more academic approach was no easy task. The Latin American specialists were highly aware of the need for proposals for improvement in existing tourism developments in each country of the region, together with the requirement for innovation. However, the universities where tourism was on the curriculum did not fully grasp the importance of scientific research with tangible results, working rather at the level of hypothesis, of how a certain natural or cultural resource could be made into a tourist attraction or, equally hypothetically, of how to improve efficiency within the business sector (Bertoncello, 2002).

The first issues, as a result, covered a wide range of subjects and styles, from essays based on personal considerations and interpretations of like-minded authors through to brief descriptions of equally brief fieldwork, passing almost invariably through the bibliographical research produced by the World Tourism Organization on the country or region in question.

In the beginning, mainly during the first five years of the *Revista Latinoamericana en Turismo/Estudios y Perspectivas en Turismo*, the subjects varied widely and covered articles as diverse as how tourists are viewed under the customs code of Argentina (Gerlero, 1991), employment in Mexico's four and five-star hotels (Rodríguez

Woog and Hiernaux Nicolás, 1992), tourism impact in Mexico, whale watching in Patagonia (Martínez Rivarola *et al.*, 1995) and reviews of events in tourism. Since the idea was to cover the whole of Latin America's problems in the sector, there were also articles on extra-regional demand and human resource management difficulties.

However, some common features soon became clear from the beginning, such as the need for preservation of the environment and the importance of ecotourism. These were produced in all parts of Latin America but, above all, in Argentina, by the professors of the national universities of Comahue and Patagonia (Ushuaia, the Tierra del Fuego campus). These were of immense importance, above all in the case of the National University of Patagonia, where the preservation of the environment was extended to include the cultural characteristics and identity of the first settlers on Tierra del Fuego. The articles received from the National University of Comahue touched upon matters within their region, in the south-west of the country, home to the main national parks and tourist attractions. These articles included fieldwork designed on the basis of theory and aimed at further theoretical development, with studies also carried out by researchers from outside the region.

We should also highlight that this is the period when experts from the English-speaking world began to be published in the journal (Pearce, 1993; Jafari, 1994; Bar-On, 1995; Riley, 1995; Wall, 1995), together with specialists from Spain (Bote Gómez, 1993; Requejo Liberal, 1993; Marchena Gómez y Velasco Martin, 1995; Chirivella Caballero, 1995) with a clear focus on the socio-cultural impacts of tourism. Even though these contributions did not reflect the problems of the region, they made an important theoretical contribution towards the knowledge of tourism at a time when, due to lack of funding, there were scarce possibilities of accessing this type and amount of information from outside the region. Later these contributions were not encouraged so often, since the main libraries in the USA, the United Kingdom and Spain threatened to cancel their subscriptions on the grounds that they expected a Latin American journal to deal with Latin American matters written by Latin Americans.

Even though in 1996 no mention had yet been made of impact factors of articles and journals, the authors were, logically, concerned with respect to the diffusion of their articles. Slowly, the indexation of journals began to be a real concern for more members of the academic world. In the beginning, the impact factor was calculated according to number of issues printed, number of subscribers, the physical location of the publishers, and the number of university libraries and international organizations with regular subscriptions.

The inclusion of Spanish journals into the indices was a challenge since the index system was designed for publications written in English. Nevertheless, Mexico led the way, creating two indices for Latin American journals: REDALYC (Red de Revistas Científicas de América Latina y el Caribe, España y Portugal – www.redalyc.com/mx) and LATINDEX (Sistema Regional de Información en Línea para Revistas

Científicas de América Latina, el Caribe, España y Portugal –www.latindex.unam.mx), as did Argentina, where the UNIRED was created, under the auspices of the Ministry of Finance, to partially cover the problem.

Notwithstanding this progress, researchers began to realize the need for their work to be frequently quoted which produced a new problem: the need to publish in English in internationally renowned journals. This task was not simple at all, since the author was faced with the imposition of writing an article as if s/he were a native English speaking person, a major challenge for many researchers. The positive side of this negative perspective was that international standards of presentation had also to be adopted, leading to more case studies working within more elaborate theoretical frameworks.

Although ecological matters continued to be of interest, as of 1996 greater interest was shown for subjects relating to business, such as marketing, human resources management and service quality, a trend which lasted around ten years. These aspects were most focused on by Mexican experts, especially from the University of the Americas – Puebla (Domínguez et. al., 1997), and from the National University of Comahue, Argentina (Boschi, 1998; Otero and González, 1998), as well as by researchers residing outside the region, mainly from Turkey (Aksu, 2004).

During the same timespan, more and more articles were received from Latin America and Spain which focused basically on rural tourism, to such an extent that a special issue on the subject was published in January 2001. Due to the characteristics of the printed journal, similar to that of a book, this special issue was extremely successful in the market, clearly demonstrating the great interest in the subject and the lack of relevant literature at the time. Other recurrent subjects over the years were: crime, food security, risk perception and terrorism, subjects which, inexplicably, lost force after 9/11, with the exception of one article which appeared shortly afterwards, referring to the impact suffered by the Mexican hospitality industry as a consequence of said tragic attack (Domínguez et al., 2003).

Until the year 2000, there were very few articles published by anthropologists, but this situation changed with the special issue on *Anthropology and Tourism in Brazil* with Margarita Barretto, of the University of Caxias do Sul, Brazil, as guest editor. Barretto presented a collection of work of extremely important anthropologists, all of whom analysed tourism from the anthropological perspective. The quality of the articles, together with the longstanding reputation of the journal, opened the doors to QUALIS (the Brazilian journal index) for Tourism Studies and Perspectives to QUALIS, and, thus, noticeably changed the profile of the future authors of *Estudios y Perspectivas en Turismo*, strengthening the presence of articles submitted in Portuguese to such an extent that it came to be called a Brazilian journal written in Spanish. New authors were also incorporated, and theoretical and empirical articles began to flow in.

Notwithstanding the marked presence of articles 'made in Brazil', contributions from other Latin American countries continued but with a clear downturn in articles from within Argentina, due to a growing preference on the part of 'traditional' authors to publish in 'e-journals' or so called 'open journals', such as the Spanish PASOS–On Line (www.pasosonline.org), at the University of la Laguna, Tenerife, or *Cuadernos en Turismo*, at the University of Murcia (http://revistas.um.es/turismo). Even though *Cuadernos* has a limited paper-edition, its real presence is 'on line'. On the other hand, articles sent in by Spanish authors in search of greater projection on the Latin American market became more frequent.

The beginning of 2007 marked an important change for *Estudios y Perspectivas en Turismo*, when it was included in the Basic Core of Argentinean Scientific Journals by the CONICET (National Council of Scientific and Technical Research) which opened the doors to its being incorporated in the index of SciELO (Scientific Electronic Library Online), a virtual bookstore with the full texts of Ibero-American scientific journals, and kudos for researchers published in the same (www.scielo. org.ar/scielo.php). The inclusion of *Estudios y Perspectivas en Turismo* (www.estudiosenturismo.com.ar) in SciELO led to articles of great quality, by researchers in various different fields, parts of a project financed by the major research agencies.

Another kind of article began to be received, indicating a new research trend towards anthropology, sociology and the social sciences in general. Poverty mitigation through tourism in Latin American countries (Font, 2008), econometric analyses of tourism, modelling in order to determine international tourist flows, and the impact of tourism on archaeological sites were the main trendsetters with interest in ecotourism and nature conservation gradually dropping off. Likewise, gastronomy and wine became important as fields to be researched. As regards research design, exploratory research gave way to descriptive research design, with surveys as the staple research tool.

The participation in SciELO also requires journals to have their own website with back issues of at least three volumes, and the commitment to reflect online all the former issues. It is also suggested that the articles be published in their original language, as well as in Spanish, to make them available to a wider readership. That is how *Estudios y Perspectivas en Turismo* has kept its faithful contributors but has drawn specialists from the world over, who have only become acquainted with the journal since it was included in SciELO, through browsing for specific subjects. Given the importance of this network in Brazil, the number of articles originating from this country has continued to grow, as indeed have the numbers of articles from other countries. The most evident change, however, has been the increased contribution by Argentineans from different areas such as anthropology, geography and history. This journal has moved from struggling to produce three or four articles every three months, 20 years back, to a bi-monthly publication, with double the number of contributions, of greater complexity and more designed for specialist readers.

Final comments

Bearing in mind our goal, to analyse the last 20 years of tourism research in Latin America through the evolution of an academic journal, we can say that the trend is indicative of what occurred in the region as a whole. We can see how trends in tourism research have evolved over the years, thanks to the bolstering effect of the journal. The end of the 20th century and the early 21st century show that tourism has matured as a field of research, moving from the fixed black and white photos of the past, either positive or negative, to the colourful and dynamic productions of the presentday.

We have seen how the journal has risen to the ever greater standards of evaluation and appraisal, with the consolidation of tourism research and know-how in educational institutions and scientific or technical organizations. In many cases, such as in Argentina, this happened slowly and somewhat ambiguously but was understood, nevertheless, as a priority (Bertoncello, 2005).

The shift from the perception of tourism exclusively as an economic activity, to tourism as a social practice in the broadest possible sense, led to the inclusion of theoretical frameworks borrowed from the various disciplines of the social sciences. This multidisciplinary perspective enriched the discourse of and on tourism, allowing for more ambitious methodologies and broader-reaching conclusions and results.

Tourism education nowadays generally recognizes the need to produce research in order to advance. The curriculum also integrates research projects and their results into the syllabus. The results are visible. Tourism, as a field of research, is in full bloom, incorporating new concepts and methodological developments. A whole body of knowledge on the subject has evolved which allows us to overcome the restrictive and short-sighted black or white perspectives of the past.

Nobody doubts any longer that tourism is an academic field in its own right, incorporating a myriad of perspectives, quite a different picture from the past. But the future holds challenges for tourism. How will the financial crisis affect it, for example? If tourism drops off, will the interest of social scientists drop off accordingly?

Looking to the future, we are optimistic with respect to tourism research. On the one hand, it would seem now that knowledge-based research is an integral part of scientific institutions which now consider tourism to be an important field of study. At the same time, an increasing number of scholars work in the field and receive recognition for the same from their peers, something which did not happen in the past. More and more research and researchers focusing on tourism make for more and more academic papers available for further studies, not only for those interested in tourism but for other related fields.

Then again, research is more and more oriented towards subsidies or action-based (both for policy making or management and planning). This has broadened the scope and the horizons of tourism. General concerns, such as sustainability or community involvement, have become part of tourism development studies, and other wider social concerns such as poverty reduction. Tourism and development are no longer considered to be exclusive of one another, since it is now clear how tourism can enhance the potential to attract foreign investment and produce employment. The negative impacts of tourism are more visible now in the concerns pertaining to identity, through socio-territorial development, citizen involvement and education. Another positive aspect is the concern with respect to quality tourism that is no longer only restricted to the business as such but now factors in the quality of life of the local population as well as the enrichment of the tourist experience.

The growth of tourism research in Latin America is also shown by the increase in tourism related conferences organized by universities and researchers' associations. While older journals like *Gestión Turística* (Chile) and *Aportes y Transferencias* (Argentina) are still alive, new journals come into being, mainly in Mexico (*El Periplo Sustentable, Culinaria*) and Brazil (*RBTur, CulTur*), benefiting from the capacity of the new technologies to reduce cost and increase visibility. Moreover, conferences, like the annual reunion of the MERCOSUR anthropologists, also now have special sessions dedicated to tourism studies.

References

Aksu, A.A. (2004) 'Evaluación de las necesidades de capacitación en el nivel gerencial. Un ejemplo de la región de Antalya, Turquía', *Estudios y Perspectivas en Turismo*, **13**, 24-34.

Bar-On, R.R. (1995) 'Desarrollo del turismo y las inversiones en Israel', *Estudios y Perspectivas en Turismo*, **4** (2), 127-146.

Bertoncello, R. (2002) 'Turismo y territorio. Otras practicas, otras miradas', *Aportes y Transferencias*, **6** (2), 29-50.

Bertoncello, R. (2005) 'Documento de base y síntesis del Panel del "Sector Turismo". Bases para un plan estratégico de mediano plazo en ciencia, tecnología e innovación (Argentina, Ministerio de Educación, Ciencia y Tecnología de la Nación)', *SECYT*, Buenos Aires: Anexo 4 Paneles estratégicos II, pp.133-167.

Boschi, A.M. (1998) 'Efectos ambientales del turismo en el sendero a la cascada Chaichín: Parque Nacional Lanín, Argentina', *Estudios y Perspectivas en Turismo*, 7, 47-62.

Bote Gómez, V. (1993) 'El turismo y la conservación y rehabilitación del patrimonio rural en España', *Estudios y Perspectivas en Turismo*, **2** (1), 65-77.

Chirivella Caballero, M. (1995) 'Desarrollo de nuevos productos turísticos en Gran Canaria', *Estudios y Perspectivas en Turismo*, **4** (3), 181-200.

De Kadt, E. (1979) *Tourism. Passport to Development? Perspectives on the Social and Cultural Effects of Tourism in Developing Countries*, New York: Oxford University Press.

Domínguez, P., Burguete, E. and Bernard, A. (1997) 'El empowerment como estrategia de liderazgo para reducir la rotación voluntaria de personal', *Estudios y Perspectivas en Turismo*, **6**, 17-37.

Domínguez, P., Burguete, E. and Bernard, A. (2003) 'Efectos del 11 de septiembre en la hotelería mexicana. Reflexión sobre la monodependencia turística', *Estudios y Perspectivas en Turismo*, **12**, 335-348.

Font, X. (2008) 'Sostenibilidad y alivio de la pobreza en países en vías de desarrollo. El papel del hotelero y del investigador', *Estudios y Perspectivas en Turismo*, **17**, 7-28.

Gerlero, M. (1991) 'Régimen de equipaje. El turista en el Código Aduanero Argentino', *Revista Latinoamericana en Turismo*, **1** (2), 120-129.

Guevara Ramos, R., Molina, S. and Tresserras, J. (n.d.) 'Hacia un estado de la cuestión en investigación turística', available from http://web.ujat.mx/dip/estudios _multidisciplinarios_turismo (accessed March 2009).

Hiernaux Nicolás, D. (2000) 'La fuerza de lo efímero. Apuntes sobre la construcción de la vida cotidiana en el turismo', in Alicia Lindón (ed.) *La Vida Cotidiana y su Espacio*-temporalidad, Mexico City: Anthropos, pp. 95-122.

Jafari, J. (1994) 'La cientifiación del turismo', *Estudios y Perspectivas en Turismo*, **3** (1), 7-36.

Leal, S.R. (2006) 'Madurez en la investigación científica en turismo en Brasil y el mundo', *Estudios y Perspectivas en Turismo*, **15**, 81 – 92.

Marchena Gómez, M.J. and Velasco Martín, A. (1993) 'La región Caribe como espacio turístico', *Estudios y Perspectivas en Turismo*, **2** (2), 130-149.

Martínez Rivarola, M., Tagliorette, A. and Campagna, C. (1995) 'Impactos del turismo sobre el comportamiento de las ballenas', *Estudios y Perspectivas en Turismo*, **4** (3), 226-242.

Mathieson, A. and Wall, G. (1990) *Turismo. Repercusiones económicas, físicas y sociales*, México City: Editorial Trillas.

Otero, A. and González, R. (1998) 'Umbrales ambientales límites para actividades turísticas. Parque Nacional Lanín, Argentina', *Estudios y Perspectivas en Turismo*, **7**, 111-129.

Pearce, D. (1991) *Desarrollo turístico. Su planificación y ubicación geográfica*, México City: Editorial Trillas.

Pearce, D. (1993) 'Patrones de viajes turísticos e impactos regionales. Aspectos y ejemplos de Nueva Zelanda', *Estudios y Perspectivas en Turismo*, **2** (4), 301-320.

Requejo Liberal, J. (1993) 'El papel de la planificación en la resolución de los conflictos entre agricultura y turismo en el litoral y sus efectos sobre el medio ambiente', *Estudios y Perspectivas en Turismo*, **2** (1), 54-64.

Riley, M. (1995) 'Análisis del desarrollo del turismo en las Islas Malvinas', *Estudios y Perspectivas en Turismo*, **4** (2), 93-100.

Rodríguez Woog, S. and Hiernaux Nicolás, D. (1992) 'Turismo y absorción de la fuerza de trabajo: el caso de México', *Estudios y Perspectivas en Turismo*, **1** (1), 21–43.

Schlüter, R. (1985) 'Tourism studies at Argentine universities', *Tourism Management*, **6** (1), 70.

Schlüter, R. (1988) 'In search of cultural identity. Latin American tourism literature', *Annals of Tourism Research*, **15** (2), 285-288.

Schlüter, R. (1991) 'Creación del CIETAL: Acapulco, México, 14 de junio 1991', *Revista Latinoamericana de Turismo*, **1** (4), 291–292.

Schlüter, R. (1992) '2° Curso interamericano de actualización para la gestión turística', *Estudios y Perspectivas en Turismo*, **1**, 56-66.

Schlüter, R. (1993) 'Tourism and development in Latin America', *Annals of Tourism Research*, **20** (2), 364-367.

Schlüter, R. (1998) 'Tourism development: a Latin American perspective', in W. Theobald (ed.), *Global Tourism*, 2nd edn, Oxford: Butterworth Heinemann, pp. 216-230.

Schlüter, R. and Winter, G. (1993) *El fenómeno turístico. Reflexiones desde una perspectiva integradora*, Buenos Aires: Editorial Docencia.

Sebreli, J.J. (1984) *Mar del Plata, el ocio represivo*, Buenos Aires: Editorial Leonardo Buschi.

Veblen, T. (1992) *Teoría de la clase ociosa*, México City: Fondo de Cultura Económica.

Wall, G. (1995) 'Turismo y patrimonio. Necesidad de estudios comparados', *Estudios y Perspectivas en Turismo*, **4** (4), 340-350.

12 Tourism and hospitality research in Mainland China: trends from 2000 to 2008

Cathy H.C. Hsu, Jue Huang, and Songshan (Sam) Huang

Introduction

Accompanying three decades of rapid economic growth, the tourism industry in China (which refers to mainland China in the present study) has experienced momentous development. In 2006, China ranked as the world's number four and number five tourism destinations based on international tourist arrivals and tourism receipts, respectively (UNWTO, 2007). With a gradual loosening of policies by the central government allowing Chinese citizens to travel abroad, China has also become the biggest outbound tourism market in Asia, with travellers reaching 40.95 million in 2007. Domestic tourist arrivals reached 1.61 billion in 2007, more than double the figure in 2001 (China National Tourism Administration, 2008). Undoubtedly, China's tourism industry has emerged as a major force in the global tourism market.

While the tourism industry in China has caught much attention both domestically and internationally, tourism research in China still remains as a relatively unfamiliar activity to the international research community. Due to language barriers and resource constraints, opinions and research findings of indigenous Chinese scholars have hardly been exposed to the outside world (Zhang, 2003). Several books on China's tourism (e.g. Lew and Yu, 1995; Zhang et al., 2005) have been published in English and dozens of articles discussing China's tourism issues can be found in international journals (e.g. Pine, 2002; Xiao, 1997; Zhang et al., 1999). However, most of the authors are overseas scholars and thus cannot represent their counterparts' activities in China. Furthermore, among the limited work in English on China's tourism, few have pictured the overall development of tourism research in China. The term 'tourism' is used in the rest of the chapter to represent both tourism and hospitality unless otherwise noted.

Tourism research in China progressed concomitantly with the development of the tourism industry in the country. From the founding of People's Republic of China in 1949 until the economic reform in 1978, tourism was nothing more than a tool of foreign affairs under the direct control of the government. In the late 1970s, tourism was advocated as an economic activity as part of the government's opening-up policy, and early tourism research efforts concentrated on introducing the concept of tourism and its related economic activities to policy-makers and the general public (Zhang, 2003). The industrial position of tourism was gradually established in the 1980s, and in 1986 tourism was included in China's national plan for social and economic development for the first time. Research during this period focused on 'what to do' and 'how to do', which laid the grounds for the government's formulation of tourism development strategies and policies (Zhang, 2003: 72). The most influential tourism research journals sprang up in the late 1980s (e.g. *Tourism Tribune* started publication in 1986, *Tourism Science* in 1987, and *Journal of Guilin Institute of Tourism* in 1989), signalling the proliferation of tourism research in China as well as the dissemination of research findings.

Since the 1990s, tourism research has been passionately debated among researchers in China. However, much of the work was published in Chinese with a few exceptions (e.g. Zhang, 2003). Li and Zhao (2007) commented that tourism research in China adopted basically a conservative closed-door practice without much international intercourse. Most research was government-directed, which had two manifestations. First, shifts in government policies often brought waves of 'research fever', focusing on issues of policy priorities (Xie, 2003). Second, government agencies and officials often have research publications related to their administrative functions. However, publication by government agencies and officials is gradually declining, and more research by scholars from universities is appearing. For example, in Zhao's (2000) review of publications in *Tourism Tribune* from 1990 to 1999, authorship from government agencies and universities was 26 per cent and 47 per cent, respectively, and was 13.3 per cent and 71.6 per cent respectively in Zhang and Lu's (2004) review of the same journal from 1999 to 2003. A similar pattern was found by Wu *et al.* (2001) for authorship comparison between 1986–92 and 1993–99 periods.

Research methods used were predominantly descriptive, speculative, and qualitative (Zhang and Lu, 2004; Zhu and Liu, 2004), and research topics covered were mainly related to tourism as an economic activity, with trade/industrial administration, corporate management, tourism resources development, and tourism planning on top of the list (Zhang, 2002; Zhao, 2000; Zhu and Liu, 2004). However, accompanying the shift in authorship, theoretical research (Zhao, 2000) and studies using more advanced qualitative and quantitative methods (Zhang and Lu, 2004) have been conducted by scholars.

Research objectives and methods

Prior studies about the status of tourism research in China mainly investigated research themes/topics and researcher background (e.g. Zhao, 2000, Wu *et al.*, 2001; Zhang, 2002). Very few studies have conducted a comprehensive examination of research methods employed (e.g. Zhang and Lu, 2004; Zhu and Liu, 2004). Comparative studies that examined tourism research in China and abroad were even fewer (e.g. Xie, 2003; Zhu and Liu, 2004).

Based on an extensive review of the literature, this study has two purposes. First, it aims to provide an overview of academic research activities in tourism in China, and to reveal the trends of their development since the beginning of the 21st century. Second, the study compares publications on China's tourism in leading journals in China (in Chinese) and in international journals (in English) to reveal similarities and differences between the two sources.

Ten mainland Chinese researchers from five cities were asked to name and rank the top tourism and hospitality journals in China. *Tourism Tribune* and *Tourism Science* were unanimously selected as the top two. All full articles published in the two journals from 2000 to 2008 were reviewed. Written discussions, conference reviews, industry reports, and book reviews were excluded from the analysis. A total of 1511 papers were identified.

Research about China's tourism industry in international journals for the same period was represented by publications in three tourism journals (*Annals of Tourism Research*, *Tourism Management*, and *Journal of Travel Research*) and three hospitality journals (*Cornell Hotel and Restaurant Administration Quarterly*, *International Journal of Hospitality Management*, and *Journal of Hospitality & Tourism Research*), based on McKercher *et al.*'s (2006) ranking. The study searched for papers that contained 'China' or 'Chinese' in the abstract, keyword, and full text. The resulting papers were examined to identify those related to China's tourism issues. Altogether, 62 papers were found.

Content analysis of the chosen papers focused on their background disciplines, research topics/themes, and research methods. To reveal the composition of the research community, authorship information including authors' age, gender, and institutional affiliations was analysed. Cross-tabulations were also conducted to disclose relationship between authors' research approaches and their background as well as to identify characteristics of the research community. Authorship analysis was restricted to Chinese papers because demographic information for authors of English papers was unavailable. Two researchers worked together to perform the content analysis; any ambiguities or disputes regarding the coding were resolved after discussion with an experienced researcher.

Results

Background disciplines

Because tourism embraces virtually all aspects of society, tourism research has been approached through a variety of disciplinary perspectives. Goeldner and Ritchie (2009) listed 21 disciplinary inputs to the study of tourism, a list that was used as the coding guide in this study. Two of the 21 categories (architecture and kinesiology) were absent in all papers. However, literature review was added as a category for papers that discussed the overall status of tourism research in China (e.g. Wu *et al.*, 2001).

Table 12.1 lists the disciplines that together contributed to over 91 per cent of the 1511 Chinese papers. Approximately 55 per cent of the papers were informed by the top four disciplines of business, urban and regional planning, economics, and marketing. Other disciplines that were scantly represented and not shown in Table 12.1 included agriculture, geography, political science, history, anthropology, entrepreneurship, and transportation.

The 62 English papers represented 12 disciplinary inputs. Interestingly, the 12 most popular disciplines in Chinese papers mostly overlapped with those of the English papers. Thus, the two streams of research appeared to draw on similar disciplinary inputs, although with different priorities.

Table 12.1: Background disciplines of the reviewed papers

Chinese papers			English papers		
Background disciplines	N	%	Background disciplines	n	%
Business	247	16.35	Hotel and restaurant administration	14	22.58
Urban and regional planning	226	14.96	Psychology	13	20.97
Economics	189	12.51	Business	7	11.29
Marketing	167	11.05	Parks and recreation	6	9.68
Hotel and restaurant administration	102	6.75	Political science	5	8.06
Parks and recreation	99	6.55	Sociology	4	6.45
Psychology	95	6.29	Marketing	3	4.84
Sociology	78	5.16	Urban and regional planning	3	4.84
Literature review	55	3.64	Economics	3	4.84
Environmental studies	49	3.24	Anthropology	1	1.61
Law	46	3.04	Environmental studies	1	1.61
Education	28	1.85	Law	1	1.61
Other disciplines	130	8.61	Education	1	1.61
Total	**1511**	**100.00**	**Total**	**62**	**100.00**

Research themes

The Chinese papers covered a wide range of research areas. Table 12.2 lists the most popular research themes that each has 40 or more papers published. Collectively, they accounted for nearly 54 per cent of the papers. Tourism resources/attractions/product development, management, and protection was the most often researched topic. This stream of research focused on the development of tourism resources (e.g. natural and cultural resources), attractions (e.g. scenic areas, ethnic towns), and products (e.g. itinerary design). Other topics debated under this theme included strategies and modes of tourism development, property rights and operating rights of resources/attractions, attraction interpretation system, and admission ticket pricing.

Hotel management also attracted much research attention and included issues such as industry development status and trends, marketing, financial management, customer service, hotel group development, and development of diverse accommodation facilities (e.g. economy hotel, hostel). Studies on tourism marketing and market analysis were primarily for different places (e.g. scenic areas, administrative regions) and market segments (e.g. domestic tourists, self-drive tourists).

Tourist behaviour research focused predominantly on tourist satisfaction and decision-making. Other issues included tourist motivation, perception/experience, and travel characteristics of different markets. A few papers examined tourists' complaint behaviour and online travel community. MICE (meetings, incentives, conferences and exhibitions) studies focused on industry status and trends, development conditions, and strategy for different cities or events (e.g. 2008 Beijing Olympics). Several papers investigated MICE attendees' perception and decision-making as well as the impact of MICE. In addition to those shown in Table 12.2, topics that were less popular but nevertheless received considerable attention included urban tourism, rural tourism, law and regulation, heritage tourism, travel agency management, tourism education and research, e-business, social and cultural impact, and community participation.

Table 12.2: Top research themes of the Chinese papers

Themes	N	%
Tourism resources/attractions/product development, management and protection	183	12.11
Hotel management	100	6.62
Tourism marketing and market analysis	84	5.56
Tourist behaviour	75	4.96
MICE	70	4.63
Tourism economics	57	3.77
Destination management	56	3.71
Regional tourism cooperation and development	55	3.64
Human resources management	47	3.11
Tourism planning	44	2.91
Ecotourism	42	2.78
Other themes	698	46.19
Total	1511	100.00

Compared with Chinese papers, English papers covered fewer topics, which could be attributed to the limited number of publications reviewed. Tourist behaviour and hotel management were the most popular topics, with 12 and 9 papers, respectively. Other topics examined were similar to those in the Chinese papers, with one or two articles on each topic.

Research methods

Research methods were coded into three broad categories of qualitative, quantitative, and mixed-methods. Papers that used both qualitative and quantitative methods but were mainly informed by one method were categorized as either qualitative or quantitative. A study was classified as 'mixed-methods' only when both methods made substantial contribution to the research findings and conclusions (e.g. Yang *et al.*, 2007). Qualitative papers were further classified into two levels. Level One referred to those that did not possess a clearly defined methodology; most often they were discussion or opinion essays about a topic. Papers classified as Level Two provided information about the research methods used, based on which results were disclosed and conclusions drawn.

Table 12.3: Distribution of research methods in the Chinese papers (2000–08)

Research methods	2000		2001		2002		2003		2004	
	n	%	n	%	n	%	n	%	n	%
Qualitative, Level 1	119	97.54	123	89.13	114	88.37	117	89.31	127	82.47
Qualitative, Level 2	0	0.00	1	0.72	0	0.00	1	0.76	3	1.95
Quantitative	1	0.82	14	10.14	11	8.53	9	6.87	21	13.64
Mixed	2	1.64	0	0.00	4	3.10	4	3.05	3	1.95
Total	**122**	**100.00**	**138**	**100.00**	**129**	**100.00**	**131**	**100.00**	**154**	**100.00**

Research methods	2005		2006		2007		2008		Total	
	n	%	n	%	n	%	n	%	n	%
Qualitative, Level 1	134	77.46	158	63.71	127	53.59	76	42.46	1095	72.47
Qualitative, Level 2	0	0.00	8	3.23	5	2.11	8	4.47	26	1.72
Quantitative	34	19.65	77	31.05	93	39.24	86	48.04	346	22.90
Mixed	5	2.89	5	2.02	12	5.06	9	5.03	44	2.91
Total	**173**	**100.00**	**248**	**100.00**	**237**	**100.00**	**179**	**100.00**	**1511**	**100.00**

Table 12.3 shows the distribution of research methods for the Chinese papers from 2000 to 2008. Percentages of Level One qualitative papers decreased steadily over the years, while those of other methods experienced conspicuous growth. In 2000, 97.5 per cent of the papers belonged to Level One. By 2008, 42.5 per cent fell into

this category. In contrast, the percentage of papers with quantitative method increased from 0.8 per cent in 2000 to 48 per cent in 2008. The distribution of Level One, Level Two, quantitative, and mixed-methods for the English papers for the nine years combined was 11.29 per cent, 25.81 per cent, 48.39 per cent, and 14.52 per cent, respectively. The numbers were not analysed by year due to the small sample size ($n = 62$). Compared with Chinese papers, English articles had much lower percentage for Level One and higher percentages for the other categories.

The following sections present more detailed information about the research methods used. As discussed previously, papers coded as Level One did not provide any information about the methods used. Thus the following findings about data collection and analysis were based on the remaining papers, which included 416 Chinese and 55 English papers.

Data collection

The majority of Chinese papers (83.9 per cent) used a single method to collect data, with questionnaire surveys and the use of secondary data being the most frequently employed techniques (Table 12.4). About 16 per cent used mixed methods with a combination of techniques, such as interview, questionnaire, Delphi, and observation. Techniques used in English papers were similar to those of Chinese papers, except that English papers had a higher percentage using mixed methods.

Table 12.4: Methods of data collection

Chinese papers			English papers		
Data collection	n	%	Data collection	n	%
Single method	349	83.89	Single method	37	67.27
Questionnaire	200	48.08	Questionnaire	23	41.82
Secondary data	124	29.81	Secondary data	8	14.55
Interview	10	2.40	Interview	6	10.91
Literature review	8	1.92			
Delphi	4	0.96			
Web search	3	0.72			
Mixed methods	67	16.10	Mixed methods	18	32.73
Interview, questionnaire	27	6.49	Interview, questionnaire	3	5.45
Questionnaire, secondary data	7	1.68	Interview, questionnaire, Secondary data	3	5.45
Delphi, questionnaire	5	1.20	Interview, observation, secondary data	2	3.64
Questionnaire, observation	4	0.96	Interview, secondary data	2	3.64
Others	24	5.77	Others	8	14.55
Total	416	100.00	Total	55	100.00

Data analysis

Of the Chinese papers, 39.2 per cent utilized only one statistical method to analyse data (Table 12.5), and descriptive statistics were the most commonly used single method (32.2 per cent). There were 34.6 per cent using assorted statistical methods. Besides descriptive statistics, which were most often used in combination with other methods, exploratory factor analysis (EFA), linear and non-linear regressions, and Cronbach's alpha were used frequently. Other less popular methods included correlation, *T*-tests, ANOVA, cluster analysis, structural equation modelling (SEM), confirmatory factor analysis (CFA), and chi-square test.

Among the 416 Chinese papers, 26.2 per cent used methods other than statistics as the main techniques for data analysis, although some types of statistical analysis were used as auxiliary methods. Researchers apparently were keen on constructing various evaluation indicators or indices (e.g. competitiveness index, customer satisfaction index), accounting for 13.9 per cent of the papers. For qualitative studies, content analysis was the most commonly used method. Other methods such as tourism trends forecasting, artificial neural network model, and importance-performance analysis (IPA) were used less frequently.

Among the 55 English papers, 11 used only descriptive statistics (20.0 per cent) and 22 used assorted statistical methods (40.0 per cent), similar to those found in Chinese papers. For methods other than statistics, the most commonly used was content analysis, found in 16 papers (29.1 per cent).

Table 12.5: Methods of data analysis

Data analysis methods	Chinese papers		English papers	
	n	%	n	%
Single statistical method	163	39.18	11	20.00
Descriptive analysis	134	32.21	11	20.00
Regression	15	3.61		
EFA	6	1.44		
Correlation	4	0.96		
Cronbach's alpha	4	0.96		
Assorted statistical methods	144	34.62	22	40.00
Other methods besides statistics	109	26.19	22	40.00
Evaluation index construction	58	13.94	1	1.82
Content analysis	12	2.88	16	29.09
Tourism trends forecasting methods	6	1.44	1	1.82
Artificial neural network model	6	1.44		
IPA	5	1.20	2	3.64
Other methods	22	5.29	2	3.64
Total	416	100.00	55	100.00

Authorship information

A total of 1654 individuals contributed to the 1511 Chinese papers. They reported affiliation with organizations in 29 provinces/municipalities/autonomous regions as well as 10 overseas countries/regions. The top three places were Beijing, Shanghai, and Guangdong, which together accounted for about 42 per cent of the authors. For the 116 individuals who authored the 62 English papers, 34 were from Hong Kong, 23 from the USA, 20 from China, and the remaining from seven other countries/regions.

Among the 1654 contributing authors of the Chinese papers, 1357 provided information on age and gender. Authors were divided into five age groups (Table 12.6). The main force of the research community constituted authors born in the 1960s, 1970s, and 1980s, accounting for 84.1 per cent. Moreover, when examining the gender distribution across age groups, it was evident that the percentages of females in younger age groups were progressively increasing. The chi-square test was significant with $X^2(4) = 115.26$, $p<.001$.

Table 12.6: Age group and gender cross-tabulation

Gender	Birth year	1920-40s	1950s	1960s	1970s	1980s	Total
Female	Count	7	36	105	236	161	545
	% within age group	10.29	24.32	28.38	47.01	59.85	-
Male	Count	61	112	265	266	108	812
	% within age group	89.71	75.68	71.62	52.99	40.15	-
Total	Count	68	148	370	502	269	1357
	% of total	5.01	10.91	27.27	36.99	19.82	100.00

Table 12.7: Age group and research method cross-tabulation

Birth year	Research methods	Level 1	Level 2	Quantitative	Mixed methods	Total
1920-50s	Count	208	0	42	5	255
	% within age group	81.57	0.00	16.47	1.96	100.00
1960s	Count	308	10	103	10	431
	% within age group	71.46	2.32	23.90	2.32	100.00
1970s	Count	284	14	137	17	452
	% within age group	62.83	3.10	30.31	3.76	100.00
1980s	Count	69	2	51	8	130
	% within age group	53.08	1.54	39.23	6.15	100.00
Total	Count	869	26	333	40	1268
	% of total	68.53	2.05	26.26	3.15	100.00

Table 12.7 shows the cross-tabulation between research method used and age group (based on the first author's birth year). As authorship changes from older to younger age groups, the use of Level One method declines, while use of other methods increases. The chi-square test was highly significant with $X^2 (9) = 49.21$, $p<.001$, indicating the use of more sophisticated methods by younger authors.

The Chinese paper authors' affiliations were classified into five types, namely enterprise, government, press, research institute, and university. Cross-tabulation between publication year and institutional type (based on 2572 author name exposures) revealed that the contribution from enterprises, government organizations, and the press witnessed a gradual decline over the years, while that from universities increased from 77.6 per cent in 2000 to 93 per cent in 2008. The share of contributions from research institutes remained relatively unchanged.

Authors from different institutional types seemed to have their own preferences for research methods. The Level Two method was not used by authors with enterprise, government, and press affiliations. Moreover, authors from enterprises and government organizations did not use mixed-methods, and authors from the press did not use quantitative methods. In other words, only authors from research institutes and universities employed all four types of methods shown in Table 12.3.

Discussion

Research about China's tourism industry draws on a wide range of disciplinary inputs. However, the top five disciplines that underlie 62 per cent of the Chinese papers were business or economics related, suggesting that tourism was often investigated for its economic values. Nevertheless, studies from alternative perspectives have emerged recently in Chinese papers. For example, among the 95 papers from a psychological perspective, 84 appeared after 2003. Similarly, 54 of the 78 papers from a sociological perspective appeared after 2004. The findings support Aramberri and Xie's (2003) view that the future direction of research is likely to shift from the current economic-oriented mentality towards investigations with multiple disciplinary inputs and priorities.

In terms of research themes, tourism researchers in China were mainly interested in topics such as tourism resources/attractions/product development, hotel management, tourism marketing and market analysis. The results were generally consistent with those of previous studies (e.g. Zhao, 2000; Zhang, 2002; Zhu and Liu, 2004). Although the popularity of these topics remains largely unchanged over the study period, other themes are beginning to gain recognition. For example, most studies on topics such as tourism impacts, tourist behaviour, community participation, leisure and recreation, and rural tourism emerged after 2004 or 2005. This paralleled the emerging shift in disciplinary inputs discussed above, in view of the fact that these newly emerging topics were mainly examined from psychological or sociological viewpoints.

The dominance of an economic/business orientation among researchers in China suggests that studies in China largely reflect single-minded advocacy voices for the economic potential of tourism. This represents the first stage of the scientification journey of tourism as a field of investigation (Jafari, 2002). Nevertheless, changes in research topics as well as their underlying background disciplines in recent years suggest that research in China generally follows the route experienced in many western countries. The shift from an economic/business perspective to a more social science perspective indicates an emerging holistic and multidisciplinary understanding of tourism, where tourism is treated not only as an array of economic activities but also as a set of sociocultural practices (Jafari, 2002). However, an increasing range of tourism research, other than that within the narrow boundaries of the economic/business field, calls for innovative theoretical and methodological approaches (Tribe, 2005). While new approaches suggest that, internationally, tourism research is at an important turning point in its development (Tribe, 2005), the theoretical and methodological aspects of tourism research in China are less mature.

Concerning research methods, the majority of Chinese papers (72.47 per cent) were discussion or opinion essays devoid of any research methodology. As a result, the conclusions made are at best untested hypotheses that await further investigation (Ma, 2007). This contrasts sharply with the English papers that have about 11 per cent coded as Level One. Excluding Level One papers, techniques for both data collection and analysis employed in the remaining Chinese papers are comparable to those in English papers, although the latter more often utilize mixed techniques for data collection and methods other than statistics for data analysis.

This study also identified quite a number of Chinese papers introducing tourism related theories and methodologies from abroad to the indigenous audience (e.g. Dai and Bao, 2003). However, fewer studies were found that expanded or contributed to the existing international knowledge base. Researchers in China may not yet have realized the research potential of many unique problems that the world's largest socialist developing country confronts (Xiao, 2005), or they may be unable to capitalize on the opportunities because of theoretical or methodological deficiency (Ma, 2007).

Although the rigour of academic research in China still lags behind that of the international scholarly work, the future of tourism research appears to be optimistic due to the following findings. First, the mainstay of the research community in China constitutes authors born between the 1960s and 1980s, and these younger researchers are more likely to employ methods other than Level One qualitative research. This supports Ma's (2007) comments that the older generation mainly relies on personal experience and reflection to produce research work. Second, consistent with previous studies (e.g. Wu *et al.*, 2001), authorship of non-academic backgrounds (i.e. enterprise, government, and press) has steadily shrunk over the study period, and that with university affiliation is increasing. The latter group constitutes authors who are more likely to utilize more sophisticated research methods (e.g. Level Two and mixed-methods), a finding that is comparable to that of Zhang and Lu

(2004). Thus, with more members of the younger generation and of university affiliation joining the research community, China's tourism research should gradually catch up with the international academic practice.

The limited but promising publications by researchers from mainland China in English journals and by those from overseas scholars in Chinese journals suggests increasing academic exchange and collaboration across geographic regions. Most of these publications are co-authored by researchers from within and outside China. Such collaboration appears to be a recent phenomenon. Among the 29 name exposures of researchers from mainland China in English journals, 25 appeared after 2005. Similarly, of the 67 overseas researchers' names that appeared in the Chinese journal database, 52 appeared after 2004. In addition, 55 of the 62 English papers related to China's tourism issues appeared after 2004, which indicates that scholarly discourse about China's tourism development has recently been brought to an international forum. After decades of economic reform and opening-up, tourism research in China can no longer be conducted with doors closed.

Based on the above discussion, a few issues seem to be fundamental to the advancement of tourism research in China. First, it is imperative to equip upcoming generations of researchers with advanced methodological skills. Chinese universities could undertake joint research degree programmes with overseas institutions. Bringing in skilled researchers from abroad (either overseas Chinese or foreigners) and entrusting them with the education of research students may be another approach.

Second, although there are a number of hospitality oriented journals in China, they have not yet been widely recognized in the academic community. This study also found an increasing number of articles on leisure and recreation since 2004 in the two journals reviewed, indicating that leisure studies are still in the embryonic stage in China because leisure-oriented journals are presently non-existent in the country. Internationally, studies on tourism, hospitality, and leisure each have their own established research track and clearly demarcated outlets for publication. Upgrading tourism research in China also necessitates the establishment of credible academic journals. Although Chinese researchers are encouraged to publish in English journals, it is still necessary to provide credible publication outlets in Chinese due to language barriers. This calls for institutional support and dedication from journal editors and reviewers.

The rapidly developing tourism sector as well as its increasingly complex social, economic, and environmental impacts indicate that rigorous and ongoing research efforts are imperative for laying a sound foundation for the future development of tourism in China. The establishment of the China Tourism Academy (CTA) in 2008 under the National Tourism Administration signified the importance attributed to tourism research on a national level. One of the key responsibilities of the CTA is to undertake research on basic theoretical and policy issues as well as on fundamental and focal problems. The founding of CTA may well herald the coming of a new age for tourism research in China if CTA can effectively take up a leadership role through collaborative strategies between researchers from various organizations (e.g. government agencies, universities, and the industry) to address the nation's tourism research imperatives.

References

Aramberri, J. and Xie, Y. (2003) 'Multi-vision and China's tourism research – comment on the domestic and foreign relevant literature', *Tourism Tribune*, **18** (6), 14-20.

China National Tourism Administration (2008) *China Tourism Statistics Bulletin 2007*, available from www.cnta.gov.cn (accessed on 20 March 2009).

Dai, G. and Bao, J. (2003) 'On the concept, content and method of research on Event and Event Tourism (E & ET) In Western countries and its enlightenment', *Tourism Tribune*, **18** (5), 26-34.

Goeldner, C.R. and Ritchie, J.R. (2009) *Tourism: Principles, Practices, Philosophies*, 11th edn, Hoboken, NJ: John Wiley & Sons.

Jafari, J. (2002) 'Tourism's Landscape of Knowledge. ReVista: Tourism in the Americas', available from http://www.drclas.harvard.edu/revista/articles/view/35 (accessed on 25 May 2009).

Lew, A. and Yu, L. (eds) (1995) *Tourism in China: Geographic, Political, and Economic Perspectives*, Boulder, CO: Westview.

Li, X. and Zhao, W. (2007) 'Progress in international tourism research on China: evidence from *Annals of Tourism Research*, *Tourism Management*, and *Journal of Travel Research*', *Tourism Tribune*, **22** (3), 90-96.

Ma, C. (2007) 'From concept to empirical study: the future of tourism research in China', *Tourism Tribune*, **22** (3), 6-7.

McKercher, B., Law, R. and Lam, T. (2006) 'Rating tourism and hospitality journals', *Tourism Management*, **27** (6), 1235-1252.

Pine, R. (2002) 'China's hotel industry: serving a massive market', *Cornell Hotel and Restaurant Administration Quarterly*, **43** (3), 61-70.

Tribe, J. (2005) 'Editorial: new tourism research', *Tourism Recreation Research*, **30** (2), 5-8.

UNWTO (2007) 'Tourism Highlights 2007 Edition', available from www.unwto.org (accessed on 23 August 2008).

Wu, B., Song, Z. and Deng, L. (2001) 'A summary of China's tourism research work in the past fourteen years – academic trends as reflected in *Tourism Tribune*', *Tourism Tribune*, **16** (1), 17-21.

Xiao, H. (1997) 'Tourism and leisure in China: a tale of two cities', *Annals of Tourism Research*, **24** (2), 357-370.

Xiao, H. (2005) 'The tradition of social sciences and future of tourism research', *Tourism Tribune*, **20** (5), 6-7.

Xie, Y. (2003) 'Tourism and hospitality industry studies: a comparative research between China and the overseas countries', *Tourism Tribune*, **18** (5), 20-25.

Yang, Y., Bai, L. and Su, Z. (2007) 'A comparative study on the structured and unstructured measurements of tourist destination image: a case of Yangshuo, Guilin', *Tourism Tribune*, **22** (4), 53-57.

Zhang, G. (2003) 'Tourism research in China', in A. Lew, L. Yu, J. Ap and G. Zhang (eds), *Tourism in China*, New York: Haworth Hospitality Press, pp. 67-82.

Zhang, H. and Lu, L. (2004) 'An initial analysis of tourism research methods in China', *Tourism Tribune*, **19** (3), 77-81.

Zhang, H. Q., Chong, K. and Ap, J. (1999) 'An analysis of tourism policy development in modern China', *Tourism Management*, **20** (4), 471-485.

Zhang, H.Q., Pine, R. and Lam, T. (2005) *Tourism and Hotel Development in China: From Political to Economic Success*, New York: Haworth Hospitality Press.

Zhang, J. (2002) 'Analysis and thoughts on China's tourism research literature', *Journal of Huaqiao University (Philosophy and Social Science)*, **1**, 52-57.

Zhao, Y. (2000) 'A preliminary statistics and analysis of the documentary library of *Tourism Tribune* from 1990-1999', *Tourism Tribune*, **15** (4), 57-63.

Zhu, H. and Liu, Y. (2004) 'Viewing the difference and trend of Chinese and foreign tourism researches by comparing the articles published on *Tourism Tribune* and *Annals of Tourism Research*', *Tourism Tribune*, **19** (4), 92-95.

13 A 20-20 vision of tourism research in Bali: towards reflexive tourism studies

Shinji Yamashita

Introduction

Bali in Indonesia is well known as an international tourist site. Historically, Balinese tourism dates back to the 1920s when it was discovered as 'the last paradise' by Western artists and scholars. Hickman Powell's travel book, originally published in 1930, was subtitled, *An American's discovery of Bali in the 1920s* (Powell, [1930] 1986). Under such a 'tourist gaze' (Urry 1990), Balinese culture was re-created for Western audiences. In the words of the historian Adrian Vickers (1989), Bali was 'a paradise created'.

After Indonesia's independence, the first five-year development plan began in 1969 under the Suharto regime. In this plan, tourism was seen as an important source of foreign currency earnings for Indonesia, and Bali was designated as the most important of Indonesia's international destinations. The Balinese Provincial Government adopted the policy of tourism development with a special emphasis on cultural tourism. Since then, Bali has grown successfully as the most important international tourist destination in Indonesia to the extent that Bali and tourism may be considered inseparable.

This chapter reviews tourism research in the context of the development of tourism in Bali for the past 20 years, especially in terms of cultural tourism from a mainly anthropological point of view. In so doing, the chapter provides a new outlook on tourism research, 'reflexive tourism studies', and attempts to rethink tourism research. While focusing only on the single site of the island of Bali, the chapter intends to contribute to the theoretical development in tourism research beyond Bali as well, especially in terms of the relationship between tourism and culture. The examination of changing research on tourism in Bali over a 20-year period will develop a research agenda of tourism studies for the next 20 years as the age of 'reflexive modernization' (Beck *et al.*, 2005) .[1]

Culture in the contexts of tourism: cultural tourism

Direct foreign tourist arrivals in Bali over the past 40 years have increased from 11,278 in 1969 to 1,801,864 in 2008 (Figure 13.1). Growth was particularly rapid in the first half of the 1990s: the number of international visitors increased from 490,729 in 1990 to 1,015,314 in 1995.[2] In recent years, however, the number of visitors has remained stagnant due in part to Indonesia's political instability after the collapse of the Suharto regime in 1998, terrorist bombings, and natural disasters (such as earthquakes and tsunami).

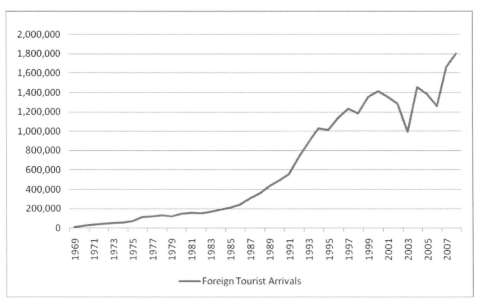

Figure 13.1: Foreign tourist arrivals in Bali 1969-2008. Source: Bali Government Tourism Office. The figures indicate the number of direct foreign tourists' arrivals in Bali.

When tourism development policy was introduced to Bali, there was concern amongst Balinese intellectuals that the island would become a 'second Waikiki' (McKean, 1989: 120). Accordingly, the strategy that they used to handle this problem was to invert the idea that 'Bali exists for the benefit of the tourists' into a philosophy that 'tourism exists for the benefit of Bali', intending thereby to protect the local residents from any threat of 'cultural pollution' by foreign visitors. 'To prevent such a fatal outcome', Picard (2009: 122) writes, 'the Balinese authorities devised a policy of "cultural tourism" (*pariwisata budaya*), which was intended to develop tourism without debasing Balinese culture, by using culture to attract tourists while fostering culture through the revenue generated by tourism'.

Picard also has observed that 'the doctrine of cultural tourism succeeded in merging the promotion of culture with the development of tourism, to the point of entrusting the fate of Balinese culture to the interested care of the tourist industry', pointing out that

> *this was achieved by splitting Balinese culture into two distinct conceptions: whereas before the advent of tourism their culture was for the Balinese 'heritage' which they preserve, it now became, in addition, a 'capital' which they could exploit for profit.*

(Picard, 1995: 55).

'Culture' then has been a key concept for Balinese tourism research. From the early work of McKean (1973) to the latest work by Picard (2009), tourism research in Bali has revolved around the concept of culture. In conventional anthropology, culture is defined as 'a way of life' rooted in a region or a society from generation to generation. However, Balinese culture is being continually re-created within the framework of tourist development as well as Indonesian state cultural policy. In fact it is even an 'invented tradition' under a tourist gaze that dates back to the Dutch colonial period (Yamashita, 2003: Chapters 3–4).

Picard (1995, 1996) has made an important contribution to the study of cultural tourism in Bali by paying attention to the concept of 'tourist culture', that is, the culture 'created' in the process of tourism development, rather than the 'previously existing' culture which is 'preserved' for cultural tourism. He points out that 'tourism had neither polluted Balinese culture, nor brought about its renaissance, but rendered the Balinese self-conscious of their culture: thanks to tourism the Balinese realize they possess something valuable called culture' (Picard, 1995: 60). This view leads to the problem of 'identity' rather than that of 'influence' – whether bad or good – in the study of tourism. The real issue to be researched under the name of cultural tourism, therefore, is that of the dynamics of identity. As Lanfant *et al.* (1995) have demonstrated, this can be observed in many other parts of the world. I have also discussed the case of the Toraja, Sulawesi, Indonesia, and Tono in Northeastern Japan (Yamashita, 2003: Chapters 9 and 11).

Methodologically, the anthropologist Edward Brunner's 'ethnographer/tourist' approach is quite relevant in terms of the participant observation of cultural tourism. He discussed his experiences serving as a tour guide to Indonesia for affluent Americans. As an ethnographer working as a guide for tourists, he was led 'to reflect on the similarities and differences between ethnography and tourism' (Bruner, 1995: 225). This is a strategic method to understand, in a qualitative way, the tourist's experience of 'culture'. In his later work (2005), he developed this method, a 'mobile approach', in various settings ranging from safari excursions in Kenya, East Africa, to cultural tourism Bali, to a mountain fortress in Israel, and to Abraham Lincoln heritage in Illinois, USA.

The dilemma of cultural tourism: Besakih Temple as a World Heritage site contested

However, the dilemma of cultural tourism is that even while tourists are in search of culture, that culture itself can be threatened by the very act of tourism. This dilemma comes to the fore in heritage tourism; particularly with regard to UNESCO's World Heritage sites (see Chapter 15). In Indonesia there are seven World Heritage sites, including the famous Borobudur and Prambanan Temple Compounds in Java, the Tropical Rainforest Heritage of Sumatra, and the Komodo National Park in Flores. Bali, however, does not have any World Heritage sites. Instead there has been a heated debate over the possible nomination of the Besakih Temple, the most important Hindu temple in Bali, as a UNESCO World Heritage site.

According to Darma Putra and Hitchcock (2005: 230), proposals to nominate Besakih as a World Heritage site have emerged on three occasions. The first of these took place in 1990. At that time, the Hindu Council *Parisada* rejected the proposal, objecting to the term *warisan* (heritage) because it seemed to imply that the people had to abandon Besakih. They did not want Besakih to be treated like Borobudur where ritual activities had been regulated.[3] Two years later in 1992, controversy resurged when the national government issued a law on heritage conservation (*cagar budaya*) which would make it possible for Besakih and other temples to be listed as national heritage. Again, the Hindu Intellectual Forum persuaded the government not to include Besakih as either national heritage or world heritage. Despite these two rejections, a third proposal appeared in 2001. This time, I Gde Ardika, the then Minister of Culture and Tourism who was a Balinese, played an important role. This new initiative stemmed from an international conference on cultural heritage conservation in Bali in 2000. Prior to the conference, a feasibility study was undertaken for drafting the proposal to nominate other sites, namely Taman Ayun and the Jatiluwih rice terrace. But, after a heated debate, the nomination of Besakih was halted again.

An important reason for Balinese Hindus' reluctance over accepting the Besakih as a national or a world heritage site is that they would have to hand over the protection and conservation of their temples not only to the world community but also to the Indonesian state, in which Muslims constitute a majority. Furthermore, under the post-Suharto regime since 1998, the resistance may relate to structural changes in Indonesia, with the devolution of power from the centre to the periphery and regional autonomy. This has accelerated the complex identity politics within many parts of Indonesia, including Bali.

In spite of repeated local resistance, the Indonesian government recently proposed the 'cultural landscape of Bali province' at the World Heritage Committee meeting held at Quebec City, Canada, in 2008. In this proposal three 'cluster sites' were listed for World Heritage recognition: (1) the Jatiluwih rice field terraces, traditional villages in the Tabanan region together with its surrounding rice terraces, (2) Taman

Ayun, the island's main temple complex, and (3) a group of eight temples along the Pakerisan River valley. This concept of 'cultural landscapes' is rather new, having been first introduced at the 1992 World Heritage committee meeting. As the combined works of man and nature, they express a longstanding and intimate relationship between peoples and their natural environment, while revealing the Hindu-Balinese cosmology concept of *tri hita karana* – the interlinking of god, human being and natural environment.[4] However, the proposal was not adopted but postponed for further revision.

World Heritage tourism has become popular in the recent tourism market. To be listed as a World Heritage site, a destination is recognized to have 'outstanding touristic value' with an expectation that visitor numbers will increase. However, this possible economic benefit from increased tourism does not necessarily materialize nor coincide with benefits to the local people. As a result, World Heritage becomes an essentially political question: who is to make use of a heritage for whom, and with what purpose? (Harrison and Hitchcock, 2005). This is particularly the case with what is called 'living heritage' such as Liajiang, Yunnan, China, and Shirakawago in Central Japan (Yamashita, 2009a: Chapter 4).

The study of sustainability in the acceleration of tourism development

Until the 1980s, Balinese tourism had been confined to the southern part of Bali (Badung and Gianyar regencies), but in the last 20 years it has spread to places in all parts of Bali, including the regencies of Karangasem (Candidasa) in the east, Buleleng (Lovina) in the north, Tabanan (Tanah Lot) in the west, and Jambarana (Negara) in the north. In addition, the neighbouring islands – including Lombok, Flores and Komodo – in eastern Indonesia are being added to the tourist map as an 'extension' of Bali.

Additionally, in recent years there has been an acceleration of commercialization. This is particularly evident in the rise of the price of land in tourist areas. In some tourist zones in Kuta, for instance, in the 1990s land prices rose to ten times their former level. The reason for the rise in the land price was the influx of outside capital from Jakarta and elsewhere. Aditjondoro (1995: 1) has gone so far as to say that Bali is a colony of Jakarta. Many of the people running the rows of shops on the main street in Kuta are thus non-Balinese and some are even foreigners. Similar conditions now extend to Ubud in the interior, which has become known as the 'second Kuta'.

The acceleration of tourism development has also awoken concerns about sustainable development in Bali. The international Bali Sustainable Development Project (BSDP), a collaborative venture between the Faculty of Environmental Studies, University of Waterloo, Canada, and Gajah Mada University in Yogyakarta, Indonesia, with assistance from Udayana University in Bali, was carried out from 1989 to 1994. The project aimed to formulate a sustainable development strategy for the unique environment of Bali under pressure of a rapidly expanding tourism industry. According to the project leader, Geoffrey Wall (1992: 571), the Balinese concept of sustainable development can be expressed in terms of three features: the continuity of natural resources and production, the continuity of culture and the balances within culture, and development as the process that enhances the quality of life. These, in turn, are the sources of sustainable development criteria that serve as the connection between concept and action. The project produced a book (Martopo and Mitchell, 1995), which emphasizes traditional Balinese culture as the foundation of sustainable community planning and development in response to emerging issues of tourism and regional growth (Ringer, 1997: 485). It is interesting to observe that the latest sustainability model goes back again to 'the traditional Balinese culture' which is considered to be built on the balance of environment, economy and culture.

In this regard, village tourism focusing on traditional Balinese culture may offer an exemplary model for sustainable tourism. To explore this possibility, a research team based at Gadjah Mada University carried out research towards a master plan for Balinese tourism in this new era (Universitas Gadjah Mada, 1994: 1). This research resulted in a proposal for a type of tourist village called *desa wisata terpadu*, or 'integrated tourist village'. According to the then governor of Bali, Ida Bagus Oka, this was an attempt to develop sustainable tourism in Bali and to push forward the frontiers of tourist development on the island (Oka, 1992: 127). These integrated tourist villages are not villages created for tourist use, but ordinary 'traditional' villages which present their 'living culture' to tourists. They give 'model culture' for sustainable development.

Three villages were selected for a pilot project: Jatiluwih in Tabanan regency, Sebatu in Gianyar regency, and Penglipuran in Bangli regency. Each of these three villages has its own local colour. Jatiluwih is a village with beautiful rice terraces. Sebatu is a craft village famous for wood carvings, with an ancient Hindu temple called Gunung Kawi. Penglipuran preserves the 'traditional' village spatial structure in the layout of the houses. The selling point of village tourism is 'traditional Balinese culture' but we have to note here again that this is not simply tradition which has been unconsciously transmitted from long ago, but rather it is culture being manipulated and re-created within the contemporary economic, social, and cultural context. In fact the current appearance of Penglipuran is the result of repairs made for a planned visit by the then President Suharto in 1991, though the visit never took place.

I have discussed the case of Penglipuran village based on my 1995 field research (Yamashita, 2003: Chapter 8). The village has been classified as *desa tertinggal*, 'a village left behind'. For this reason, the Bangli regency government plans to place the district in the forefront of present-day development by turning Penglipuran village into 'an integrated tourist village'. Tourism in Penglipuran is thus an exercise in village development, allowing it to adapt itself to the new age while conserving Bali's traditional culture. From the viewpoint of sustainable tourism, the case of Penglipuran is interesting in the sense that even though development has been carried out under government leadership, it has actively involved the local people. Entry tickets for the village and car park are an important source of income, 60 per cent of which goes to Bangli regency, and 40 per cent to Penglipuran. Therefore, this is a sort of 'community based tourism' as well.

This pattern of regional development based on participation of the residents is quite relevant to the theme of *daerah otonomie*, regional autonomy, which has been promoted in recent years under the post-Suharto regime in parallel with the devolution of the various functions of central government to the regions. Furthermore, especially after the Kuta Bombing in 2002, the revision of future development strategy is proposed to balance the uneven development of Balinese tourism: (1) promote greater equity in the distribution of the benefit of tourism, (2) develop an environment supportive of investment, (3) support other sectors to mitigate against the inherent risks of the tourism sector and (4) create effective rural development politics that benefit those not benefiting directly from tourism (UNDP/World Bank, 2003: 66 cited in Picard, 2009: 112). Interestingly, the bombing was taken by the Balinese 'as a warning that something must be out of balance in Bali, that all was not well on the island of the gods' (Picard, 2009: 99), as we will examine in the next section.

After terrorist bombings: the politics of identity to maintain Balineseness

For the last ten years Balinese tourism has experienced serious challenges through such negative incidents as the Asian economic crisis in 1997, the political instability caused by the collapse of the Suharto regime in 1998, the bombings in the Balinese resort of Kuta in 2002 and 2005, the SARS epidemic in 2003 and the recent spread of bird flu in Asia, as well as the increasing international distrust of Garuda Indonesia Airlines. As a result, tourism in Bali has entered a period of uncertainty which cannot be described by a simple developmental model.

Darma Putra and Hitchcock (2006) analyse the Bali tourism crisis caused by bombings with reference to Butler's tourism development cycle: exploration, involvement, development, consolidation, stagnation and rejuvenation or decline (Butler, 1980, 2004). Although the bombings had a great impact on international tourism, they concluded, the subsequent strong resurgence in international arrivals suggests that the destination has not yet reached the consolidation stage of Butler's hypothesis, but rather that the strength of the resurgence owes much to the underlying trend of the development phase. In fact, in 2008 international arrivals amounted to 1.8 million, the highest figure in the history of tourism in Bali.

What is interesting about the cultural process after the bombings is what Hitchcock and Darma Putra (2005: 71-72) have called 'local cultural strategies', a series of inter-faith measures which include joint prayer to promote inter-religious harmony. They report that '[t]hese commenced with a prayer for world peace, *Doa Perdamainan Dunia dari Bali*, on the auspicious full moon afternoon of 21 October 2002, which was attended by the minister of religious affairs, who is Muslim'. The bombing was interpreted by Balinese as an expression of the anger of the gods, a consequence of bad *karma*. Therefore, the following month, a huge ceremony, involving the most powerful priests, was carried out on 15 November 2002. This huge demonstration helped to cleanse the trauma of the bombing and enabled the Balinese to put the terrible incident behind them and to contribute to the emerging recovery strategy.

Hitchcock and Darma Putra (2005: 73) further point out that the current crisis coincides with and adds greater significance to the emerging debate on Balinese identity, regional autonomy, and a growing discourse of multiculturalism among the Balinese intelligentsia. As was already mentioned, with the development of tourism, Bali was invaded by Jakartan investment money and non-Balinese Muslim migrants from Java and other islands. Prior to the bombings, many locals feared that Bali was inevitably heading toward serious inter-ethnic tension and even conflict (Couteau, 2003: 42). After the bombing there was widespread support for the anti-migrant movement and the implementation of restrictions on inter-island migration, especially from Java. The *Bali Merdeka* (independent Bali) movement against Jakarta may be interpreted as another expression of this kind of tension.

Couteau (2003: 43) has discussed that the bombing provides an unexpectedly good way of evaluating the evolution of the political situation in Bali. In other words, the bombing has brought local people back to their own, traditional, Balinese frame of reference, namely ritual, as we have seen. The recent slogan of *ajeg Bali* ('maintaining firmly Bali' or 'Bali standing strong') reflects this direction (Kumbara, 2008). International tourist globalism could soon encounter tension with this new Balinese politics of identity that seeks for 'Bali for the Balinese' – an earlier slogan which actually existed at the outset of Balinese tourism in the late 1960s, and even dates back to the colonial period, when Dutch administrators and orientalists, Christian missionaries, American anthropologists, Western artists and tourists impelled the Balinese to be Balinese (Picard, 2009: 114). The Balinese macro developmental cycle of tourism seems to have got back to its starting point.

The paradox of cultural tourism: towards reflexive tourism

In the paper mentioned above, Couteau (2003: 52), referring to Picard (2000), argued that '[m]odern Balinese identity ... came to be constructed in terms of *adat* [custom], religion (*agama*) and, increasingly, culture (*budaya*), foreign categories which the Balinese have successively bargained for, appropriated and reinterpreted for their own purposes'. Nowadays, there is a cultural situation in Bali in which, as Picard (2000: 109) observes, 'with their *adat* secularized and their *budaya* touristified, *agama* Hindu has become the emblem of *Kebalian* [Balinese identity]'. Through this process, culture has become an asset, 'cultural capital' to use Bourdieu's term, which may be owned, managed and controlled by outsider – Jakartan or international – money, out of the reach of Balinese hands. Even the Hindu religion, the emblem of current Balinese identity, has been commercialized by outsider money, exemplified by the Garuda Wisinu Project, launched in 1993, and the Bali Nirwana Resort project in Tanah Lot in the same year, as Couteau (2003: 54) observes.

This is the paradox that Balinese cultural tourism faces today. Cultural tourism started so that the Balinese could control their own culture, but as a result of its practice, their culture has started moving beyond their control. In this sense I observe that Bali stands at a crossroads in the path of what Beck *et al.* (2005) have called 'reflexive modernization'. 'Reflexive modernization', according to Beck, means the creative self-destruction for an entire epoch: that of industrial society. He writes:

> If simple (or orthodox) modernization means, at bottom, first the disembedding and second the re-embedding of traditional social forms by industrial social forms, then reflexive modernization means first the disembedding and second the re-embedding of industrial social forms by another modernity... This new stage, in which progress can turn into self-destruction, in which one kind of modernization undercuts and changes another, is what I call the stage of reflexive modernization.
>
> *(Beck et al., 2005: 2)*

Some would say that Bali was an isolated society enjoying an unchanging tradition that has only recently come under external modernizing influences. However, as Howe (2005) argues, this is wrong. Bali has always been part of larger changing political and economic structures, and thus it has been part of the modern world system. As an extension of its modern history, I am arguing that Bali too is entering into this stage of reflexive modernization.

The grand narratives of development are said to be finished. As described above, what the Bali bombings have revealed are the signs of a reflexive kind of tourism, in which risk management for the local environment, society and culture engenders its own 'creative self-destruction'. As Beck points out, the other side of the obsolescence of the industrial society is the emergence of the 'risk society'. Tourism too must come to be concerned about risk management. 'Sustainable tourism' could be regarded as part of this project. In this reflexive framework, things are not so clear-cut. The influence of development on the local society cannot be seen simply as either 'good' or 'bad'. In the risk society, the production of 'goods' produces 'bads' (or 'risks') as well (Beck *et al.*, 2005: 6). Reflexive modernization contains such uncertainty and we must deal with this kind of new ambivalence. In this reflexive vein, I am proposing 'reflexive tourism' as a key concept for the next 20 years of Balinese tourism.

The blurring of the distinction between tourism and migration: redefining tourism

Furthermore, I would like to add the fact that the distinction between tourism and migration in recent Balinese tourism is blurring. I noticed this phenomenon for the first time when I was doing research on Japanese tourists in Bali in 1995. I came across more than 200 young Japanese women who had married Balinese men after repeated visits to Bali as tourists. [5] After their marriages they stayed in Bali as I have discussed elsewhere (Yamashita, 2003: Chapter 7, 2009b: 192-194). These travellers represent what Machiko Sato (2001) has called 'lifestyle migrants'.

There is also an emerging type of tourism/migration called 'long-stay'. 'Long-stay', the term Japanese use for international retirement migration, has come to the fore in the recent Japanese tourist market. Against the background of a falling birth rate, increasing life expectancy, the high cost of living in Japan, and worry over life after retirement, an increasing number of elderly Japanese have been moving abroad to locales such as Hawaii, Australia, and particularly Southeast Asian countries. There they seek more meaningful lives with a lower cost of living and a warmer climate. Bali has become one of the most popular destinations for Japanese retirees (Yamashita, 2008, 2009a: Chapter 7).

This phenomenon of a blurred distinction between tourism and migration leads us to the redefinition of modern tourism. In her now classic editorial work on the anthropology of tourism, Valene Smith defines a tourist as 'a temporarily leisured person who voluntarily visits a place away from home for the purpose of experiencing a change' (Smith, 1989: 1). In this definition, tourism is a non-routine experience away from the everyday life to which tourists will return. However, this definition cannot necessarily be applied to life-style tourism/migration in which the distinction between tourism and migration has become blurred. Therefore, in studying this new kind of tourism it has become necessary to link tourism and migration studies (Hall and Williams, 2002).

Conclusions: a proposal for future tourism research

We are living in a continuously changing world. In this chapter I have examined the changing nature of research on Balinese tourism over the past 20 years, a period in which the world as a whole has changed radically with increased globalization. In this transition the definition and forms of tourism must change as well. In conclusion, therefore, I would like to propose a new tourism research agenda for the next 20 years, what I would call 'reflexive tourism studies'.

'Reflexive modernization', as suggested above, is a process to replace one modernity with another. For example, an industrial modernity may be replaced by a post-industrial one. In this transition, concerns about the sustainability of the globe rather than industrial development will come to the fore, reflecting a move towards a post-industrial modernity with a low carbon society and green economy. In the tourism sector too, over the past 20 years, we have observed the emergence of environmentally as well as culturally sustainable forms of tourism such as responsible tourism and ecotourism. To develop this direction further, I am proposing 'reflexive tourism studies' which examine the form of tourism development to obtain a balance between the 'goods' and 'bads' (benefits and costs) which modern tourism industry has produced. I should stress that the process of reflexive modernization is not necessarily straight but often circuitous – going forwards and backwards. As we have seen, the latest model of sustainability in Bali goes back to the 'traditional Balinese culture' which was built on a balance of environment, economy and culture. 'Reflexive tourism studies' I am proposing, therefore, will attempt to devise a possible way forward for tourism in a flexible and sometimes indirect path towards a new modernity.

Notes

1   In this chapter, I have re-used some parts of my earlier book on Balinese tourism (Yamashita, 2003), updating the data for the current purpose.

2   In 1991, the first 'Visit Indonesia Year' campaign was carried out to promote international tourism to Indonesia. Total international arrivals to Indonesia as a whole increased to 1.1 million in 1987, 2.1 million in 1990, 4.3 million in 1995, and 5.5 million in 2007.

3   However, this was based on a misunderstanding, as there are examples of what are sometimes called 'living' World Heritage sites.

4   UNESCO World Heritage Centre: http://whc.unesco.org/en/tentativelists/5100/.

5   The number of international marriages between Japanese women and Balinese/Indonesian men keeps increasing. Currently it is presumed that such marriages number over 400.

References

Aditjondoro, G. (1995) 'Bali, Jakarta's colony: social and ecological impacts of Ja-karta-bade conglomerates in Bali's tourism industry', Working Paper No. 58, Perth: Asia Research Centre, Murdoch University.

Beck, U., Giddens, A. and Lash, S. (2005) *Reflexive Modernization: Politics, Tradition and Aesthetics in the Modern Social Order*, Cambridge: Polity Press.

Bruner, E. (1995) 'The ethnographer/tourist in Indonesia', in M.-F. Lanfant, J.B. Allcock and E.M. Bruner (eds), *International Tourism: Identity and Change*, London: Sage Publications, pp. 224-41.

Bruner, E. (2005) *Culture on Tour: Ethnographies of Travel*, Chicago: University of Chicago Press.

Butler, R.W. (1980) 'The concept of a tourist area cycle of evolution: implications for management of resources', *Canadian Geographer*, **24** (1), 5-12.

Butler, R.W. (2004) 'The tourism area life cycle in the twenty-first century', in A.A. Lew, C.M. Hall and A.M. Williams (eds), *A Companion to Tourism*, Oxford: Blackwell Publishing, pp. 159-169.

Couteau, J. (2003) 'After the Kuta bombing: in search of the Balinese soul', *Antropologi Indonesia*, **70**, 41-59.

Darma Putra, I.N. and Hitchcock, M. (2005) 'Pura Besakih: a World Heritage site contested', *Indonesia and the Malays World*, **33**, 225-237.

Darma Putra, I.N. and Hitchcock, M. (2006) 'The Bali bombings and the tourism development cycle', *Progress in Development Studies*, **6**, 157-166.

Hall, C. M. and Williams, A. M. (eds.) (2002) *Tourism and Migration: New Relationships between Production and Consumption*, Dordrecht, Boston and London: Kluwer Academic Publishers.

Harrison, D. and Hitchcock, M. (eds) (2005) *The Politics of World Heritage: Negotiating Tourism and Conservation*, Buffalo, NY and Toronto: Channel View Publications.

Hitchcock, M. and Darma Putra, I.N. (2005) 'The Bali bombings: tourism crisis management and conflict avoidance', *Current Issues in Tourism*, **8**, 62-76.

Howe, L. (2005) *The Changing World of Bali: Religion, Society and Tourism*, London: Routledge.

Kumbara, A.A. Ngr. Anom (2008) 'Ajeg Bali dalam pusaran arus globalisasi: Kritik epistimis [Ajeg Bali in a swift current of globalization: An epistemological criticism]', in I Wayan Aridika *et al.* (eds), *Dinamika social masyarakat Bali dalam lintasan sejarah [Social Dynamics of the Balinese Society in Historical Process]*, Denpasar: Universitas Udayana, pp.196-211.

Lanfant, M.-F., Allcock, J.B. and Bruner, E.M (eds) (1995) *International Tourism: Identity and Change*, London: Sage Publications.

Martopo, S. and Mitchell, B. (eds) (1995) *Bali: Balancing Environment, Economy and Culture*, Department of Geography Publication Series 44, Waterloo, Canada: University of Waterloo.

McKean, P. (1973) 'Cultural involution: tourists, Balinese, and the process of modernization in an anthropological perspective', unpublished PhD thesis, Providence: Brown University.

McKean, P. (1989) 'Toward a theoretical analysis of tourism: Economic dualism and cultural involution in Bali', in V.L. Smith (ed.), *Hosts and Guests: The Anthropology of Tourism*, Philadelphia: University of Pennsylvania Press, pp. 93-108.

Oka, I.B. (1992) 'A sub-system of cultural tourism in Bali', in Wiendu Nuryanti (ed.), *Universal Tourism: Enriching or Degrading Culture?*, Yogyakarta, Indonesia: Gadjah Mada University Press, pp. 123-131.

Picard, M. (1995) 'Cultural heritage and tourist capital: Cultural tourism in Bali', in M.-F. Lanfant, J.B. Allcock and E.M. Bruner (eds), *International Tourism: Identity and Change*, London: Sage Publications, pp. 44-66.

Picard, M. (1996) *Bali: Cultural Tourism and Tourist Culture*, Singapore: Archipelago Press.

Picard, M. (2000) 'Agama, adat, budaya: the dialogic construction of kebalian', *Dialog*, **1** (1): 85-124.

Picard, M. (2009) 'From "kebalihan" to "ajeg Bali": tourism and Balinese identity in the aftermath of the Kuta bombing', in M. Hitchcock, V.T. King and M.J.G. Parnwell (eds), *Tourism on Southeast Asia: Challenges and New Directions*, Copenhagen: Nias Press, pp. 99-131.

Powell, H. ([1930] 1986) *The Last Paradise: An American's "Discovery" of Bali in the 1920s*, Singapore: Oxford University Press.

Ringer, G. (1997) '(Book Review) Bali: balancing environment, economy and culture', *Annals of Tourism Research*, **24** (2), 485-487.

Sato, M. (2001) *Farewell to Nippon: Japanese Lifestyle Migrants in Australia*, Melbourne: Trans Pacific Press.

Smith, V.L. (ed.) (1989) *Hosts and Guests: The Anthropology of Tourism*, Philadelphia: University of Pennsylvania Press.

UNDP/World Bank (2003) *Bali, beyond the Tragedy: Impact and Challenges for Tourism-led Development in Indonesia*, Jakarta: UNDP/USAID/The World Bank.

Universitas Gadjah Mada (1994) *Penyusunan rencana pengbangunan desa wisata di Bali:Laporan terakhir [Village tourism plan in Bali: A final report[*, Yogyakarta: Fakultas Teknis, Universitas Gadjah Mada.

Urry, J. (1990) *The Tourist Gaze: Leisure and Travel in Contemporary Societies*, London: Sage.

Vickers, A. (1989) *Bali: A Paradise Created*, Berkeley, CA and Singapore: Periplus Editions.

Wall, G. (1992) 'Bali sustainable development project', *Annals of Tourism Research*, **19** (3), 569-571.

Yamashita, S. (2003) *Bali and Beyond: Explorations in the Anthropology of Tourism* (translated by J.S. Eades), New York and Oxford: Berghahn Books.

Yamashita, S. (2008) 'Here, there, and in-between: lifestyle migrants from Japan', paper presented at the Wenner-Gren workshop Wind over Water: An Anthropology of Migration from an East Asian Setting, 17-18 November, Institute of East Asian Studies, University of California at Berkeley.

Yamashita, S. (2009a) *Kankô jinruigaku no chôsen [The Challenge of the Anthropology of Tourism]*, Tokyo: Kôdansha.

Yamashita, S. (2009b) 'Southeast Asian tourism from a Japanese perspective', in M. Hitchcock, V.T. King and M.J.G. Parnwell (eds), *Tourism in South East Asia Revisited*, Copenhagen: NIAS Press, pp.189-205.

Part IV

Emerging themes

14 Charting a journey: from refugee to tourism employee and tourism entrepreneur?

Tom Baum and Geri Smyth

Introduction

The development of international tourism since the middle of the 20th century has seen a process of continuity but, more fundamentally, progressive and accelerating change in terms of consumers and their expectations; the products and services that they consume; the social, political and economic environment within which international tourism is located; and the impact of technology in the marketing and distribution of tourism products and services. Changes such as these have rendered international tourism unrecognisable today from its counterpart some 60 years ago.

A parallel process can be seen with respect to work within the tourism sector, both at the level of the firm and the individual and in terms of the macro labour market, national and international, within which the sector is located. In quantitative terms, a tourism sector which has grown hugely over the past 60 years requires a far greater number of people at all levels to deliver its services. The nature of the industry has created a significantly greater range of employment categories within tourism than was the case in the past, driven by the changing nature of tourist activities and the technologies used to service them. At the same time, a rather more limited range of roles in tourism have decreased in importance or disappeared altogether. Finally, it is important to recognise that the geographical spread of tourism to encompass most communities in both the developed and less developed world has created employment opportunities within the sector in locations that previously had little or no contact with commercial travel and tourism.

Notwithstanding such change, many aspects of tourism work have remained similar over the timeframe of the past 60 years. Baum (2007: 1385), in reviewing tourism work from the early 1930s to the present day, concludes that 'there is, therefore, little evidence, notwithstanding exceptional best practice examples by some organisations from across the industry, that working conditions in tourism have improved significantly'. Baum's reference here is primarily to low skills work in the accommodation and food service sub-sectors of tourism where the impact of technology and productivity enhancements have been limited, especially within smaller operations. However, all sectors of tourism include work which is labour intensive, widely described as requiring low skills and relatively unchanging in the nature of the work and skills required over the past half century such as front-line service work, cleaning functions, estates functions and baggage handling. Tourism and related service work has traditionally and widely been characterised as low skills although this stereotype is challenged by a number of authors (Baum, 1996, 2002, 2006a; Burns, 1997) on the basis that this represents both a technical and western-centric perception of work and skills. There is a dominant if not universal view that much work undertaken within the sector can be described as low value, demanding few, if any, conceptual or knowledge-driven attributes.

Demographic change, economic development and the growth of tourism demand in all mature western economies have created shortages within all low skills sectors, wherein current and anticipated demand for labour far exceeds that available within the locality of most businesses. As a consequence, the tourism industry in many developed countries has relied on a combination of productivity enhancement and sourcing new supplies of low skills labour in order to meet its staffing needs. A widespread response to staff shortages in the sector has been through the recruitment of migrant labour, whether from elsewhere in the country or from international sources. Many countries in Europe (e.g. Ireland, Switzerland, and the UK) and elsewhere are now heavily dependent on migrant labour for the delivery of core tourism services (Baum *et al.*, 2007a; Devine *et al.*, 2007). While migration for work in tourism is by no means a new phenomenon, the scale of contemporary migration is unprecedented and has implications which challenge the delivery of traditional services and tourism experiences (Baum *et al.*, 2007b).

Employment in tourism-related businesses, alongside similar weak labour market sectors such as agriculture and construction, is frequently the first step towards economic independence taken by newly arrived migrants to a host country, whether their status is one of choice or that of refugee. A diversity of employment requirements at low and semi-skilled levels, stochastic demand patterns and the wide geographical dispersal of the tourism sector combine to create opportunities for 'incomers' to find ready access to work within both the legitimate and the grey economies of most developed countries. This work is frequently based upon low pay and exploitative conditions, within what Jayaweera and Anderson (2008) describe as 'vulnerable employment'. Migrants and refugees are also widely under-employed in terms of the skills set that they often have gained in their country of origin and find accessing employment commensurate with their qualifications difficult. At the same time, the tourism context provides significant opportunities for entrepreneurial activity by migrants and refugees in areas such as ethnic cuisine, arts, crafts, and wider cultural presentation.

This chapter draws on a number of conceptual strands, notably those relating to the impact of migration on tourism work (e.g. Devine *et al.*, 2007) and builds upon the work of the authors in addressing issues of refugee integration, including economic integration through access to employment. This multidisciplinary study considers the refugee experience of community integration in terms of social and cultural, educational and employment dimensions, calling on the work of Spencer (2006) among others. Refugees also embody a juxtapositional and extreme 'otherness' alongside tourist mobility (Baum *et al.*, 2008), frequently occupying similar space to their tourist counterparts on the sea (cruise ships and boat people) and in the air (shared flights and destinations between vacationers and failed asylum seekers). These challenging parallels are similar to those posed by Diken (2004) when he contrasts refugee spaces with other more desirable 'camps', such as gated communities. His ideas would be equally applicable to a contrast between refugee camps and tourism locations such as holiday camps, all-inclusive resorts and sun-belt retirement communities. In a similar vein, Bauman (1999) employs the metaphors of the 'tourist' and the 'vagabond' in contradistinction to each other, in order to demonstrate the differential mobilities of people in the context of post-modern consumer society. The refugee is eminently substitutable for the vagabond in this context, in both social and economic senses. Finally, Gibson (2003), building on Derrida's contrast of unconditional hospitality and hospitality-as-economy, considers the use of hotels as accommodation for asylum seekers in the United Kingdom and how this practice poses challenges in our interpretation of the conventional use of such facilities by tourists.

This chapter explores tourism employment as a contributory factor in refugee integration in developed countries and considers the specific conditions of work within the tourism sector as providing opportunities but also real challenges in supporting such integration.

Tourism's changing labour markets

The diversity, structure, organisation, and geographical dispersal which characterise the tourism sector in most countries create conditions which are readily accessible to potential employees with non-standard experience profiles, qualifications, and general employability skills. The sector comprises work at a wide variety of levels, demanding a plethora of skills types within the context of businesses that range from micro to global in scale. This sector environment, in the words of Vaugeois and Rollins (2007: 645), 'allows a diversity of individuals to choose where and how they would like to fit into the labour market'. The industry's heterogeneity, geographical spread and stochastic demand cycle provide both opportunity and challenge in terms of mapping these against the aspirations and expectations of those attracted into the tourism industry, either as new entrants to the labour force or in the context of change opportunities within their working lives. Szivas *et al.* (2003: 66) summarise these characteristics when they note that:

> *tourism is an accommodating industry as it offers a wide range of jobs with diverse human capital requirements. Different tourism sectors contain*

organizations of diverse form and size, each with different skill requirements and thus different forms of employment, whereby contracts, working conditions and pay vary considerably.

The transitory nature of much tourism work in temporal and spatial terms has a myriad of impacts on these key stakeholders and, of course, on the tourism employees themselves. The impact of temporal factors, seasonality in particular, as an illustration of the transitory nature of tourism work, is well documented in the literature. Therefore, the focus becomes the dimension of employee mobility and the ways in which current discourse provides insights and problematises the mobility of these tourism workers and their relations to customer service, place, experience and performance.

Tourism is a sector with a strong tradition of diversity in its workforce across many dimensions (Baum *et al.*, 2007a), notably in terms of the role that migrant staff have played within the sector since the early development of commercial hospitality. Baum (2006b) traces examples of vocational mobility in the sector in Europe back to the 13th century and discusses the important role that, primarily, southern Europeans played in developing the culture and character of tourism operations in industrialised Europe in the 19th and much of the 20th centuries. Williams and Hall (2000: 8) refer to the era of 'the Grand Tour, when aristocratic visits from northern to southern Europe, provided the economic basis for attracting immigrants from the countries of origin to provide specialized services for these niche national markets'. More recently, economic migration to post-industrial economies of North America, Europe, Australia and the Middle East has seen the tourism and hospitality sector utilise incomer employees across the workplace spectrum as a cheap and accessible source of what is seen to be low skills labour. This new migration has stimulated debate about its impact upon the form, quality and authenticity of interactive service delivery. As Bianchi (2000: 117) notes:

> *The labour-intensive and casual nature of the tourism and hospitality sectors has therefore accentuated the role of these sectors as magnets for immigrant labour, both in the major 'world cities' of western Europe and North America, and increasingly, in the mass tourism destinations of southern Europe.*

Within the mobility of their travel, long periods of immobility occur and the freedom of (im)mobility for this group of travellers gives rise to a circulatory movement, where citizens of one nation can go and work/live/travel abroad for a period of time before returning home (see Findlay, 1995; Conradson and Latham, 2005). Consequently, it is not just individuals who develop through transnational opportunities but the relations within and between wider social networks also become more mobile, complex and fluid through transnational practices and experiences. What is also necessary to recognise is that, within these same social and economic networks, informal pathways can be established that encompass:

> *the precarious routes of refugees, asylum seekers and guest workers. Multiple interacting systems and networks of mobility are appearing, and groups as diverse as*

backpackers and students, migrants and cosmopolitan professionals are more likely than ever to merge and intersect in various ways, shaping, changing and impacting on 'local' communities.

(Allon et al., 2008: 73)

The tourism sector, therefore, has traditionally provided a weak labour market climate which is conducive to relatively open access. Szivas *et al.* (2003: 65-66) talk about tourism employment in terms of its accessibility and the part this plays for new entrants from outside of the sector in:

> *the adaptation process, so socialization into a new industry involved opportunity as well as motives and human capital. The ease of accumulating skills and knowledge and the ease of finding a job were also found to be part of the motivational element of adaptation.*

Likewise, Vaugeois and Rollins (2007) address the concept of labour mobility and the extent to which tourism acts as a refuge by attracting people who have been displaced from other lives. Their discussion is primarily focused on the economically displaced but is equally applicable to the political context faced by refugees.

Riley's (1996) analysis of the tourism labour market environment differentiates between the structural features of strong and weak internal labour markets and this differentiation goes some way in explaining the characteristics of easily accessible employment within many sub-sectors of the tourism industry in developed countries. It is Riley's contention that the labour market within tourism in developed countries meets most of the criteria for 'weak' status. Central to the characteristics of a weak labour market is the notion of open access, with few hurdles to entry on the basis of either qualifications or experience. This environment provides ready labour market access for new migrants, including those of particular social and economic vulnerability, refugees and, indeed, those who have been denied such status or have not sought to obtain it after entering a country without formal sanction. Szivas *et al.* (2003) rightly point out that the very accessibility of tourism employment also simultaneously devalues the occupation by lowering its social and economic status. However, in the context of refugees and other migrants, it is this very 'attractiveness vacuum' which provides opportunity and a toehold towards integration.

Refugees and refugee integration

Defining refugee status is, at one level, quite simple but, in reality, presents considerable challenges in its application. Article 1A (2) of the United Nations Convention Relating to the Status of Refugees (1951) is widely cited and, on the face of it, clear.

> *The term 'refugee' shall apply to any person who[,]. . .owing to well-founded fear of being persecuted for reasons of race, religion, nationality, membership of a particular social group or political opinion, is outside the country of his*

nationality and is unable or, owing to such fear, unwilling to avail himself of the protection of that country; or who, not having a nationality and being outside the country of his former habitual residence as a result of such events, is unable or, owing to such fear, is unwilling to return to it.

As Shacknove (1985: 274) points out, this:

predominant, generation-old conception advanced by international instruments, municipal statutes, and scholarly treatises identifies the refugee as, in essence, a person who has crossed an international frontier because of a well-founded fear of persecution.

But, he goes on to argue that, 'given such broad agreement, the conceptual problem would appear to be resolved. But these appearances are deceptive'. It has remained impossible to define refugees in such a way that legal, ethical, and social scientific meanings of the term can be aligned.

The notion of refugee integration is equally problematic, in definitional and interpretation terms, as that of refugees in themselves. Robinson (1998: 118) argues 'that "integration" is a chaotic concept: a word used by many but understood differently by most'. Robinson goes further to argue that the concept is 'individualized, contested and contextual' and sees little prospect for a unifying definition. This is a view supported by Castles *et al.* (2001: 12) when they argue that 'there is no single, generally accepted definition, theory or model of immigrant and refugee integration. The concept continues to be controversial and hotly debated.' In the UK context, the Home Office (2006: 3) defines refugee integration as

the process that takes place when refugees are empowered to achieve their full potential as members of British society, to contribute to the community, to access public services and to become fully able to exercise the rights and responsibilities that they share with other residents of the UK.

In an earlier analysis, the Home Office (2004) proposed three indicators of integration:

1. Achieve public outcomes in employment, housing, education, health, etc. equivalent to those achieved by host community.

2. Socially connected with members of specific (national, ethnic, cultural religious, etc.) community with which they identify.

3. Linguistic competence, cultural knowledge, etc. to be able to confidently engage in society.

Integration in terms of the above indicators can be seen in terms that include cultural, social, and economic dimensions. However, central to the issue of differing interpretations of refugee status and refugee integration is the role and status of employment. 'To me integration is work, if we work we are integrated' (ECRE 1999: 42), a point reiterated by Feeney (2000: 343), when she states that 'finding employment is the single most significant barrier to the successful integration of refugees into British society'. This is a well researched area and, as Ager and Strang (2008: 170), note:

> *employment has consistently been identified as a factor influencing many relevant issues, including promoting economic independence, planning for the future, meeting members of the host society, providing opportunity to develop language skills, restoring self-esteem and encouraging self-reliance.*

Refugees face significant barriers in seeking to enter the labour market. In the UK context, Feeney (2000: 343-344) identifies that these can include:

♦ lack of adequate spoken and written English

♦ lack of work experience gained in the United Kingdom

♦ non-recognition of qualifications obtained overseas

♦ lack of information about employment and training services (including job centres)

♦ lack of information about refugee support networks and organisations

♦ lack of knowledge about job search culture and the labour market

♦ cultural barriers to effective job seeking, e.g. suspicion of application forms

♦ employers' lack of understanding over immigration status

♦ racial discrimination by employers

♦ lack of childcare provision.

The consequences of these barriers are clearly evident. Again, in the context of the UK, Hurtsfield *et al.* (2004: 1) note that:

> *although refugees have full employment rights, they face major barriers in the labour market. Indicators of their disadvantage include disproportionately high levels of unemployment and underemployment. At around 36%, their unemployment rate is around six times the national average.*

Moving through tourism employment

The tourism sector is able to utilise or exploit, depending on the perspective adopted, the frequently high level of skills and qualifications which refugees bring to the labour market and which, for a variety of reasons already enunciated, are not formally valued within the host economy. The skills they frequently do bring to the tourism workplace, however, fall into a bundle of attributes which are relatively intangible and are rarely formally credited. These include a range of 'soft' or 'generic' attributes, including communications, emotional (e.g. Hochschild, 1983; Bryman, 2004) and aesthetic skills (refer to Warhurst *et al.*, 2000; Nickson and Warhurst, 2007) which may be absent in more traditional recruitment pools for low skills work in the industry.

Hall (2008: 418) addresses the issue of the skills set which new migrants (and refugees) bring to the tourism workplace and stresses the training and development implications of recruitment from such sources.

This raises questions of how tourism quality is affected by such employee diversity and what mechanisms are in place to assist the necessary adaptation and socialization processes to accompany or precede training and education. New entrants to the sector bring experience that may be different from their tourism employment requirements.

In addition, the effect of the low access threshold of the weak labour market combined with other legal constraints, has wider business implications within the sector. Boswell and Straubhaar (2004: 4) highlight this when they argue that for

some industries – such as agriculture, construction, hotel and catering, tourism, or cleaning – the restriction of legal labour migration opportunities since the 1970s and a lack of supply of indigenous workers willing to do low-status, low-paid or seasonal work gives them little option but to hire illegal immigrants.

Embellishing this discussion of 'illegal' workers but with clear parallels to refugees, Chesney and Hazari (2003: 260) note that:

in France it is reported that 70% of the unskilled labour force used in smaller hotel establishments comprises illegal workers who are willing to work for a wage less than that of the local workers. These unskilled illegal migrants help to maintain and/or lower the relative price of the non-traded goods that the tourists consume, thereby helping tourism by making high-wage countries competitive in the world tourism market. High wage countries become competitive because, by using cheap illegal migrants, they can lower the prices of goods consumed by tourists.

There is some evidence that tourism employment can act as a transitory phase within refugee and wider migrant integration. In terms of more general migrant aspirations, Devine *et al.* (2007) note that a significant proportion of such employees in the hotel sector aspire to employment commensurate with their previous working lives, both in relation to skills and their employment status. This can be within the sector (such as through promotion) but also may be elsewhere in the economy. Given the wealth of skills and experience across other sectors of the economy which many refugees bring to the tourism workplace, such ambition is hardly surprising. Opportunity, however, may be determined by their ability to assimilate into the workplace culture of the industry in their 'host' country, their capacity to take aboard key skills requirements such as language but, equally, the extent to which employers are willing and able to recognise what may be unorthodox talent within their workforce and support its development and enhancement.

Entrepreneurial outcomes are also high on recent migrant lists of aspirational goals, both within tourism and beyond. The sector, particular in terms of food or retail-related businesses, demands a relatively low capital entry threshold and is therefore attractive as a business entry point for intending entrepreneurs. Refugees have a higher than average propensity for self-employment and entrepreneurial activity. Kirk (2004), in the UK context, reports that 32 per cent of refugees were engaged in self-employment prior to their arrival in the country. This correlation between wider forms of migration and high levels of self-employment and entrepreneurial activities is widely recognised (Bonacich and Modell, 1980; Light, 1984). Altinay and Altinay (2006) illustrate the propensity of Turkish migrants to develop entrepreneurial businesses in the catering sector and note increasing formalization of business structures as the operations mature. Entrepreneurialism among the South Asian community is seen to be due to culturally-specific entrepreneurial characteristics and values combined with 'privileged access' (Watson *et al.*, 2000: 72) to ethnic communal resources (Srinivasan, 1995; Metcalf *et al.*, 1996; Basu, 1998).

Concluding remarks

Our discussion, thus far, has demonstrated how a changing tourism sector in most developed countries and a linked impact on the sector's labour markets has provided an opportunity for the employment of migrants and, in particular, refugees. Such employment may be legal or illegal. We also note how tourism employment is a readily accessible vehicle to support the integration of refugees and other migrants into their adopted societies. It is clear, from this analysis, that the potential for ready access to the labour market combined with the benefits of such work (and its attendant learning opportunities) can provide a springboard for refugees to progress in their employment within the sector, beyond the sector and through the establishment of self-employment opportunities, again both within and outside tourism. This is a very optimistic scenario achieved by the minority of refugees. The reality, of course, is that such seamless progression is only within the grasp of a minority of those accorded refugee status in many countries. We have seen evidence of the challenges facing refugees in their access to the labour market; less than half of those seeking work in many countries actually attain it within the short to medium term.

A further difficulty reflects the notion of ghettoisation that exists within low wage and low opportunity sectors such as tourism. Toynbee (2003) addresses the hopelessness of low paid work in the UK in terms of both wages and working conditions and gives clear recognition to these as structural impediments to access alternative (and frequently preferable) employment. Her discussion focuses primarily on those working within the sector from the 'mainstream' population. Notwithstanding the positive attributes which many refugees can bring to workplaces in tourism, structural barriers can appear to be even higher when we are referring to these entrants to this labour market.

Therefore, the notion of refugee mobility from outsider to integrated tourism employee presents a number of problems when set alongside perhaps rather more simple forms of tourism mobilities, those of tourists and of those workers who travel for choice-driven economic or lifestyle motivations. Notwithstanding the potential to achieve otherwise, most refugees in developed countries have few choices with regard to where they find themselves, in geographical, cultural or employment terms. Their journey to integration is rarely one of choice and the destination they seek may be difficult if not impossible to attain. Few refugees aspire to working lives in tourism in an alien environment, perhaps acting as a hospitality proxy on behalf of the host community, but are faced with limited choices in this regard.

The sustained growth of international tourism is likely to take place against a background of demographic flux in developed countries, centred on an ageing and, in some instances, a declining population. This context provides one of the major challenges for tourism's development over the next 20 years (Baum, 2009) in a business as well as a social sense and is, arguably, an issue that is infrequently the subject of serious debate and, as a consequence, is under-researched. There are a number of 'local' measures that can be put in place in response to this challenge. These focus on attracting non-traditional employees into the tourism workforce (older workers, those with disability) as well as productivity-driven measures, based on more extensive application of technology within the low skills workplace. However, drawing on external sources of labour to supplement declining local supplies will continue to be an inevitable response by the tourism sectors of many countries faced with this challenge. This, in turn, creates opportunities for a specific group within the wider migrant community, refugees, with either legal or illegal status, to avail themselvesof employment opportunities within tourism. However, refugees working in tourism remains a community about which little is currently known. A preliminary research agenda to establish a more comprehensive understanding of this group could address the following:

- The numbers of refugees involved in tourism-related work in key host countries
- The nature of work in tourism undertaken by both refugees with legal status in their host country and those working within the grey economy
- The educational and experience profile of these workers
- The career progression, perceived prospects and barriers to advancement experienced by these tourism workers
- Entry to entrepreneurial activity in tourism and the experience of those engaged
- Impact of refugees and other migrant workers on the perceived 'authenticity' of the local tourism product and experience.

This is an area which, at policy and research levels, will increase in its significance in response to constantly changing political, economic and demographic pressures. Therefore, responding to the challenges that are posed is important for both policy makers and researchers.

References

Ager, A. and Strang, A. (2008) 'Understanding integration: a conceptual framework', *Journal of Refugee Studies*, **21** (2), 166-191.

Allon, F., Anderson, K. and Bushell, R. (2008) 'Mutant mobilities: backpacker tourism in "global" Sydney', *Mobilities*, **3** (1), 73-94.

Altinay, L. and Altinay, E. (2006) 'Determinants of ethnic minority entrepreneurial growth in the catering sector', *Service Industries Journal*, **26** (2), 203-221.

Basu, A. (1998) 'An exploration of entrepreneurial activity among Asian small businesses in Britain', *Small Business Economics*, **10** (4), 313-326.

Baum, T. (1996) 'Unskilled work and the hospitality industry: myth or reality?', *International Journal of Hospitality Management*, **15** (3), 207-209.

Baum, T. (2002) 'Skills and training for the hospitality sector: a review of issues', *Journal of Vocational Education and Training*, **54** (3), 343-363.

Baum, T. (2006a) 'Reflections on the nature of skills in the experience economy: challenging traditional skills models in hospitality', *Journal of Hospitality and Tourism Management*, **13** (2), 124-135.

Baum, T. (2006b) *Human Resource Management for Tourism, Hospitality and Leisure. An International Perspective*, London: International Thomson.

Baum, T. (2007) 'Human resources in tourism: still waiting for change', *Tourism Management*, **28**, 1383-1399.

Baum, T. (2009) 'Demographic change and labour supply in global tourism to 2030: A tentative assessment of implications for Ireland', in proceedings of 5th Annual Tourism Research in Ireland Conference, Dublin: Dublin Institute of Technology.

Baum, T., Devine, F., Dutton, E., Hearns, N., Karimi, S. and Kokkranikal, J. (2007a) 'Cultural diversity in hospitality work', *Cross Cultural Management*, **14** (3), 229-239.

Baum, T., Hearns, N. and Devine, F. (2007b) 'Place, people and interpretation: issues of migrant labour and tourism imagery in Ireland. Special Edition on "Interpretation"', *Tourism and Recreation Research*, **32** (3), 39-48

Baum, T., Devine, F. and Hearns, N. (2008) 'You won't have your names when you ride the big airplane, All they will call you will be "deportees"', paper presented at the CAUTHE conference Migration, Transport and Tourism: a Reflection on the Coalescence of Experience, February, Gold Coast, Australia.

Bauman, Z. (1999) 'The burning of popular fear', *New Internationalist*, **310** (March), 20–23.

Bianchi, R. (2000) 'Migrant tourist-workers: exploring the "contact zones" of post-industrial tourism', *Current Issues in Tourism*, **3** (2), 107-137.

Bonacich, E. and Modell, J. (1980) *The Economic Basis of Ethnic Solidarity*, Berkeley CA: University of California Press.

Boswell, C. and Straubhaar, T. (2004) 'The illegal employment of foreign workers: an overview', *Intereconomics*, January–February, 4-7.

Bryman, A. (2004) *The Disneyfication of Society*, London: Sage.

Burns, P.M. (1997) 'Hard-skills, soft-skills: undervaluing hospitality's "service with a smile"', *Progress in Hospitality and Tourism Research*, **3**, 239-248.

Castles, S., Korac, M., Vasta, E. and Vertovec, S. (2001) *Integration: Mapping the Field*, Report of a project carried out by the Centre for Migration and Policy Research and Refugee Studies Centre, University of Oxford.

Chesney, M. and Hazari, B. (2003) 'Illegal migrants, tourism and welfare: a trade theoretic approach', *Pacific Economic Review*, **8** (3), 259-268.

Conradson, D. and Latham, A. (2005) 'Escalator London? A case study of New Zealand tertiary educated migrants in a global city', *Journal of Contemporary European Studies*, **13** (2), 159-172.

Devine, F., Baum, T., Hearns, N. and Devine, A. (2007) 'Cultural diversity in hospitality work: the Northern Ireland experience', *International Journal of Human Resource Management*, **18** (2), 333-349.

Diken, B. (2004) 'From refugee camps to gated communities: biopolitics and the end of the city', *Citizenship Studies*, **8** (1), 83-106.

ECRE (1999) 'Bridges and Fences to Integration: Refugee Perceptions of Integration in the European Union. Task Force on Integration', available from http://www.refugeenet.org/pdf/bridges_fences.pdf (accessed on 25 May 2009).

Feeney, A. (2000) 'Refugee employment', *Local Economy*, **15** (4), 343-349.

Findlay, A.M. (1995) 'Skilled transients: the invisible phenomenon?', in R. Cohen (ed.), *The Cambridge Survey of World Migration*, Cambridge: Cambridge University Press, pp. 515-522.

Gibson, S. (2003) 'Accommodating strangers: British hospitality and the asylum hotel debate', *Journal for Cultural Research*, **7** (4), 367-386.

Hall, D. (2008) 'From "bricklaying" to "bricolage": transition and tourism development in Central and Eastern Europe', *Tourism Geographies*, **10** (4), 410–428.

Hochschild, A.R. (1983) *The Managed Heart: Commercialization of Human Feeling*, Berkeley: University of California Press.

Home Office (2004) *Indicators of Integration: Final Report*, Home Office Development and Practice Report 28. London: Home Office, available from http://www.homeoffice.gov.uk/rds/pdfs04/dpr28.pdf (accessed on 25 May 2009).

Home Office (2006) *A New Model for National Refugee Integration Services in England*, Consultation Paper. London: Home Office, available from http://www.ukba.homeoffice.gov.uk/sitecontent/documents/aboutus/consultations/closedconsultations/nationalrefugeeintegration/consultation_document.pdf?view=B (accessed on 25 May 2009).

Hurtsfield, J., Pearson, R., Hooker, H., Ritchie, H. and Sinclair, A. (2004) *Employing Refugees: Some Organisations' Experiences*, Brighton: Institute for Employment Studies.

Jayaweera, H. and Anderson, B. (2008) 'Migrant workers and vulnerable employment: an analysis of existing data', London: TUC Commission on Vulnerable Employment, available from http://www.vulnerableworkers.org.uk/wp-content/uploads/2008/08/ analysis-of-migrant-worker-data-final.pdf (accessed on 8 September 2008).

Kirk, R. (2004) *Skills Audit of Refugees*, London: Home Office Online Report 37/04.

Light, I. (1984) 'Immigrant and ethnic enterprise in North America', *Ethnic and Racial Studies*, 7, 195-216

Metcalf, H., Modood, T. and Virdee, S. (1996) *Asian Self-Employment: The Interaction of Culture and Economics in England*, London: Policy Studies Institute.

Nickson, D. and Warhurst, C. (2007) 'Open Pandora's Box: aesthetic labour and hospitality', in C. Lashley, P. Lynch and A. Morrison (eds), *Hospitality. A Social Lens*, Oxford: Elsevier, pp. 155-172.

Riley, M. (1996) *Human Resource Management in the Hospitality and Tourism Industry*, Oxford: Butterworth-Heinemann.

Robinson, V. (1998) 'Defining and measuring successful refugee integration', Proceedings of CRE International Conference on Integration of Refugees in Europe, Antwerp, Brussels: ECRE.

Shacknove, A. (1985) 'Who is a refugee?', *Ethics*, **95** (2), 274-284.

Spencer, S. (ed.) (2006) *Refugees and Other New Migrants: a Review of the Evidence on Successful Approaches to Integration*, London: The Home Office, available from http://www.compas.ox.ac.uk/publications/papers/Refugees_new%20migrants-Dec06.pdf (accessed on 8 September 2008).

Srinivasan, S. (1995) *The South Asian Petty Bourgeoisie in Britain*, Aldershot: Avebury.

Szivas, E., Riley, M. and Airey, D. (2003) 'Labour mobility into tourism. Attraction and satisfaction', *Annals of Tourism Research*, **30** (1), 64-76.

Toynbee, P. (2003) *Hard Work: Life in Low-pay Britain*, London: Bloomsbury.

United Nations (1951) *Convention Relating to the Status of Refugees*, New York: United Nations.

Vaugeois, N. and Rollins, R. (2007) 'Mobility into tourism refuge employer?', *Annals of Tourism Research*, **34** (3), 630-648.

Warhurst, C., Nickson, D., Witz, A. and Cullen, A.M. (2000) 'Aesthetic labour in interactive service work: some case study evidence from the "New Glasgow"', *Service Industries Journal*, **20** (3), 1-18.

Watson, R., Keasey, K. and Baker, M. (2000) 'Small firm financial contracting and immigrant entrepreneurship', in J. Rath (ed.), *Immigrant Businesses: The Economic, Political and Social Environment*, Basingstoke: Macmillan, pp. 70-89.

Williams, A. and Hall, C.M. (2000) 'Tourism and migration: new relationships between production and consumption', *Tourism Geographies*, **2** (1), 5–27.

15 The tourism destiny of World Heritage cultural sites

Myriam Jansen-Verbeke and Bob McKercher

Setting the scene

In the wide spectrum of interesting and emerging research tracks in tourism studies, our focus is on the structural role of cultural resources in shaping tourism landscapes and attractions. Understanding the dynamics of the cultural tourism market starts with the identification of cultural resources and their territorial embedding (Jansen-Verbeke, 2009). The objective of this chapter is to open a discussion on the particular role of world heritage sites as cultural resources for the development of a global and dynamic tourism market and as economic resources for local and regional development. Our main hypothesis is that tourism is one way of capitalizing on cultural resources in situ, looking at tourism as a proactive agent in the process of conservation and of building cultural identities for territories and their communities, rather than tourism as a destroyer of the past and of the uniqueness and beauty of places.

The most crucial agency in this global process of cultural awareness and identity building, in designing conservation policies and eventually launching cultural tourism has been UNESCO (United Nations Education, Scientific and Cultural Organization) This global organization ratified *The Convention Concerning the Protection of the World Cultural and Natural Heritage*, more commonly known as the World Heritage Convention, in 1972 to establish a system to identify and conserve cultural and natural heritage of outstanding universal value (UNESCO, 2009a). The World Heritage list now includes some 878 properties considered as having 'outstanding universal value', including 679 cultural, 174 natural and 25 mixed cultural and natural sites (UNESCO, 2009b). World Heritage Sites (WHS) can range from single monuments, such as the Taj Mahal or the Statue of Liberty, through to entire cities and sites or cultural landscapes that extend across international boundaries.

WHS bear a unique and important testimony of the past to the future generations. Prospective sites must meet at least one of ten criteria, of which six apply specifically to cultural sites (UNESCO, 2009c). Tourism does not feature in this list, yet it is widely recognized that the 'International Top Brand' benefits, affiliated with designation, potentially open significant tourism opportunities for communities in or adjacent to designated sites (Buckley *et al.*, 2004). It is for this reason that gaining designation is a coveted prize that can act as a focal point for national marketing campaigns (Li *et al.*, 2008). This duality of designation criteria that exclude tourism and the reality of tourism as an underlying rationale for seeking designation has generated a lively discourse on whether and how the two can be managed in a holistic and mutually beneficial manner. Ideally, tourism should be a complementary activity. The experience of rediscovering the past is a clear 'leitmotiv' for places to tell their story with tourism providing the vehicle to do so. But, tourism and tourists' demands on sites, real and perceived, have become a source of antagonism (Shackley, 1998; Harrison and Hitchcock, 2005). The issue has gained more prominence with the emergence of cultural tourism as a much sought-after commodity.

Cultural differences between places and communities have been a source of inspiration for writers, painters and artists, and a key motive for travellers since ancient times. Some people have long travelled to experience different cultures and many destinations have promoted their heritage as tourist attractions for centuries (Prentice, 1993). It was only in the late 1970s and early 1980s, though, that 'cultural tourism' emerged as a discrete product category (Tighe, 1986). Indeed, cultural tourism remains an evolving idea (Timothy and Boyd, 2003; see also Chapter 13). Some academics tend to look at cultural activities as an exponent of life style and interests in the context of the usual environment rather than a category of travel motivations, therefore regarding this a subject of interdisciplinary social analysis. Others define cultural tourism differently, reflecting ongoing trends and changes in values, placing more emphasis on the use of cultural resources for tourism (Jansen-Verbeke *et al.*, 2008), on the cultural context, motives and activities of tourists (Richards and Wilson 2006) or on the dynamics of a 'new' market niche (McKercher and du Cros, 2002).

The academic investigation into the relationship between tourism and WHS is largely fragmented, involving individual case studies that make broad generalizations about site-specific issues (Shackley, 1998). The perception that tourism's impact is negative marks much recent research work. Yet tourism has a multidimensional impact, and if managed in an intelligent way can be beneficial to many sites. The challenge is to develop a deeper understanding of the underlying forces that affect tourism sustainability and to understand how these interact in a site-specific context. This chapter presents some critical reflections on past research of tourism and cultural resources, World Heritage sites in particular, and seeks to identify key issues for a future research agenda.

Cultural heritage: valued and shaped by tourism

Looking at studies over the past 20 years, on the relationship between tourism and heritage – including tourism at heritage sites – three interrelated lines of enquiry can be traced: supply-side issues relating to characteristics of the site in view of identification of tourism potential and eventually the launching of successful tourism; demand-side issues relating to developing a deeper understanding of the market trends and alliances; and third, the most debated line focuses on sustainability issues and tends to emphasize unsustainable practices and management responses.

Supply-side issues: attributes of tourism success

This first line explores the anticipated or ongoing transformation process from cultural asset to tourism product, in general, and on understanding critical factors of successful tourism development in particular. An assumption is typically made that World Heritage designation brings with it an 'automatic' influx of tourists. Yet, empirical support for the proposition is ambiguous. Certainly some sites witness increased visitor numbers, but many others have seen little or no increment in visitors and likely never will. Research into Hungarian sites (Rátz and Puczkó, 2003) conclude that those near the national capitals are drawing visitors, but that other sites are little known and receive no benefits from designation. Studies in the United States (Hazen, 2008) and New Zealand (Hall and Piggen, 2002) conclude that WHS status has had little effect on visitation, while a UK study of 86 sites revealed that 51 saw no increase in visits, 13 had small increases and only 22 had large increases (PWC, 2007).

Indeed, the issue of why some heritage sites benefit more than oters from tourism has not been studied widely (Graham *et al.*, 2000). Fame and image of the site prior to designation play a more important role than designation itself (Evans, 2003; Buckley *et al.*, 2004). Already popular places will become more popular, while unpopular, remote or contested sites will likely gain few additional visitors. Other studies have identified a range of spatial issues that appear to be correlated directly with tourism demand. Concentration of cultural heritage assets either with other WHS or with a critical mass of other tourist attractions (Caffyn and Lutz, 1999) and grounded by an icon (Tufts and Milne, 1999) further helps to induce visitation (Li *et al.*, 2008). Likewise, synergy between tourist and other activities and clustering of tourist attractions with supporting facilities such as shops, restaurants, festivals, events, explains the dynamics of tourism in specific areas. The emerging tourismscapes in historical urban settings catch the attention of researchers, urban planners and tourism marketers (Jansen-Verbeke, 2007), rather more frequently than similar processes of touristification – at different scale levels – in rural or more remote areas (Jansen-Verbeke *et al.*, 2008). Clearly, sites located in or adjacent to large urban populations or major destination areas are more likely to experience increased visitation after designation (DCMS, 2008), whereas remote, isolated attractions may have difficulty in drawing visitors, especially if they are located in socially marginal areas (Caffyn and Lutz, 1999).

The Tourism Council of Australia (TCA, 1998) suggests further that factors relating to potential competitive advantages over existing products, life-cycle expectancy and the size of the investment required influence success. Size, scale and theming can also make a difference, with sites with a clear market identity, icon attraction and which are spatially easy to navigate having an advantage over those lacking such attributes. Ultimately, the differences in tourism benefits relate primarily to the appeal of the tourist opportunity spectrum. A number of models have been developed to assess tourism potential, but they have not been tested widely yet (du Cros, 2001; McKercher and Ho, 2006). A more holistic understanding in multiple contextual settings is required to develop a research-based indication of tourism potential and this for the broad spectrum of WHS.

Demand-side studies: visiting the past

Early demand-side research tended to be descriptive, since data on cultural tourists (profile and origin, motivation, activities, time space behaviour patterns and expenditures) were scarce. The intention was to identify the size of the market, often without recognizing its highly differentiated nature and hybrid structure. Much of this research was based on the discredited method of analysing activity questions in departing visitor surveys to infer causation and thus market size (McKercher and Chan, 2005). This approach resulted in the production of fantastic figures that overstated the size of the market by many times (examples include Antolovic, 1999 and Keefe, 2003).

Slowly, though, the understanding of the market is being supplanted by more sophisticated research that recognizes a continuum of cultural tourists exists based on the importance of heritage motives in the overall trip decision-making process (Silberberg, 1995; McKercher, 2002). This type of research also recognizes differences in the willingness and ability of tourists to engage cultural assets (Stebbins, 1996), which in turn means that different types of tourists seek different experiences from the attractions they visit (Prentice *et al.*, 1998). It suggests further that the archetypal 'deep' cultural tourist only represents a small minority of the total market. Instead, most cultural tourists travel largely for rest, relaxation and escapist motives and visit sites primarily for their educational and entertainment values (McKercher and du Cros, 2003). Timothy's (1997) research is influential, for he identifies four levels of heritage tourism attractions based on an individual's level of connectivity to the site. Some World Heritage attractions may draw large masses of tourists that invoke feelings of awe but do not invoke feelings of personal attachment. By contrast, national, local, and personal sites engender progressively stronger feelings of personal connectivity and likely facilitate deeper experiences by the visitor.

Visitation motives at heritage sites seem to be linked to the tourists' perception of the site in relation to their own heritage and their willingness to be exposed to an emotional experience (Poria *et al.*, 2003). Reasons for visiting heritage sites were classified into three groups: 'heritage experience', 'learning experience', and 'recreational experience'. Results of a more recent study in Amsterdam (Poria *et al.*, 2006) indicate a distinct relationship between tourists' perceptions of a site relative to their own heritage and the motivations for visiting the site.

The recently introduced concept of *experiencescapes* (O'Dell and Billing, 2005) adds significantly to the understanding of cultural tourism, for it recognizes that the very nature of tourism development has shifted from pushing products onto tourists to encouraging them to enjoy experiences. This shift, in turn, has increased the demand for innovation and creativity (Richards and Wilson, 2006) in what could be appreciated as an attractive tourist setting. It also challenges many beliefs about the type of experience tourists seek at WHS, how the sites need to be presented and managed and, even who – tourism or cultural heritage experts – should take a lead in managing the sites. These observations may explain why some tourists are described as icon collectors rather than having a more meaningful experience (Buckley *et al.*, 2004).

This shift from a supply-driven approach in cultural tourism to a more demand-oriented focus has its impact on the emerging tourism research agenda. The replacement of well known and intensively studied patterns of tourists' observed behaviour by a much less understood phenomenon of tourists' experiences has met some resistance, for it does not easily fit into the traditional tourism studies kaleidoscope and implies an interdisciplinary approach. Understanding the hidden and often complex agenda of visitors and tourists to cultural destinations (motives – expectations – experiences – and satisfaction) is indeed a major challenge for both qualitative and quantitative research in tourism.

Sustainability, impact and inclusion: critical issues

The third line of research in this field focuses on an increasingly wide range of critical issues of which sustainability is the most pronounced one. The academic research track is primarily interested in how potentially competing and conflicting value sets can be managed in a cohesive manner that maximizes the benefits to all stakeholders, while minimizing or mitigating impacts. Ironically, while the assessment of benefits and costs of tourism at WHS sites has gained the most attention among the research community (especially the cultural heritage community), the quality of much of this research is highly variable, even questionable. Benefits tend to be stated in generic terms relating primarily to revenue generation, job creation and the power of tourism to displace other more damaging industries. Yet, little evidence is provided to support these claims. Impacts of tourism are documented more precisely, but research results tend to be fragmented and site-specific, although generalizable conclusions are drawn. In fact, impact studies could address a wide range of processes inducing changes. Yet the focus tends to be mainly on three themes: over-use, under-use and misuse. These aspects are indeed most crucial in designing a site-specific management model.

Over use

Over use impacts have drawn the most public attention. UNESCO has established its own list of '*sites at risk*' with some 30 sites currently listed, of which only three identify tourism directly or indirectly as a cause (UNESCO, 2009d). The Global Heritage Fund has documented a range of over-use impacts, while the World Monuments Watch List also publishes a list of the '*100 most endangered sites*' that includes many WHS. In most cases, sites are 'overwhelmed' by tourist numbers that far exceed desired carrying capacity either in totality or as a result of intense pulse visits during peak holiday periods, resulting in damage to the site and a reduced quality of experience for visitors (Bennett, 2005).

Overcrowding is often spatially and temporarily uneven, with crowding at peak moments and site deterioration in specific areas, while other areas may register small numbers of visitors (Russo, 2002). Although this issue of unequal pressure in time and space occurs commonly, it is not yet researched or monitored systematically. Shifting demand from high-density to low-density areas is a significant management challenge since the average tourist prefers to capture icon sites. Intelligent and innovative visitor management strategies, based on empirical research of visitors' time and space behaviour – in situ – are now being explored with advanced technology of registration (Shoval and Isaacson, 2007).

Under use

Under-use, uneven use and misuse may actually be more prescient issues. Under-use is much harder to address, for it tends to reflect a fundamental lack of touristic appeal that cannot be overcome easily, if at all. This issue is especially relevant where sites have invested heavily in tourism infrastructure in anticipation of large numbers of visitors that do not materialize, for it can result in the insufficient generation of revenue, badly needed for conservation and a loss of local support for maintaining the attraction.

Misuse

Misuse is another misunderstood, but vitally important issue. It occurs when visitors behave in a manner other than that expected or desired by the site's managers. Brooks (2003) notes 'visitors who show little respect for the sanctity of spiritual places, practices and traditions can have an adverse impact on those places and communities'. It is most likely to occur in dissonant or contested heritage sites, where different interest groups with competing values promote or encourage divergent behaviours (Ashworth and Hartmann, 2005; David and Oliver, 2006; Ashworth, 2008). Alternatively, it can occur as a result of an information void due to poor transmission of desired messages or interference by gatekeepers that fail to define how to behave. The level of cultural insensitivity shown by such actions leads to conflict (Robinson and Boniface, 1998), can disrupt local communities, breed antagonism towards tourists and lead to less support for tourism.

Misuse of WHS also relates to the broader issue of presentation, authenticity and storytelling. A lack of appropriate presentation and communication about the significance of the place can hinder understanding of cultural values, while improper or inequitable balance of information can lead to a narrow understanding of the cultural heritage in the mind of the consumer (Brooks, 2003; Hartmann, 2009). Cultural sites, in particular, are not value-free. As much as some people would like to believe absolute histories exist, in reality, multiple, contested histories often share the same physical locale (Graham *et al.*, 2000). Jamal and Kim (2005: 58) note that

> the 'past' is the focus of this tourism type but the politics of identity, representation and preservation that arise in the instrumental use of the past influence the physical, social cultural and spiritual well-being of people and the sustainability of their cultural goods, places and environments (built and natural).

The question of whose story to tell becomes an important political consideration (Harrison and Hitchcock 2005; Ashworth, 2008; Stone and Sharpley, 2008), with tourism playing a significant role in the (re)construction and conveyance of identities (Hampton, 2005).

Use concerns, presentation and other issues that affect sustainability ultimately relate back to the presence or absence of appropriate management structures, which in turn relate to governance issues. One of the controversies of World Heritage status is that while sites are given the imprimatur as places of outstanding universal value, in reality, designation does not afford any special protection status, unless signatory economies pass relevant legislation. Critics complain that designation alone is incapable of protecting endangered sites. Obviously governance is a key agent for sustainability (Usborne, 2009). Interestingly, a large number of WHS do not seem to have formalized management plans. Empirical and systematic research in each of the cultural WHS is required in order to substantiate this debate (Poria and Ashworth, 2009).

Research findings suggests that effective management is much easier to achieve when there is a single overriding agency responsible for the entire site, or even better for the tourist destination as a coherent territorial unit. However, this becomes increasingly difficult where multiple agencies exist or where no single dominant agency is recognized (DCMS, 2008). Countries where central governments take leadership roles and are supported by strong legislation, generally have encountered fewer problems than those where management is devolved to the local level and/or not supported strongly by legislation (Harrison and Hitchcock, 2005). The risks of corrupt behaviour are especially high in developing economies where poor governance has led to a trade in stolen or illicit cultural property (Brooks, 2003). Even more alarming is the widespread corruption in the granting of exclusive management contracts at WHS for the benefit of developers and political leaders. This leaves little revenue for site management, with all its known consequences (Covington, 2004).

A research-based management agenda for cultural WH sites: the way forward

Since every WHS is unique and has its own set of challenges, effective management must be site-specific. No universal 'blue print for tourism development' exists, just as a 'one size fits all' management approach cannot work. However, researchers have identified a number of issues that appear to be common to many sites, even though this research has been historically fragmented, case-based and not integrated. The authors began this chapter by calling for the development of a deeper understanding of the underlying forces that affect tourism sustainability at WHS, and in doing so, to propose an integrated agenda to help direct research initiatives. Figure 15.1 identifies a range of critical issues that have been identified in the literature over the past 20 years that affect the sustainable use of WHS. These issues are ordered thematically according to three different, yet connected structural dimensions of heritage sites (Jansen-Verbeke, 2007):

◆   *The hardware* or tangible, physical assets of the site and its surrounds, core attractions of the site – monuments – complexes, etc. – and the supporting tourism infrastructure (roads, hotels, etc.);

◆   *The software*, or the skills to attract visitors, via strategic imaging and marketing and to deliver positive tourism experiences;

◆   The *'org-ware'*, referring to the type, power and network of organizations and management structures involved in creating a sustainable tourismscape.

The way forward requires two complementary tasks. The first task is to communicate effectively what is already known about tourism and world heritage in a more effective and unbiased manner to challenge many of the myths about tourism. These myths range from positive assumptions about automatic increases in tourism numbers and resultant economic development as well as negative perceptions that tourism is an inherently negative activity. The truth lies somewhere in between, where given the right conditions, tourism can benefit some sites, while given poor management, tourism can damage some other places. Communication needs to be directed at government officials, tourism bodies and cultural heritage managers.

The second task is to continue to expand the body of knowledge, focusing on processes rather than on 'ad hoc' perceptions and descriptions of impacts and threats. This approach suggests a critical assessment of the characteristics of the *hardware*; issues of conservation and development, also taking into account location and robusticity or ability to withstand increased visitation. This exercise needs to be conducted in various contexts (urban, peripheral, rural, remote), in different locales and types of sites. This implies not only an integrated site analysis, but also an assessment of the situational contexts, including existing tourism activities and conditions for sustainable tourism development.

Hardware

Location	Spatial characteristics	Robustness
Solitary and isolated to integrated into an urban landscape	Size of WHS – individual monument to multi-national scale	Fragility of tangible asset
Part of a contiguous destination area or isolated	Internal spatial structure of WHS (compact or dispersed, single or multiple nodes)	Risk that tourism pressure may compromise cultural values
Access considerations (easy vs. difficult)	Presence or absence of iconic feature	Ability to manage impacts
Proximity to other WHS sites	Presence or absence of buffer zone around WHS	
Connection with main tourism gateways		

Software

Tourist appeal	Experiencescape
Place in attraction's hierarchy (primary vs. secondary)	Type of tourist attracted to site / type of experience sought
Fame prior to designation	Type and quality of interpretation and which story / stories to be told presentation
Realistic assessment of tourism potential	Theming and desired message(s)
Possess necessary attributes for success	Tourist connectivity to the site
	Focus on 'edutainment' or education.

Orgware

Organisation	Policy	Management	Stakeholders
Single overriding agency vs. multiple agencies vs. no dominant agency	Pursuit of WHS status for conservation or tourism goals?	Presented as is with little commodification vs. heavily commodified	Single stakeholder with a clear focus vs. multiple stakeholders with mixed foci
Ownership public, private or a mix of public and private ownership	Presence or absence of effective national legislation	WHS site management structure - public sector, public / private partnership or leased to private sector	Direct and pragmatic vs. indirect and ideologically driven stakeholders
	Level of government management of WHS devolved to (local of federal)	Presence or absence of formal conservation or management plan and its effectiveness	Power balance between stakeholders
		Revenue source for conservation (presence / absence; reliance on tourism to provide funding)	Level / efficacy of stakeholder consultation
		Perceived role of tourism (primary use vs. ancillary use)	

Figure 15.1: Key issues in tourism at World Heritage Sites

The analysis of context variables of a heritage site and its territory can then be addressed in order to design an anticipatory plan for tourism, including how/if to transform the site for visitation by developing appropriate *software*. The transformation of cultural resources into attractive tourist experiences requires more research to understand the values, characteristics and meanings of the site from a tourism-use perspective and how tourism could impinge on other site values.

Process analysis seeks ways to integrate these findings with governance, stakeholder and other policy issues ('*org-ware*'). Here more inter-disciplinary research is required integrating anthropological, sociological and human geographical approaches to develop a deeper understanding of the dynamics of tourism and the involvement of local communities in the commodification of heritage (tangible and intangible). In addition, a more critical understanding of the role of politics and the implementation of policies is necessary to understand the process of change that is likely to occur at heritage sites in different contexts.

Successful implementation of this agenda is also dependent on developing formal or informal multinational networks of researchers who can set agreed-upon agendas to examine the range of issues identified in a comprehensive manner to develop a definitive set of knowledge about tourism and WHS. Importantly, such research must seek to test the universality of certain concepts, determine which issues are site-specific and adopt an unbiased approach to tourism. Ideally, these groups would consist of both tourism and cultural heritage experts. Some evidence of the emergence of such groups is already beginning to appear.

References

Antolovic, J. (1999) 'Immovable cultural monuments and tourism', *Cultural Tourism session notes XII Assembly*, Mexico: ICOMOS, pp. 103-118.

Ashworth, G. (2008) 'Heritage: definitions, delusions and dissonance', *World Heritage and Sustainable Tourism, Vol. 1*, in Amoeba *et al.* (eds), Barcelos, Portugal: Green Lines Institute, pp. 3-9.

Ashworth, G.J. and Hartmann, R. (2005) *Horror and Human Tragedy Revisited: The Management of Sites of Atrocities for Tourism*, New York: Cognizant Communication Corporation.

Bennett, O. (2005) 'Are we loving our heritage to death?', *The Guardian*, 30 April 2005, reproduced on the Global Heritage Fund, available from http://www.globalheritagefund.org/news/conservation_news/loving_heritage_to_death_guardian_4_30_05.asp (accessed on 11 May 2009).

Brooks, G. (2003) *Heritage at Risk from Tourism*, ICOMOS, available from http://www.international.icomos.org/risk/2001/tourism.htm (accessed on 11 May 2009).

Buckley, R., Bramwell, B. and Lane, B. (2004) 'The effects of World Heritage listing on tourism to Australian national parks', *Journal of Sustainable Tourism*, **12** (1), 70-84.

Caffyn, A. and Lutz, J. (1999) 'Developing the heritage tourism product in multi-ethnic cities', *Tourism Management*, **20** (2), 213-221.

Covington, R. (2004) 'Rescuing Angkor. Global Heritage Fund', available from http://www.globalheritagefund.org/news/conservation_news/rescuing_angkor_feb_04.asp (accessed on 11 May 2009).

David, B. and Oliver, C. (2006) 'Contested identities: the dissonant heritage of European town walls and walled towns', *International Journal of Heritage Studies*, **12** (3), 234-254.

DCMS (2008) 'World heritage for the nation: identifying, protecting and promoting our world heritage – a consultation paper', available from http://www.culture.gov.uk/images/publications/whconsultation_engversion.pdf (accessed on 11 May 2009).

du Cros, H. (2001) 'A new model to assist in planning for sustainable cultural heritage tourism', *International Journal of Travel Research*, **3** (2), 165-170.

Evans, G. (2003) 'Hard-branding the cultural city - from Prado to Prada', *International Journal of Urban and Regional Research*, **27** (2), 417-440.

Graham, B., Ashworth G.J. and Turnbridge, J. (2000) *A Geography of Heritage: Power, Culture and Economy*, London: Hodder Arnold.

Hall, C.M. and Piggen, R. (2002) 'Tourism business knowledge of world heritage sites: a New Zealand case study', *International Journal of Tourism Research*, **4**, 401-411.

Hampton, M. (2005) 'Heritage, local communities and economic development', *Annals of Tourism Research*, **32** (3), 735–759.

Harrison, D. and Hitchcock, M. (eds) (2005) *The Politics of World Heritage. Negotiating Tourism and Conservation*, Clevedon: Channel View Publications.

Hartmann, R. (2009) 'Tourism to places with a difficult past. A discussion paper on recent research trends and concepts: heritage tourism, dissonant heritage tourism, thanatourism, dark tourism, Holocaust tourism', available from www.dark-tourism.org.uk.

Hazen, H. (2008) '"Of outstanding universal value": the challenge of scale and applying the World Heritage Convention at national parks in the U.S.', *Geoforum*, **39**, 252 – 264.

Jamal, T. and Kim, H. (2005) 'Bridging the interdisciplinary divide towards an integrated framework for heritage tourism research', *Tourist Studies*, **5** (1), 55–83.

Jansen-Verbeke, M. (2007) 'Cultural resources and the tourismification of territories', *Acta Turistica Nova*, **1** (1), 21-41.

Jansen-Verbeke, M. (2009) 'The territoriality paradigm in cultural tourism', *Tourism/ Turyzm*, **19** (1/2), 25-31.

Jansen-Verbeke, M., Priestley, G.K. and Russo, A.P. (eds) (2008) *Cultural Resources for Tourism: Patterns, Process and Policies*, New York: Nova Science.

Keefe, C. (2003) *History and Culture Significant and Growing Part of the US Travel Experience*, Travel Industry Association of America, available from http://www.hotel-online.com/News/PR2003_2nd/Jun03_HistoryCulture.htm (accessed on 6 April 2004).

Li, M., Wu, B. and Cai, L. (2008) 'Tourism development of world heritage sites in China: a geographic perspective', *Tourism Management*, **29** (2), 308–311.

McKercher, B. (2002) 'Towards a classification of cultural tourists', *International Journal of Tourism Research*, **4**, 29–38.

McKercher B. and Chan, A. (2005) 'How special is special interest tourism', *Journal of Travel Research*, **44** (1), 21–31.

McKercher, B. and du Cros, H. (2002) *Cultural Tourism: The Partnership between Tourism and Cultural Heritage Management*, Binghamton, NY: Haworth Press.

McKercher, B. and du Cros, H. (2003) 'Testing a cultural tourism typology', *International Journal of Tourism Research*, **5** (1), 45–58.

McKercher, B. and Ho, P. (2006) 'Assessing the tourism potential of smaller cultural attractions', *Journal of Sustainable Tourism*, **14** (5), 473–488.

O'Dell, T. and Billing, P. (eds) (2005) *Experiencescapes: Tourism Culture and Economy*, Copenhagen: Copenhagen Business School Press.

Poria ,Y. and Ashworth, G. (2009) 'Heritage tourism – current resources for conflict', *Annals of Tourism Research*, **36** (3), 522-525.

Poria, Y., Butler, R. and Airey, D. (2003) 'The core of heritage tourism: distinguishing heritage tourists from tourists in heritage places', *Annals of Tourism Research*, **30** (2), 238–254.

Poria, Y., Reichel, A. and Biran, A. (2006) 'Heritage site perceptions and motivations to visit', *Journal of Travel Research*, **44** (3), 318-326.

Prentice, R. (1993) *Tourism and Heritage Attractions*, Routledge: London.

Prentice, R.C., Witt, S.F. and Hamer, C. (1998) 'Tourism as experience: the case of heritage parks', *Annals of Tourism Research*, **25** (1), 1-24.

PWC (2007) 'The costs and benefits of UK World Heritage Site status: literature review for the Department of culture, media and sport', Price Waterhouse Coopers June 2007, available from http://www.culture.gov.uk/images/publications/PwC literaturereview.pdf (accessed on 11 May 2009).

Rátz, T. and Puczkó, L. (2003) 'A World Heritage industry? Tourism at Hungarian World Heritage Sites', in M. Gravari-Barbas and S. Guichard-Anguis (eds), *Regards Croisés sur le Patrimoine dans le Monde à l'Aube du XXIe Siècle*, Paris, France: Presses de l'Université de Paris-Sorbonne, pp.467-481, available from http://www.ratztamara.com/holloko.pdf (accessed on 11 May 2009).

Richards, G. and Wilson, J. (2006) 'Developing creativity in tourist experiences: A solution to serial reproduction of culture?', *Tourism Management*, **27** (6), 1209-1223.

Robinson, M. and Boniface, P. (eds) (1998) *Tourism and Cultural Conflicts*, Wallingford: CABI.

Russo, A.P. (2002) 'The vicious circle of tourism development in heritage cities', *Annals of Tourism Research*, **29** (1), 165-182.

Shackley, M. (ed.) (1998) *Visitor Management: Case Studies from World Heritage Sites*, Oxford: Butterworth Heinemann.

Shoval, N. and Isaacson, M. (2007) 'Tracking the tourist in digital age', *Annals of Tourism Research*, **34** (1), 141-159.

Silberberg, T. (1995) 'Cultural tourism and business opportunities for museums and heritage sites', *Tourism Management*, **16** (5), 361-365.

Stebbins, R. (1996) 'Cultural tourism as serious leisure', *Annals of Tourism Research*, **23** (4), 948-950.

Stone, P.R. and Sharpley, R. (2008) 'Consuming dark tourism: a thanatological perspective', *Annals of Tourism Research*, **35** (2), 574-595.

TCA (1999) *Our Heritage – It's Our Business – TCA Action Plan*, Sydney: Tourism Council of Australia.

Tighe, A.J. (1986) 'The arts/tourism partnership', *Journal of Travel Research*, **24** (3), 2-5.

Timothy, D.J. (1997) 'Tourism and the personal heritage experience', *Annals of Tourism Research*, **24** (3), 751–754.

Timothy, D. and Boyd, S. (2003) *Heritage Tourism*, Harlow: Prentice Hall.

Tufts, S. and Milne, S. (1999) 'Museums: a supply-side perspective', *Annals of Tourism Research*, **26** (3), 613-631.

UNESCO (2009a) *UNESCO World Heritage Convention*, New York: United Nations, available from http://whc.unesco.org/en/conventiontext/ (accessed on 11 May 2009).

UNESCO (2009b) *UNESCO World Heritage List*, New York: United Nations, available from http://whc.unesco.org/en/list (accessed on 11 May 2009).

UNESCO (2009c) *The Criteria for Selection*, New York: United Nations, available from http://whc.unesco.org/en/criteria/ (accessed on 11 May 2009).

UNESCO (2009d) *The List of World Heritage in Danger*, New York: United Nations, available from http://whc.unesco.org/en/danger/ (accessed on 11 May 2009).

Usborne, S. (2009) 'Is Unesco damaging the world's treasures?', *The Independent*, Apr 29, available from http://www.independent.co.uk/travel/news-and-advice/is-unesco-damaging-the-worlds-treasures-1675637.html (accessed on 11 May 2009).

16 Tourism research ethics: current considerations and future options

Gianna Moscardo

Introduction

Historically there has been little discussion of research ethics in the published tourism literature. In the early era of tourism studies it is likely that researchers were guided by the codes of ethical research practice of the disciplines in which they were originally trained. If most tourism researchers had higher research degrees in the disciplines of anthropology, sociology, economics, psychology, and geography and they conducted research within the ethical frameworks that existed in those disciplines perhaps there was little perceived need to discuss research ethics. But three major recent developments suggest that it may be time to reconsider this situation. First, there is the emergence of new generations of tourism researchers who have focused on tourism as a specialised area of concern in its own right and who do not have the same background in an established discipline. There appear to be no guidelines for these researchers to follow. Second, in all of the established social sciences there are ongoing debates and critical discussions of discipline and topic specific research ethics. It seems unlikely that tourism research as an area of academic concern is immune to these ethical questions and concerns. Third, much attention has been paid to the ethical issues related to the behaviours of tourists and tourism managers. While there are examples of codes of ethical conduct for tourists and tour operators there seem to be no such codes to guide the behaviour of tourism researchers. Given these historical and contemporary situations it seems timely to turn our attention to tourism research ethics.

It is the central argument of this chapter that in a discussion of the current status and future direction of tourism research, it is important to reflect on the ethics of tourism research practice and to ask if a code of tourism research ethics is necessary, and if so, what such a code might look like. The aim of this chapter is to open a discussion on these questions by:

◆ Reviewing basic principles of ethical social science research and considering how these might apply in the tourism context using scenarios to illustrate some of the ethical challenges that tourism researchers may have to address,

♦   Describing some of the ethical issues that have been identified in recent discussions in the social science disciplines that may apply in the tourism research context.

The chapter will seek to ask questions rather than suggest answers with the aim of stimulating greater awareness of research ethics and ethical conduct for tourism researchers.

Tourism research ethics: the past

There exists an ongoing debate over what tourism is and whether or not its study and growth as an identified area of teaching in universities justifies the label of discipline (Tribe, 2006). While this chapter does not seek to extend or comment on this debate, the discussion highlights three critical features of tourism research of relevance to an analysis of research ethics. First, the earliest studies of tourism were conducted within a number of established social science disciplines, especially economics, human geography, sociology, anthropology and psychology (Botterill *et al.*, 2002). But over time there has been an increasing number of researchers who are doctoral graduates from programmes outside these traditional disciplines and based in tourism-focused university units (Butler, 2004). Second, there has been a shift in the sources used in tourism studies from the foundation social science disciplines towards journals and books published solely within tourism (Xiao and Smith, 2005). While for some authors (Xiao and Smith, 2006) this is a sign of maturity for the area, an alternative view is that increasingly tourism research is conducted by individuals guided by second-hand models, concepts and theories who may not always realise the origins and challenges associated with their original development and who may be using concepts from disciplines they have no direct links to (Tribe, 2006). This leads us to the third area to be considered and that is the connections back to the original disciplines. An increasingly inward focus for tourism research may contribute to less attention paid to changes and developments in the original disciplines. It has been noted by several authors that the tourism research literature has not explicitly recognised or engaged in more recent social science debates about epistemology and methodology (Crick, 1989; Tribe, 2006). Clearly this is also the case for the area of research ethics. While earlier work was likely to have been conducted within the ethical codes and frameworks that exist in disciplines like anthropology (AAA, 1998), sociology (ASA, 1999), psychology (APA, 2002), and geography (AAG, 2005), it is not clear what codes or approaches, if any, are currently used by tourism researchers. Debates about ethical research issues are also noticeably absent from the tourism literature.

A search of the three key tourism journals, *Annals of Tourism Research*, *Journal of Travel Research* and *Tourism Management*, using the terms 'ethics', 'ethical' and 'codes of conduct', revealed very little about research ethics. Only a few papers were found that explicitly referred to tourism research ethics and in most the discussion was limited. In some only one aspect of research ethics was considered. For example, Opperman *et al.*'s (1998) opinion piece focused exclusively on citation and referencing practices, while Okumus *et al.*'s (2007) analysis only discussed ethical issues related to gaining access to organizations for research and disclosure of findings. In others, research ethics were discussed more as barriers to conducting research (Ahas *et al.*, 2008; Illum *et al.*, forthcoming) than as issues to be carefully considered. Only Schuler *et al.*'s (1999) paper placed ethical challenges at the centre of their paper about the implications of research ethics for the design of tourism research conducted with an Indigenous Australian community.

The review did, however, find considerable discussion of tourism ethics more broadly and these papers could be seen as organised around three key themes. The first key theme was research into perceptions of ethical dilemmas and conduct in tourism and hospitality workplaces. Lovelock (2008), for example, analysed ethical decisions made by travel agents, while Yaman and Gurel (2006) discussed the ethical approaches of tourism marketers. This area overlapped with the second main theme, the discussion of codes of ethical conduct for tour operators, destination development and marketing organisations and tourists (see Fennell, 2005; Fennell and Malloy, 2007, for detailed reviews and discussions of this work). This focus on codes of conduct for tourism organisations was closely linked to growing concerns about and arguments for understanding and improving the role of tourism in sustainable development (Fennell, 2005). In turn, considerations of ethics and sustainability in tourism could be linked to a longer running debate on the relationship between tourism and development (Lea, 1993; Burns, 1999; Smith and Duffy, 2003), which was the third main tourism ethics theme identified in the tourism literature.

Tourism research ethics: recent developments

The introductory section highlighted a major change in the nature of tourism research over the last 30 to 50 years – that of a shift from researchers based within and referring mainly to traditional social science disciplines to researchers emerging from tourism focused programmes referring increasingly to knowledge published within tourism literature (Butler, 2004; Xiao and Smith, 2005, 2006). One of the questions that such a shift raises is that of what research ethics codes or frameworks guide these newer generations of tourism scholars. Given the limited discussion of research ethics in key tourism journals it is unlikely that they are guided by codes that consider tourism research challenges in any detail. It is also unlikely that these researchers are cognisant of ongoing developments and debates on research ethics in the traditional social sciences disciplines as evidence generally suggests that such debates in other areas are not making much impact in the tourism literature (Ryan, 1997; Tribe, 2006). Newer generations of tourism researchers are also under considerable pressure to be taken seriously as academics, both as individuals and as part of a larger community of scholars interested in tourism. Tribe (1997) notes that in the latter case there is pressure to conduct particular types of research that are seen as more scientific and to find funding for this type of research, which in turn exerts pressure on the selection of research topics. Butler (2004) acknowledges the pressure on individuals to develop their careers by identifying and claiming niche areas resulting in an explosion of studies on different forms of tourism. Both of these types of pressures have ethical implications.

This pressure to pursue a particular tourism niche contributes to what Jafari (1990) calls the Adaptancy Platform. Jafari identified four phases or approaches to tourism research including the Advocacy Platform (based mostly on economic studies and the assumption that tourism was a positive force), the Reactionary Platform (based more on anthropology, sociology and human geography and concerned with the negative impacts of tourism for destinations), the Adaptancy Platform (character-ised by description and support for a range of particular forms of tourism) and the Knowledge-Based Platform. The latter is described as distinctive from the others in that it is driven by a scientific approach characterised by a neutral position and an appreciation of tourism as a complex system. While others have debated the value and extent to which the fourth platform is desirable and/or achievable (Macbeth, 2005), the underlying concept of the frameworks alerts us to the existence of many unquestioned assumptions and approaches taken to tourism research.

Macbeth's (2005) extension of these platforms to include an Ethics Platform rec-ognises both the rise of sustainability as a major theme in tourism research and the debate surrounding the concept of sustainable tourism versus tourism as a tool for sustainable development (Moscardo, 2008). Macbeth's (2005) discussion of ethics also explicitly raises the idea that tourism researchers are not simply neutral observ-ers describing and analysing the phenomenon but are active participants who have an obligation to move this activity towards more sustainable outcomes. Macbeth's (2005) paper and the debate over the implications of sustainability for tourism (Ryan, 2002; Saarinen, 2006) can be seen as part of an increasing awareness of the need for more critical and reflective approaches to tourism research. These discus-sions of power and tourism (Cheong and Miller, 2000; Ryan, 2002; Higgins-Desbi-olles, 2006) and critical approaches to tourism research (Crick, 1989; Tribe, 1997, 2006) raise a number of questions about the role and actions of individual tourism researchers which have implications for ethical conduct in tourism research.

In summary, the literature on tourism research platforms, tourism and sustainabil-ity, the analysis of power in tourism and the forces that act on tourism researchers raise four key questions about the role of tourism researchers and the ethical impli-cations of the way we currently approach tourism research.

♦   Why do we study some aspects of tourism but not others?

♦   Who and what is not studied and what does this mean for the welfare of those neglected?

♦   What power do tourism researchers have and how do they use it?

♦   What responsibilities do tourism researchers have and how do they seek to meet these?

These are all issues that are being discussed in social science disciplines, but rarely yet in tourism.

Tourism research ethics: current challenges

In order to understand the challenges involved in analysing tourism research ethics it is useful to briefly overview the complexity and philosophical context for research ethics in general. Macrina (2005) offers an overview of the entire set of areas related to scientific integrity or research ethics and this includes issues of choice of research areas, conduct of research with people and with animals, record keeping and data storage, publication and acknowledgement of information. Research ethics also includes managing relationships with colleagues and students, with the research institutions and other organisations, with reviewers and reviewees, as well as with participants and other stakeholders (Macrina, 2005). Kitchener and Kitchener (2009) provide an overview of the three main philosophical traditions with relation to ethics and research:

◆ A virtues approach, where the focus is on acting according to moral traits such as honesty and courage;

◆ Utilitarianism or consequentialism, where the ethical judgements focus on the consequences of actions and seek to produce the greatest good for the greatest number; and

◆ Deontology, where the properties of the action are most important and the focus is on respect for others.

(See Fennell, 2005 for a more detailed discussion of these philosophical approaches.)

Kitchener and Kitchener (2009) argue that current research ethics codes are a mixture of ideas from both utilitarianism and deontology but are most heavily influenced by a deontological stance. Wenstop and Keppang (2009) agree with this perspective and argue further that, in general, research ethics codes need to move away from deontology and a focus on strict rule adherence to having a stronger focus on consequences. Such a move would highlight the responsibility of the researcher to more proactively consider their ethical position (Wenstop and Keppang, 2009).

As noted earlier, multiple and detailed codes for research ethics and responsible research conduct exist for most traditional disciplines. Despite the multitude of codes that exist they share a common set of general principles:

◆ Research integrity and quality, where it is argued that only valid, reliable, unbiased or good research is ethical.

◆ Non-maleficence, or the concept of 'do no harm' which is often translated into the idea that researchers have a duty of care for those involved in their research.

◆ Beneficence, or the requirement to conduct research for some positive outcome, other than personal gain. This usually includes the notion of balancing risks against benefits in deciding on research actions and increasingly, a focus on the overall contribution the research makes to the welfare of the research participants.

♦   Respect for persons or research participants, which is usually translated into the two related areas of autonomy of participants and informed consent. These two rules argue that it is important the research participants are given the information required for them to make an informed decision about their participation in the research and that they are free to participate to whatever degree they wish without negative consequences.

♦   Fidelity, truth and transparency which all refer to the trustworthiness of the researcher in their dealings with all those involved in the research including participants, other stakeholders and other researchers.

♦   Justice which recognises that researchers often come from a privileged position and that their research has the potential to negatively impact on those who are most vulnerable in society. Increasingly this principle calls for a more proactive stance amongst researchers and stresses a responsibility to improve the position of these groups.

(Sources: Khanlou and Peter, 2005; Broom, 2006; Kitchener and Kitchener, 2009)

Despite considerable time and effort expended in the development and revision of the research codes that are based on these principles, there are ongoing debates that question their basic assumptions. These codes are primarily based on Western medical research models and were often put forward in response to experimental studies that were questionable in their conduct, are assumed to be universal in their application, see all research participants as independent individuals, believe researchers are neutral and research is value free, describe the researcher–researched as a simple relationship where the power is held by the researcher, and are most appropriate for research methods that are technical and quantitative (Benatar, 2002; Hoeyer *et al.*, 2005; Broom, 2006; Greenhough, 2007; Harper, 2007). Further, in practice these codes are often filtered through or interpreted by Institutional Review Boards (IRBs) or Institutional Ethics Review Committees (IERCs). These are usually mandated by law and are common in Western university, government and related research organisations. In many places researchers must formally submit applications for approval to conduct their research and the IRBs or IERCs are meant to monitor and audit research to ensure that it meets appropriate ethical standards. But as with discipline codes, these groups are limited by their context and often become more concerned with the legal and financial implications of research conduct for the institution rather than broader ethical issues (see Weijer, 2000, for a more detailed discussion of criticisms and operations of such boards or committees).

Not surprisingly there is longstanding debate about the applicability of such codes for research conducted in the social sciences in real world settings with multiple stakeholders from varying cultural and political backgrounds (see Mertens and Kinsberg's, 2009, edited volume for a detailed discussion of this debate). Criticism of these codes and their assumptions exist at two levels – challenges to specific aspects of the principles and more broad analyses of some of the core underlying assumptions of the codes. In the first category, Broom (2006) considers the principle of non-maleficence and argues that it was originally concerned with physical harm and that other forms of harm tend to be neglected. Broom (2006) argues that social harm can be serious for participants and researchers should not easily dismiss the potential for harm from social science research. In a related argument Benham and Francis (2006) suggest that it is not easy in practice to balance risks and benefits as it can be difficult to predict actual results and consequences of a specific research project. Bachrach and Newcomer (2002) and Brocklesby (2009) challenge the principle of quality research noting that there is considerable debate about issues of what constitutes quality, especially in the social science disciplines. Brocklesby (2009), in particular, argues that the unquestioning use of popular research models or techniques can be a threat to ethical research conduct and that researchers have a responsibility to select the most appropriate technique for the situation. The selection of a technique for reasons such as the likelihood of publication is not ethical, despite being common practice in some areas. But the selection of an appropriate technique is only possible if researchers have knowledge of and skills in a wide range of methodological techniques (Bachrach and Newcomer, 2002). Finally, there has been considerable discussion about the notion of informed consent, arising particularly from research in cross-cultural settings (Khanlou and Peter, 2005; Greenhough, 2007; Parker, 2007). In this case it is argued that the concept of informed consent assumes that both the researcher and the researched can have perfect knowledge of the future in terms of how research outcomes will be used and this is not likely (Greenhough, 2007). Critics of the concept also point to the need to develop a different kind of relationship in which power is shared between the researcher and the researched and that it might be better to talk about negotiated consent (Parker, 2007).

Challenges to the more basic assumptions of the existing research codes and frameworks tend to cluster around two related themes – reflexivity and the importance of context and researcher responsibility to ensure justice and to actively improve the well-being of relevant communities. These two themes both focus on questioning the assumptions that science is valuable in its own right, individuals can exist and act outside their social, historical and political context, the principles are universal and research and researchers are neutral and/or value free. Challenges to these assumptions arise both from cross-cultural research, especially with vulnerable groups (Benatar, 2002; Johnstone, 2007) and from applied research in real world settings (Lavery *et al.*, 2003; Brocklesby, 2009; Wenstop and Keppang, 2009).

Reflecting on and critically analysing contexts relevant to research can occur at several levels. First, there is the context of the individual researcher and the extent to which their own values, experiences, motives and circumstances influence their choices in terms of what to study and how to study it (Wenstop and Keppang, 2009). While the codes of ethics have in the past focused attention on how researcher characteristics can introduce bias into the research process, there has not been much explicit recognition of how the institutional context and pressure for funding and career development can influence research choices. Benham and Francis (2006) argue that conducting research solely for career development is unethical. Bachrach and Newcomer (2002) suggest that institutional pressures on researchers to get external research funding and or to engage with the private sector in their research are sources of bias that threaten the ethical integrity of research.

The second level at which the research context matters comes out of these pressures to find funding for research and is concerned with choices made about what and who gets researched and, more importantly, what and who are not researched (Bachrach and Newcomer, 2002). The third level is the context of the researched, in terms of their real autonomy and ability to make independent choices about participation and the potential for the research to make a difference to their circumstances (Benatar, 2002). These issues of context have become particularly important in work with vulnerable groups and across cultural boundaries where justice is a major issue. Johnstone (2007) outlines the issues for research with Australian indigenous communities and proposed that ethical research with such groups must be developed with an understanding of their history and previous treatment by those with power, must arise from cooperative negotiations, include local decisions and promote positive outcomes for the community including the building of community capacity in relevant areas. The importance of recognising the role of communities in research and the need to frame the research with input from communities and stakeholders has also been proposed for applied research in other areas (Benatar, 2002; Parker, 2007; Brocklesby, 2009).

Tourism research ethics: looking forward

What then are the implications of these broader debates about ethical social science research for tourism studies? First, it is important to note that these debates are about expanding the existing ethics codes in various ways to cover a wider range of situations, participants and researcher responsibilities. None of the critiques suggest removing the existing principles or rules. Tourism as a field of study does not have any existing codes or principles to begin with. Second, most tourism studies share many of the features that have been identified elsewhere as likely to contribute to ethical problems. Bachrach and Newcomer (2002) argue that bias is more likely in research projects that are externally funded and connected to private organisations and Brocklesby (2009) sees ethical challenges in multidisciplinary research in complex situations with multiple stakeholders with competing values and interests. Lavery *et al.* (2003) believe that ethical problems arise where the research has the problem of under-determination. Under-determination means that there are multiple and simultaneously plausible but conflicting interpretations of research data (Lavery *et al.*, 2003). Such a situation allows the results to be more easily manipulated to suit political agendas. Tourism research is often conducted in cross-cultural situations, with multiple stakeholders with competing interests, where research funding is often tied to the agendas of governments and private organisations with interests that may be at odds with those of the community being researched and is typically under-determined. In other words, much tourism research is particularly susceptible to challenging and difficult ethical questions.

Returning to the four key questions posed earlier:

♦　　Why do we study some aspects of tourism but not others?

♦　　Who and what is not studied and what does this mean for the welfare of those neglected?

♦　　What power do tourism researchers have and how do they use it?

♦　　What responsibilities do tourism researchers have and how do they seek to meet these?

It can be suggested that newer generations of tourism researchers may not only lack a strong connection to the wider disciplines that their tourism research relates to and a tourism specific code of conduct to pursue, but that they also operate in an academia that is increasingly pressured to perform according to externally imposed measures of quality and performance. Scott (2003) lists some of the ethical challenges that arise from these new assessment and funding regimes in universities. Add to this the challenge to present tourism as a serious academic activity and it is not surprising that tourism researchers may find themselves in increasingly difficult situations. While most discussions of power in research ethics have tended to see researchers as being the powerful actors, the changing research paradigm described above may mean that researchers increasingly face being very limited in their power and may believe that they lack the ability to address ethical issues.

Despite and because of these pressures it is important that tourism researchers more explicitly consider their research ethics. While it is not clear that a code of research ethics specific to tourism is necessary, it is clear that the debate about such a code could be useful in stimulating awareness of the issues. It might also be useful to begin such a process by recognising that the issues exist in tourism, encouraging critical reflexivity on the part of researchers, support deliberate and careful analyses of research contexts and conduct debates about the roles and responsibilities of researchers. These actions could be embedded in tourism education, recognised at tourism research meetings and tackled by existing tourism research associations. The development and dissemination of case studies on these topics could also be a useful option (Harper, 2007). Having greater knowledge of these issues can be empowering for both the researcher and the researched.

Brocklesby (2009: 1082) offers the most eloquent conclusion to this discussion of research ethics:

> adopting an ethical stance does not necessarily imply that the analyst has to act in support of the full range of interests that bear upon a particular situation. That is both utopian and in most circumstances impossible. What it does involve is acting under the clear awareness that there are alternative possibilities and that choices must be made. … Perhaps the most that can be asked is there is such awareness and that when choices are made, this happens through design rather than default.

Beginning an open dialogue amongst the tourism research community about the need for ethical guidance and frameworks for research is an important first step towards reaching this design.

References

AAA (1998) 'Code of Ethics of the American Anthropological Association', American Anthropological Association.

AAG (2005) 'Statement on Professional Ethics', Association of American Geographers.

Ahas, K., Aasa, A., Roose, A., Moark, O. and Silm, S. (2008) 'Evaluating passive mobile positioning data for tourism surveys: an Estonian case study', *Tourism Management*, **29** (3), 469-486.

APA (2002) 'Ethical Principles for Psychologists and Code of Conduct', American Psychological Association.

ASA (1999) 'Code of Ethics and Policies and Procedures of the ASA Committee on Professional Ethics', American Sociological Association.

Bachrach, C. and Newcomer, S.F. (2002) 'Addressing bias in intervention research: summary of a workshop', *Journal of Adolescent Health*, **31** (4), 311-321.

Benatar, S.R. (2002) 'Reflections and recommendations on research ethics in developing countries', *Social Science and Medicine*, **54**, 1131-1141.

Benham, B. and Francis, L. (2006) 'Revisiting the guiding principles of research ethics', *The Lancet*, **367**, 387-388.

Botterill, D., Haven, C. and Gale, T. (2002) 'A survey of doctoral theses accepted by universities in the UK and Ireland for studies related to tourism, 1990-1999', *Tourist Studies*, **2** (3), 283-311.

Brocklesby, J. (2009) 'Ethics beyond the model: how social dynamics can interfere with ethical practice in operational research/management science', *Omega*, **37** (6), 1073-1082.

Broom, A. (2006) 'Ethical issues in social research', *Complementary Therapies in Medicine*, **14** (2), 151-156.

Burns, P. (1999) 'Paradoxes in planning: tourism elitism or brutalism?', *Annals of Tourism Research*, **26** (2), 329-348.

Butler, R. (2004) 'Geographical research on tourism, recreation and leisure: origins, eras and directions', *Tourism Geographies*, **6** (2), 143-162.

Cheong, S-M. and Miller, M.L. (2000) 'Power and tourism: a Foucauldian observation', *Annals of Tourism Research*, **27** (2), 371-390.

Crick, M. (1989) 'Representations of international tourism in the social sciences: sun, sex, sights, savings, and servility', *Annual Review of Anthropology*, **18**, 307-344.

Fennell, D.A. (2005) *Tourism Ethics*, Clevedon: Channel View.

Fennell, D.A. and Malloy, D.C. (2007) *Codes of Ethics in Tourism: Practice, Theory and Synthesis*, Clevedon: Channel View.

Greenhough, B. (2007) 'Situated knowledges and the spaces of consent', *Geoforum*, **38** (6), 1140-1151.

Harper, I. (2007) 'Translating ethics: researching public health and medical practice in Nepal', *Social Science and Medicine*, **65** (11), 2235-2247.

Higgins-Desbiolles, F. (2006) 'More than an "industry": the forgotten power of tourism as a social force', *Tourism Management*, **27** (6), 1192-1208.

Hoeyer, K., Dahlager, L. and Lynoe, N. (2005) 'Conflicting notions of research ethics: the mutually challenging traditions of social scientists and medical researchers', *Social Science and Medicine*, **61**, 1741-1749.

Illum, S.F., Ivanov, S.H. and Liang, Y. (forthcoming) 'Using virtual communities in tourism research', *Tourism Management*.

Jafari, J. (1990) 'The basis of tourism education', *Journal of Tourism Studies*, **1** (1), 33-41.

Johnstone, M.-J. (2007) 'Research ethics, reconciliation, and strengthening the research relationships in indigenous health domains: an Australian perspective', *International Journal of Intercultural Relations*, **31** (3), 391-406.

Khanlou, N. and Peter, E. (2005) 'Participatory action research: considerations for ethical review', *Social Science and Medicine*, **60**, 2333-2340.

Kitchener, K.S. and Kitchener, R.F. (2009) 'Social science research ethics: historical and philosophical issues', in D.M. Mertens and P.E. Ginsberg (eds), *The Handbook of Social Research Ethics*, Los Angeles: Sage, pp. 5-22.

Lavery, J.V., Upshur, R.E.G., Sharp, R.R. and Hofman, K.J. (2003) 'Ethical issues in international environmental health research', *International Journal of Hygiene and Environmental Health*, **206** (4/5), 453-463.

Lea, J. P. (1993) 'Tourism development ethics in the Third World', *Annals of Tourism Research*, **20** (4), 701-715.

Lovelock, B. (2008) 'Ethical travel decisions: travel agents and human rights', *Annals of Tourism Research*, **35** (2), 338-358.

Macbeth, J. (2005) 'Towards an ethics platform for tourism', *Annals of Tourism Research*, **32** (4), 962-984.

Macrina, F.L. (2005) *Scientific Integrity*, 3rd edn, Washington: ASM Press.

Mertens, D.M. and Kinsberg, P.F. (eds) (2009) *The Handbook of Social Research Ethics*, Los Angeles: Sage.

Moscardo, G. (2008) 'Sustainable tourism innovation: challenging basic assumptions'. *Tourism Review International*, **8** (1), 4-13.

Okumus, F., Altinay, L. and Roper, A. (2007) 'Gaining access for research: reflections from experience', *Annals of Tourism Research*, **34** (1), 7-26.

Opperman, M., Chon, K. and Cai, L.A. (1998) 'Citation, referencing and ethics', *Tourism Management*, **19** (3), 195-197.

Parker, M. (2007) 'Ethnography/ethics', *Social Science and Medicine*, **65**, 2248-2259.

Ryan, C. (1997) 'Tourism: a mature discipline?', *Pacific Tourism Review*, **1** (1), 3-5.

Ryan, C. (2002) 'Equity, management, power sharing and sustainability – issues of the "new tourism"', *Tourism Management*, **23** (1), 17-26.

Saarinen, J. (2006) 'Traditions of sustainability in tourism studies', *Annals of Tourism Research*, **33** (4), 1121-1140.

Schuler, S., Aberdeen, L. and Dyer, P. (1999) 'Sensitivity to cultural difference in tourism research: contingency in research design', *Tourism Management*, **20** (1), 59-70.

Scott, P. (2003) 'The ethical implications of the new research paradigm', *Science and Engineering Ethics*, **9**, 73-94.

Smith, M. and Duffy, R. (2003) *The Ethics of Tourism Development*, London: Routledge.

Tribe, J. (1997) 'The indiscipline of tourism', *Annals of Tourism Research*, **24** (3), 638-657.

Tribe, J. (2006) 'The truth about tourism', *Annals of Tourism Research*, **33** (2), 360-361.

Weijer, C. (2000) 'The ethical analysis of risk', *Journal of Law, Medicine and Ethics*, **28** (4), 344-361.

Wenstop, F. and Koppang, H. (2009) 'On operations research and value conflicts', *Omega*, **37** (6), 1109-1120.

Xiao, H. and Smith, S.L.J. (2005) 'Source knowledge for tourism', *Annals of Tourism Research*, **32** (1), 275- 277.

Xiao, H. and Smith, S.L.J. (2006) 'The making of tourism research: insights from a social sciences journal', *Annals of Tourism Research*, **33** (2), 490-507.

Yaman, H.R. and Gurel, E. (2006) 'Ethical ideologies of tourism marketers', *Annals of Tourism Research*, **33** (2), 470-489.

17 Knowledge management in tourism: from databases to learning destinations

Chris Cooper and Pauline Sheldon

Introduction

The tourism industry, a natural user and producer of information, has been a late and reluctant adopter of information technology (IT), and subsequently a limited user of knowledge management (KM). This chapter will identify the major developments and fields of research in tourism-related IT and KM with a focus on the latter. The historical development of IT in tourism is already well documented and need not be re-visited here. For example, Gretzel and Fesenmaier (2009) give a thorough history of tourism IT research over the decades. Their paper shows that most research has tended to focus on the private sector; airlines (Buhalis, 2004), accommodation (O'Connor and Murphy, 2004), the use of e-commerce (Werthner and Ricci, 2004), and management information systems (Buhalis and Laws, 2008), or alternatively on the consumer. Some researchers have examined KM at the destination level, such as the use of IT in visitors' bureaux (e.g. Zach *et al.*, 2008), however a common focus of that research is improving a destination's marketing and competitiveness. The volume of literature on public sector use of IT and particularly KM is more limited.

While KM is implicit in IT and vice versa, IT developments have not always delivered transformative knowledge solutions and some have kept firms and destinations locked in old patterns (Vendelo, 2005). Therefore we see KM rather than IT as the key area to develop competitiveness and sustainability in tourism; hence it is the focus of this chapter. The goal of the chapter is to track the development of knowledge management in tourism and to examine how future research can assist destinations in becoming more sustainable learning destinations integrating knowledge into responsible planning and policy.

Knowledge in tourism

The generation and use of new tourism knowledge for innovation and product development is critical for the competitiveness of both the tourism sector and destinations. However, the tourism sector has been slow to adopt the principles of the knowledge economy and as a result, unlike many other economic sectors, tourism has not been subject to a knowledge management approach and the sector is less competitive as a result (Stamboulis and Skayannis, 2003; Cooper, 2006). Knowledge management is a relatively new approach that addresses the critical issue of organizational adaptation, survival, and competitiveness in the face of increasingly discontinuous environmental change. This pace of change underscores the fact that knowledge-based innovation is a core competency required by all tourism organizations if they are to be competitive in a changing world (Argote and Ingram, 2000). There are many definitions of knowledge management but this chapter takes the stance that it is about 'applying the knowledge assets available to [a tourism] organization to create competitive advantage' (Davidson and Voss, 2002: 32).

Tourism and knowledge management research

For tourism, there are four significant issues for the development of a knowledge management research agenda. The first is related to types of knowledge. Knowledge can be thought of as the use of skills and experience to add intelligence to information in order to make decisions or provide reliable grounds for action. Knowledge management classifies knowledge according to its ability to be codified and therefore communicated (Polanyi, 1966). This distinction is fundamental and goes a long way to explaining the failure of the tourism sector to adequately capitalise upon and manage knowledge. Simply, the conversion of tacit to explicit knowledge is critical, as there is so much tacit knowledge in the tourism sector that could benefit other organizations, destinations and governments. It is here that a knowledge management approach provides significant benefits as it focuses upon the management of tacit and explicit knowledge to create organizational learning, innovation and sustainable competitive advantage.

The second is related to the issue of scale. If knowledge management is to be utilized by tourism at the destination level, then the micro-level focus on the organization, which dominates knowledge management thinking, needs to be expanded to embrace knowledge stocks and flows within networks of organizations at the destination. Here, Hislop *et al.* (1997) provide a solution by arguing that knowledge *articulation* occurs in networks of organizations attempting to innovate and build upon knowledge. They identify two types of network. First, micro-level networks within organizations where knowledge is created and is dominantly 'tacit' and 'in-house', and a second macro-level, inter-organizational network where knowledge is transferred around a network of organizations and tends therefore to be 'explicit' in nature. Hislop *et al.*'s (1997) notion of knowledge *articulation* involves the gradual conversion of tacit knowledge at the individual organization level into explicit knowledge. This is transmitted through the wider network of organizations via the usual processes of knowledge management and the analogy with tourism destinations is clear.

The third issue focuses upon the very nature of the tourism sector itself. Researchers have to accept the nature of tourism as a complex and multi-sectoral industry if they are to develop an effective, future-facing research agenda. The sector is traditional, fragmented and populated dominantly by small and medium-sized enterprises (SMEs), with only the larger enterprises and the public sector recognizing the need for the generation and adoption of new knowledge. At the same time, those generating tourism knowledge and those adopting it form two distinctive 'communities of practice' and do not communicate well. Additionally, vocational reinforcers are evident with the tourism workforce less inclined to share and adopt knowledge because of issues related to high labour turnover, low recognition of talent, poor compensation that is not linked to ability, and weak job security.

Finally, the field of knowledge management itself remains shrouded in confusion as a concept and there is a lack of agreement over terminology (Beesley and Cooper, 2008). Effectively, a knowledge management system has to be easy to understand and to use, and if this is not the case, then implementation of the concept will be difficult (Malhotra, 2002). As a result, this has limited the extent to which the broader business community has employed deliberate knowledge management practices (de Hoog and van der Spek, 1997; Dilnutt, 2002; Malhotra, 2002; Raub and Von Wittich, 2004).

An emergent research agenda

Although the link between tourism and knowledge management research is still in its early phases, a research agenda is emerging. This began in the late 1990s with papers in the ENTER conferences that focused on knowledge management in both destinations and the hospitality sector. This was followed in the new millennium by the overt linking of knowledge management with the need for innovation in tourism, championed by international agencies including the OECD and the European Commission. These developments recognized the need for a greater crossover between generic knowledge management research and tourism. Moving forward, the emerging agenda is coalescing around four key themes (Bouncken and Sungsoo, 2002; Cooper, 2006; Hall and Williams, 2008).

Tourism, knowledge management and innovation

Innovation is key to competitive advantage and economic growth in tourism (OECD, 2000) and as such deserves to be the focus of an emerging research agenda. In broad terms, innovation incorporates new products, processes, markets, raw materials, and new forms of organization (Schumpeter, 1934; Hjalager, 2002) whilst at an organizational level it represents 'the embodiment, combination, or synthesis of knowledge in original, relevant, valued new products, processes, or services' (Luecke and Katz, 2003: 2).

Here there is recognition that the generation and transfer of knowledge is a fundamental antecedent to innovation, and research into how it is generated, disseminated, managed and applied is needed. Indeed, successful implementation of these processes will continue to be a distinguishing factor among the strongest economies (OECD, 1996; DETYA, 1999; Darroch and McNaughton, 2002). For destinations and tourism enterprises to be competitive and engage in development that is socially and environmentally sustainable, they must maximize their capacity for innovation (OECD 2004; Hall and Williams, 2008).

For tourism, Shaw and Williams (2009) apply Schumpeter's (1947) idea of innovation as disruptive. Examples of disruptive innovation include the rise of e-distribution and the business model of low-cost carriers. Hjalager's (2002) work however is more comprehensive identifying four types of tourism innovation – regular, niche, architectural and revolutionary with a corresponding increase in 'disruption' from regular to revolutionary.

Underpinning innovation is the development and transfer of knowledge and there is no doubt that tourism is still in the early stages of understanding effective mechanisms of knowledge transfer, partly for reasons identified above (Frechtling, 2004; Ruhanen and Cooper, 2005; Cooper, 2006; Shaw and Williams, 2009). In tourism, the concept of absorptive capacity of organizations, the notion of communities of practice and a clear understanding of the processes and media of knowledge transfer will be critical (Chua, 2001; Ladd and Ward, 2002). Both Hjalager's (2002) four-channel model and Hall and Andriani's (2002) classification of channels will assist the tourism sector in this process.

Research into the ability and willingness of SMEs to enter into collaborative knowledge sharing arrangements will be a focal part of the research agenda. This will include research into their absorptive capacity to apply knowledge to their operations, the skills and competencies needed to do this and the understanding of the fit between different types of knowledge and tourism business operations.

Collaborative tourism research initiatives

Collaborative research arrangements involving industry, academics, and government have become popular in tourism as a means to involve stakeholders (see for example the Australia Sustainable Tourism Cooperative Research Centre). Collaborative research initiatives remain a focus of government research and development policy (Gray, 1989; Hagen, 2002). Tourism is particularly suited to a collaborative, or knowledge sharing, approach since its inherent multi-sectoral nature means that destinations stand to benefit from collaborative ventures (Beesley, 2004a, b). Collaborative production of tourism knowledge is vital because in a knowledge-based economy, university, industry, and government are interdependent as they hold interrelated interests that necessitate that they work together (Rod and Paliwoda, 2003). The 'critical mass' formed through such collaborative arrangements is commonly referred to as 'communities of practice' (Porter, 1998; Coakes and Clarke, 2006), 'knowledge hubs' (Garrett-Jones, 2004; Owen-Smith and Powell, 2004), or 'clusters' (Porter, 1998), that are created by, and dependent upon networks and networking (Dredge, 2006; Sundbo et al., 2007). Research shows that collaboration between local authorities, education/research institutions and local SMEs is a key factor in facilitating any local innovative ventures because of the clusters that develop through the networks spawned through collaboration (Novelli et al., 2006). Examples of this can be seen through the Canadian tourism product clubs approach and Switzerland's innovation programme, 'Innotour', whereby government initiatives support consortia of mostly small businesses formed to develop new, or improve existing tourism products (OECD, 2000). Here the research agenda focuses upon how collaborative research can be made more effective through enhancing and understanding the management of the stakeholders and their expectations, the emotional aspects of collaboration, and the effectiveness of the facilitating agency.

Applying knowledge management in networks of organizations

As the knowledge-based economy has developed, governments have been faced with the need to develop policy initiatives, yet little research exists that has examined the most effective mechanisms of policy intervention. Effectively, these policies grapple with the issues surrounding the nature of knowledge as a global public good and include access to knowledge, the removal of barriers to knowledge transfer and adoption and the need to encourage private enterprise to share knowledge. Here, policy for the knowledge economy addresses the usual issues of allocation, but it also has to address the critical need for policy to encourage the optimal utilization of knowledge. A particular application of policy is the development of effective knowledge sharing networks.

Here, however, research is in the early stages of examining issues of scale. For example, tmuch knowledge management research has focused upon single organizations but for tourism, the notion of destinations as networks of organizations demands a different approach (Cooper, 2006).

There are only a small number of examples and applications of knowledge management across networks of tourism organizations (Cooper, 2008). However, recognition of the significance of the approach is growing as practitioners realize the value of knowledge sharing not just within the organization, but also through networks, and in particular the encouragement of partnerships within destinations. This new thinking has given rise to the concept of sharing *knowledge capital* and relates to the nature of knowledge as a *resource*. Knowledge itself does not deliver growth; it has to be incorporated into the production of goods and services because it is linked to human capital and labour markets. Here, networks of organizations recognize that the same knowledge can be used by more than one organization but that the cost does not increase in terms of accessing that knowledge (Scott *et al.*, 2008). This is reflected in the fact that enterprises are showing increased interest in co-operation across organizational boundaries. Effectively, the enterprise has become a networked organization and its success will depend upon the degree to which it can leverage strategic advantage from its networks.

For tourism destinations, the dominant form of organization in tourism, SMEs, best illustrates this concept. As noted above, the dominance of SMEs in the tourism sector provides a challenge for the implementation of knowledge management at the destination.

Knowledge for stewardship

Given the world-wide pressures for environmental and socio cultural sustainability in destinations, knowledge bases to foster responsible stewardship of the destination will be increasingly valuable. Few destinations measure and monitor the impact of tourism on their environmental and socio-cultural fabric despite the large body of knowledge on this topic (e.g. UNEP, 2003; UNWTO, 2004). Sustainability indicators are well conceptualized in the literature; however, their implementation at the grass roots level is rare. The Tourism Optimization Management Model (TOMM) in Kangaroo Island, Australia is one example of a knowledge management system for destination stewardship which engages a variety of stakeholders and fully integrates both indicators and monitoring processes (www.tomm.info). Such knowledge bases for stewardship may include resident sentiment indicators, environmental indicators measuring congestion and pollution, and visitor satisfaction measures that can be shared openly with all stakeholders.

Private sector contributions to destination stewardship through corporate social responsibility programmes are indicative of increasing stakeholder responsibility in the destination's future (Nicolau, 2008). Successful programmes are based on knowledge sharing with the destination community and its planners, identifying projects to which the firm can best make a contribution. This requires the development of public–private sector knowledge networks.

Learning destinations

Tourism destinations can benefit from the work of urban planning researchers seeking to understand how cities and towns 'learn'. While not all tourism destinations are towns or cities, the understanding from this literature can benefit all destinations. Campbell (2009) suggests that cities need to create a 'soft infrastructure' to become learning cities. This includes local knowledge, learning and creativity, trust, networks, conversion of tacit to explicit knowledge and both collaboration and cooperation. He also notes that a crisis often stimulates the transition for a city to value knowledge and take the initiative to gain it. Modalities of creating a soft infrastructure are keeping track of events, documenting findings, building databases, tracking performance indicators, and using the shadow economy of knowledge provided by agencies such as NGOs as foundations for their knowledge acquisition.

A crucial component of a learning destination is a network of stakeholders, formal or informal, engaged in a collective endeavour. Here, the European Union's (EU) learning destinations project provides a comprehensive manual for stakeholders demonstrating how to establish a learning destination (http://ec.europa.eu/enterprise/services/tourism/studies_and_publications.htm).

Networks based on the values of trust, identity and allegiance within and between networks in a region are critical to their success. Campbell's typology of learning cities is adapted in Table 17.1 for the tourism context and suggests how destinations can create and share knowledge through destination clusters and networks, proactive groups of destinations, and one-on-one destination pairings.

Table 17.1: A typology of learning destinations. Adapted from Campbell (2009)

Type of grouping	Characteristics of learning	Examples
Proactive destinations	Takes initiative and commits resources to outward search for knowledge. Incorporates knowledge into policy	Kangaroo Island, Australia
Destination clusters	Some networking with similar types of destinations	UNESCO World Heritage Cities
Destinations one-to-one	Agreements between destinations for exchange purposes	Sister cities; Destination pairs in proximity e.g. Spain/Portugal; Australia/New Zealand
Destination networks	Membership organizations with convening power	European Cities Network; The European Network of Cities for Sustainable Tourism

The European Network of Cities for Sustainable Tourism is an example of a knowledge network of tourism destinations. It was founded in 2001 and consists of 14 cities throughout Italy, Spain, Turkey, Greece and Israel. It is coordinated by ICLEI (the International Council for Local Environment Initiatives), some of whose objectives are:

♦   To develop and implement joint projects to pursue sustainability in the tourism sector.

♦   To develop policies and good practices for sustainable tourism.

♦   To exchange information and experiences (also organizing study visits and exchanges).

♦   To pass political messages to both the EU and to other international institutions and organizations which are relevant actors in the field of tourism.

♦   To develop common training and distance training projects for local authority officials.

♦   To develop common presentation strategies to new potential markets by taking into account the sustainability targets (www.eukn.org).

Another network, albeit focused on marketing, is the European Cities Marketing Organization. This network links city tourist offices and convention bureaux to share their expertise and knowledge and work together on business opportunities. More than 134 major cities from 32 countries belong to this network (www.europeancitiesmarketing.org) and benefit from the collaboration and cooperation. The development of similar knowledge networks in other geographic areas will be important for their destinations to be competitive.

Values-based knowledge

A major transmitter of knowledge in the tourism industry is the human workforce (Hjalager, 2002; Shaw and Williams, 2008). Human capital is the reservoir of tacit knowledge and its quality is crucial to the success of tourism enterprises and destinations. Therefore it is argued that education programmes providing human capital to destinations have a responsibility to contribute to the destination's knowledge network (see for example the British Columbia Centre for Tourism Leadership and Innovation – www.bctli.ca/).

University tourism programmes now include courses on ethics and sustainability to provide students with the knowledge to be responsible leaders and destination stewards. Much of this, however, is incremental in nature and does not represent a fundamental redesign of tourism curricula. Students entering the rapidly changing and vulnerable tourism sector need different skills, aptitudes and knowledge, implying that radical changes in educational systems are needed. Graduates who are 'philosophical practitioners' reflecting on their operational tasks from a values perspective can support this change (Tribe, 2002). The redefinition of the skills and knowledge sets learned, and the questioning of current structures and assumptions are necessary to produce a different kind of graduate.

Pressures facing destinations in the future speak to an increasing need for responsible stewardship and values-based tourism education. A recent initiative started in 2007 called the 'Tourism Education Futures Initiative' (TEFI) is rethinking the values upon which tourism education has been based, and proposes a focus on the knowledge needed to lead and transform the industry (Sheldon *et al.*, 2008). TEFI is an international consortium of tourism educators and industry members whose mission is: 'to provide vision, knowledge and a framework for tourism education programs to promote global citizenship and optimism for a better world'.

Five categories of values have been identified by TEFI to form the pillars of education for responsible leadership in tourism. These five overlapping value sets are shown in Figure 17.1: stewardship (sustainability, responsibility, service to the community), knowledge (critical thinking, innovation, networking, creativity), ethics (transparency, honesty, authenticity), mutuality (diversity, inclusion, equity, humility, collaboration, and professionalism (leadership, teamwork, partnerships, practicality, reflexivity). The value sets are permeable and overlap giving rise to different sets of values appropriate for different courses/units and for different professional and sectoral situations. TEFI continues to develop tools that support the teaching of these values such as a values inventory assessment and sample coursework (www.tourismeducationsummit.com).

Another initiative critically examining the values upon which tourism scholarship and education are based is the Academy of Hope (Ateljevic et al., 2008). 'As tourism teachers and researchers we have emotional and spiritual responsibilities to those with whom we co-create tourism knowledge, to our students and also to ourselves...' (Ateljevic *et al.*, 2008: 4). These and other attempts to influence the knowledge that university graduates transfer to their industry positions are important signs of change. However, the assumption that new graduates can transform the destination to one that is knowledge-based and values-based is at once inspiring and naïve. It will require change on the part of professionals at every level. Future research to understand the transfer of knowledge by new graduates will be important.

The Five TEFI Values

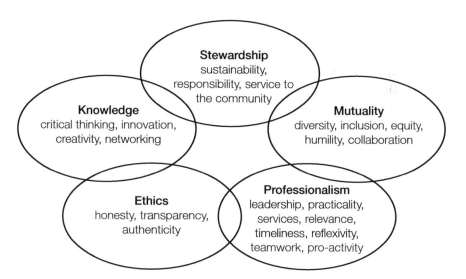

Figure 17.1: Values of the Tourism Education Futures Initiative

Future research agenda

The next 20 years of research on knowledge management in tourism can build on the foundations being laid now, and incorporate knowledge from different and allied fields. It will need to focus on knowledge stocks and flows in all aspects of tourism and understand how to manage them at the corporate level and the destination level. The smooth integration of these and other systems to transfer relevant knowledge between all destination stakeholders is a challenging task for future researchers. It has been suggested that different layers of knowledge networks at the local, regional, and state levels are needed for destinations to maximize their benefit from knowledge networks (Gretzel *et al.*, 2006). More research on the implementation of strategies for the public and private sector to share knowledge for the greater public good is needed.

One area that is particularly promising is the research on social capital and social networks. The field of tourism is rapidly proliferating knowledge from many sources. This knowledge is shared in social networks which then becomes social capital for the destination. Destinations will need to understand how to capture these various kinds of knowledge, identify best practices, and maximize their use for both sustainability and competitiveness. Customer knowledge must also be managed as the power of virtual knowledge communities in tourism expands. Social networks on the Internet, e-word of mouth (eWOM) and other customer generated knowledge content is driving much decision making today, but it can be conflicting and confusing, requiring destinations and tourism firms to take more active knowledge-provision roles (Lee *et al.*, forthcoming).

Research is also needed on how organizations can best meet the needs of the new knowledge worker. Their attraction and retention is necessary if the tourism industry is to positively transform itself. Consideration of changes in corporate and organizational cultures to foster knowledge management is a rich area for future researchers. There is also a need to understand issues of intellectual capital and organizational memory as part of a knowledge strategy. Without new organizational structures and new approaches to human resources in tourism, the sector will be stifled and not reach its full potential. In addition to managing knowledge for the environmental and socio-cultural sustainability of the destination, these are perhaps the two most important areas for future knowledge management research in tourism.

References

Argote, L. and Ingram, P. (2000) 'Knowledge transfer: a basis for competitive advantage in firms', *Organizational Behavior And Human Decision Processes*, **82** (1), 150-169.

Ateljevic, I, Morgan, N. and Pritchard, A. (2008) 'Introduction: promoting an academy of hope in tourism enquiry', in I. Ateljevic, N. Morgan and A. Pritchard (eds), *The Critical Turn in Tourism Studies*, London: Routledge, pp. 1-7.

Beesley, L.G. (2004a) 'The management of emotion in collaborative tourism research settings', *Tourism Management*, **26** (2), 261-275.

Beesley, L.G. (2004b) 'Multi-level complexity in the management of knowledge networks', *Journal of Knowledge Management*, **8** (3), 71-100.

Beesely, L and Cooper, C. (2008) 'Defining knowledge management (KM) activities: towards consensus', *Journal of Knowledge Management*, **12** (3), 48-62.

Bouncken, R.B. and Sungsoo, P. (2002) 'Introduction', in R.B. Bouncken and P. Sungsoo (eds), *Knowledge Management in Hospitality and Tourism*, New York: Haworth Hospitality Press, pp. 1-4.

Buhalis, D. (2004) 'eAirlines: strategic and tactical use of ICTs in the airline industry', *Information and Management*', **41** (7), 805–825.

Buhalis, D. and Law, R. (2008) 'Progress in information technology and tourism management: 20 years on and 10 years after the internet – the state of eTourism research', *Tourism Management*, **29** (4), 609–623.

Campbell, T. (2009) 'Learning cities: knowledge, capacity and competitiveness', *Habitat International*, **33** (2), 195–201.

Chua, A. (2001) 'Relationship between the types of knowledge shared and types of communication channels used', *Journal of Knowledge Management Practice*, **2**, Article 26.

Coakes, E. and Clarke, S. (2006) *Encyclopedia of Communities of Practice in Information and Knowledge Management*, Hershey, PA: Idea Group Reference.

Cooper, C. (2006) 'Knowledge management and tourism', *Annals of Tourism Research*, **33** (1), 47-64.

Cooper, C. (2008) 'Tourism destination networks and knowledge transfer', in N. Scott, R. Baggio and C. Cooper (eds), *Network Analysis and Tourism: From Theory to Practice*, Clevedon: Channel View, pp. 40-57.

Darroch, J. and Mcnaughton, R. (2002) 'Examining the link between knowledge management practices and types of innovation', *Journal of Intellectual Capital*, **3** (3), 210-222.

Davidson, C. and Voss, P. (2002) *Knowledge Management*, Auckland: Tandem.

De Hoog, R. and van der Spek, R. (1997) 'Knowledge management: hope or hype?', *Expert Systems With Applications*, **13** (1), V-VI.

DETYA. (1999) *Knowledge and Innovation. A Policy Statement of Research and Research Planning*, Canberra: Department of Education, Training and Youth Affairs.

Dilnutt, R. (2002) 'Knowledge management in practice: three contemporary case studies', *International Journal of Accounting Information Systems*, **3** (2), 75-81.

Dredge, D. (2006) 'Policy networks and the local organisation of tourism', *Tourism Management*, **27** (2), 269-280.

Frechtling, D. (2004) 'Assessment of tourism/hospitality journals' role in knowledge transfer: an exploration study', *Journal of Travel Research*, **43** (1), 100-107.

Garrett-Jones, S. (2004) 'From citadels to clusters: the evolution of regional innovation policies in Australia', *Organization Science*, **34** (1), 3-16.

Gray, B. (1989) *Collaborating: Finding Common Ground for Multiparty Problems*, San Francisco: Jossey-Bass.

Gretzel, U. and Fesenmaier, D. (2009) 'Information technology: shaping the past, present and future of tourism', in T. Jamal and M. Robinson (eds), *Handbook of Tourism Studies*, Thousand Oaks, CA: Sage, pp. 558-580.

Gretzel, U., Fesenmaier, D., Formica, S. and O'Leary, J. (2006) 'Searching for the future: challenges faced by destination marketing organizations', *Journal of Travel Research*, **45** (2), 116-126.

Hagen, R. (2002) 'Globalization, university transformation and economic regeneration', *International Journal of Public Sector Management*, **15** (3), 204-218.

Hall, M and Williams, A. (2008) *Tourism Innovation*, London: Routledge.

Hall, R. and Andriani, P. (2002) 'Managing knowledge for innovation', *Long Range Planning*, **35** (1), 29-48.

Hislop, D., Newell, S., Scarborough, H. and Swan, J. (1997) 'Innovation and networks: linking diffusion and implementation', *International Journal of Innovation Management*, **1** (4), 427- 448.

Hjalager, A.M. (2002) 'Repairing innovation defectiveness in tourism', *Tourism Management*, **23** (5), 465- 474.

Ladd, D.A. and Ward, M.A. (2002) 'Of environmental factors influencing knowledge transfer', *Journal of Knowledge Management Practice*, **3**, 8-17.

Lee, W., Gretzel, U. and Law, R. (forthcoming) 'Quasi-trail experiences through sensory information on destination websites', *Journal of Travel Research*.

Luecke, R. and Katz, R. (2003) *Managing Creativity and Innovation*, Boston, MA: Harvard Business School Press.

Malhotra, Y. (2002) 'Why knowledge management systems fail? Enablers and constraints of knowledge management in human enterprises', in C.W. Holsapple (ed.), *Handbook on Knowledge Management*, vol. 1, Heidelberg: Springer-Verlag, pp. 577-599.

Nicolau, J. (2008) 'Corporate social responsibility: worth-creating activities', *Annals of Tourism Research*, **35** (4), 990-1006.

Novelli, M., Schmitz, B. and Spencer, T. (2006) 'Networks, clusters and innovation in tourism: a UK experience', *Tourism Management*, **27** (6), 1141-1152.

O'Connor, P. and Murphy, J. (2004) 'Research on information technology in the hospitality industry', *International Journal of Hospitality Management*, **23** (5), 473–484.

OECD (1996) *The Knowledge Based Economy* (No. OECD/GD (96)102), Paris: OECD.

OECD (2000) *The New Economy. The Changing Role of Innovation and Information Technology in Growth*, Paris: OECD.

OECD (2004) *Innovation and Growth in Tourism*, Paris: OECD.

Owen-Smith, J. and Powell, W.W. (2004) 'Knowledge networks as channels and conduits: the effects of spillovers in the Boston biotechnology community', *Organization Science*, **15**, 5-21.

Polanyi, M. (1966) *The Tacit Dimension*, New York: Doubleday.

Porter, M. (1998) 'Clusters and the new economics of competition', *Harvard Business Review*, **76** (6), 77-90.

Raub, S. and Von Wittich, D. (2004) 'Implementing knowledge management: three strategies for effective CkOs' *European Management Journal*, **22** (6), 714-724.

Rod, M.R.M. and Paliwoda, S.J. (2003) 'Multi-sector collaboration: a stakeholder perspective on a government, industry and university collaborative venture', *Science and Public Policy*, **30**, 273-285.

Ruhanen, L. and Cooper, C. (2005) 'The use of strategic visioning to enhance local tourism planning in periphery communities', in C. Ryan, S. Page and M. Aicken (eds), *Tourism to the Limits: Issues, Concepts and Managerial Perspectives*, Oxford: Elsevier, pp. 53-64.

Schumpeter, J. (1934) *The Theory of Economic Development*, Cambridge, MA: Harvard University Press.

Schumpeter, J. (1947) *Capitalism, Socialism and Democracy*, New York: Harper and Rowe.

Scott, N., Baggio, R. and Cooper, C. (2008) *Network Analysis and Tourism. From Theory to Practice*, Clevedon: Channel View.

Shaw, G. and Williams, A. (2008) 'Knowledge transfer and management in tourism organisations: an emerging research agenda', *Tourism Management*, **30** (3), 325-335.

Sheldon, P.D. Fesenmaier, C. Cooper, K. Woeber and Antonioli, M. (2008) 'Tourism

education futures: building the capacity to lead', *Journal of Teaching in Travel & Tourism*, **7** (3), 61-68.

Stamboulis, Y. and Skayannis, P. (2003) 'Innovation strategies and technology for experience-based tourism', *Tourism Management*, **24** (1), 35-43.

Sundbo, J., Orfila-Sintes, F. and Sørensen, F. (2007) 'The innovative behaviour of tourism firms – comparative studies of Denmark and Spain', *Research Policy*, **3**, 88-106.

Tribe, J. (2002) 'The philosophic practitioner', *Annals of Tourism Research*, **29** (2), 338-357.

UNEP (2003) *Tourism and Local Agenda 21.The Role of local Authorities in Sustainable Tourism*, Paris: UNEP.

UNWTO (2004) *Indicators of Sustainable Development for Tourism Destinations. A Guidebook*, Madrid: UNWTO.

Vendelo, M.T. (2005) 'IT in knowledge processes: if the solution is the problem, is there a solution to the problem?', in P.N. Bukh, K.S. Christensen and J. Mouritsen (eds), *Knowledge Management and Intellectual Capital*, Chippenham: Anthony Rowe.

Werthner, H. and Ricci, F. (2004) 'E-Commerce and tourism', *Communications of the ACM*, **47** (12), 101–105.

Zach, F., Xiang, P., Gretzel, U. and Fesenmaier D. (2008) 'Innovation in the Web Marketing Programmes of American Convention and Visitors' Bureaux', working paper, Philadelphia, PA: National Laboratory for eCommerce in Tourism, Temple University.

18 Conclusions: trends and advances in tourism research

Douglas G. Pearce and Richard Butler

Individually, the preceding chapters have traced the path that tourism research on particular themes and in different parts of the world has taken over the past two decades and outlined some agendas for how it might develop in coming years. Collectively, the ideas, views and material presented in these reviews provide an opportunity to discuss how tourism research more generally has developed over this period and to reflect on the implications of these broader trends. The 17 chapters, of course, could not hope to cover and encapsulate all possible themes and trends. In particular, there is an under-representation of work from a social science perspective and, with the exception of Butler's discussion of carrying capacity (Chapter 5), environmental issues are only touched upon here although they have been addressed more fully in earlier Academy volumes (Cooper and Wanhill, 1997). Moreover, the literatures reviewed are predominantly, though not exclusively, based on English language references. Finally, the authors are mainly established senior scholars whose views on what is important, especially with regards to future agendas, no doubt differ from those of a newer generation of forward-looking researchers. Nevertheless, by way of conclusion, an attempt is made here to draw out and discuss some general trends with the aim of stimulating further debate and perhaps providing more focus for future research in this field.

Trends

Five basic and interrelated trends in tourism research emerge from an overview of the preceding chapters. First, the growth in the volume of tourism studies has been accompanied by an increasingly wide range of topics being researched. This is evident at various levels. At one level, Aramberri (Chapter 2) has discussed broader disciplinary approaches reflected in the split between the *how to* of the business-oriented studies and the more critical *why* type approaches of the social sciences. The reviews of Latin America and China (Chapters 11 and 12) also trace the growing diversity of research being undertaken in those countries where tourism research has been more recently established as a field of study, where studies on the economic aspects of tourism are being progressively complemented by social and other considerations. The chapters in Part IV illustrate how new themes emerge as awareness of particular phenomena develops, for example refugees and tourism employment (Chapter 14), or the relevance of broader issues to tourism is recognized, as with ethics and knowledge management (Chapters 16 and 17). Within particular themes, the scope and coverage of research has also changed and widened, as is demonstrated in such chapters as those dealing with tourism and development (Chapter 4), tourism SMEs (Chapter 7) and distribution (Chapter 8). At the same time, as these latter studies in particular have shown, coverage remains variable, the focus has not always been on the most important topics and considerable scope for further research remains.

Second, changes have occurred in the way in which tourism is viewed and research has been done. However, the nature and extent of these changes varies and the overall picture that emerges is one of continuity and incremental change; there is little evidence of any major paradigm shift. Frechtling and Smeral (Chapter 6), for instance, reviewed changing methodologies for measuring the economic impact of tourism as limitations were recognized in existing techniques and new issues assumed greater importance. Perdue, Tyrell and Uysal (Chapter 10) illustrated how the conceptual foundations of the value of tourism have diverged among stakeholders over time. Yamashita (Chapter 13) accounted for changing concepts of cultural tourism in Bali as the phenomenon itself and perceptions of it evolved. Other contributors, such as Shaw and Williams (Chapter 7), identified recurrent themes with regard to particular topics. In other instances, issues raised echo those made at earlier Academy meetings (Chapter 1) and elsewhere. Foremost among these is the need for greater theorization, a point set in context by Smith and Lee's very useful attempt (Chapter 3) to develop a typology of theory in tourism and to systematically assess changing applications of theory in tourism studies. Crompton (2005: 38) argues: 'The seminal papers in the tourism literature are conceptual; they are not empirical... Conceptualization precedes empiricism....without it there cannot be any long-term effective research contribution'. Chapter 3 showed progress was being made in this domain but much more could be done. At the same time, Harrison, who discussed tourism and development against the changing backdrop of development theories (Chapter 4), called for more empirical work to test and substantiate theories and claims. His and other chapters (10, 11, 13, and 15) highlight the ongoing tension noted in Chapter 1 involved in balancing more systematic and theoretical approaches against case studies stressing contextual factors.

Third, little common purpose and no great sense of direction are evident amongst these changes and within this diversifying coverage. Although the body of tourism research has substantially increased over the past two decades it appears not to have been driven by the pursuit of core questions under the umbrella of any unifying set of theories leading to a structured, cumulative body of knowledge. Rather, we are witnessing an increasingly large and fragmented literature, or sets of literature, as studies proliferate in a largely piecemeal fashion. As was noted with regard to tourism distribution (Chapter 8), there have been relatively few sustained contributions whereby tourism researchers pursue particular topics over time or engage in multi-year projects that not only provide breadth but also add greater structure and depth of understanding.

Fourth, much, perhaps the bulk, of tourism research now being undertaken is being disseminated in specialized tourism journals, books and conferences. The extent to which this is happening is difficult to measure given the tendency for quantified content analyses to focus on a limited number of journals (Chapters 3 and 12) but it would appear that much tourism research is now distanced from, or not well integrated with, related work in other sectors. Although studies on tourism and development have been dealt with in terms of both sets of literature (Chapter 4), in other cases, for example tourism SMEs (Chapter 7) and distribution (Chapter 8), the tourism research has been characterized by a marked lack of engagement with the broader literature. Elsewhere, Jafari (2005: 5) refers to 'the inbreeding and walling in of tourism itself'. Complementary reviews in key disciplines also show tourism scarcely occupies a mainstream position there. Gibson (2008: 418), for example, observes 'tourism geography still somehow appears to occupy a liminal position in the discipline', a point borne out by the relatively small number of tourism articles published in leading international geography journals. Ioannides (2006) asserts that while tourism researchers are well aware of recent trends in economic geography, mainstream economic geographers largely ignore tourism. Detailed analysis of researcher affiliations in a wide range of publications is needed to substantiate the pattern but it would appear that most of the work on tourism is now being done by researchers specializing in tourism, rather than by disciplinary-based researchers focusing on tourism to explore themes of broader interest.

Nevertheless, this 'field of study' approach to tourism research and the development of specialized tourism programmes has not yet generated a lot of truly interdisciplinary research which the subject is seen to call for (Przeclawski, 1993).

This is unfortunate, not only from the point of view of a resulting narrow, if not isolated, focus in much tourism research, but also because many research funding agencies are calling for an increased emphasis on multi- and interdisciplinary research, meaning that tourism research may be missing out on potential mainstream research interest and support. A narrow focus on one aspect of one discipline leaves tourism (as other perceived 'minor' areas of research) particularly vulnerable to missing out on research funding and priority support from agencies, both national and international. One might cite the examples of treatment (or rather non-treatment) of tourism, by the British government during the outbreak of foot-and-mouth disease in 2001, and the relative lack of concern for the impacts on tourism of SARS or H1N1 virus in more recent years. While the former has attracted some research interest, the effect of and subsequent responses to flu pandemics on tourism have been minimal in published research. Comprehensive and effective research on these topics would require truly interdisciplinary efforts and these have not been forthcoming from tourism researchers.

Language barriers, or an unwillingness to look beyond one's own cultural setting, are another dimension by which tourism research is 'walled in'. This is not a new phenomenon, nor is it one that is limited to English-speaking researchers as accounts of tourism research in France and Germany show (Lazzarotti, 2002; Kreisel, 2004). However it is becoming an increasingly important issue as tourism expands throughout the world and more research is undertaken in new destinations and markets (Chapters 11 and 12). It is not yet clear what, if any, distinctive characteristics tourism research in Latin American and Chinese research is developing but if the pattern elsewhere is followed where particular national or regional schools have emerged (Pearce, 1999; Lazzarotti, 2002; Kreisel, 2004) then the literature as a whole will be poorer if new findings, concepts and methods from scholars there and in other regions are not widely disseminated and incorporated into more general discourses. By analysing citations in English and other languages, Dann (2009) provides an interesting assessment of just how international earlier publications of the Academy have been. His analysis shows much scope to increase the dialogue between researchers publishing in different languages. In the first six books resulting from the Academy meetings, 13 per cent of the references in chapters contributed by English-speaking authors were in a language other than English, compared with 35 per cent for those contributors for whom English was not their mother tongue. As global issues such as the current economic depression, climate change, political reorganization, terrorism and health issues assume ever-increasing importance, it can be expected that much research will be conducted in languages of the countries affected by such problems, not all of which will appear in English or in English language publications.

Advancing tourism research

Individual chapters have outlined agendas for research on particular topics. Common points that emerge from these, together with the trends just outlined, suggest that several basic issues cut across much tourism research and must be addressed if work in this field is to advance more effectively.

First, we need to address the increasing fragmentation of tourism studies, develop a more concerted approach to identifying key issues and build a more cumulative body of knowledge. To do this we need more structure and a greater sense of direction. Several of the chapters have shown how this might be done. In Chapter 8, Pearce demonstrated how a strategy design process model (Figure 8.1) might be used to develop relevant questions and frame a research agenda on tourism distribution. In a similar fashion, Jansen-Verbeke and McKercher use Figure 15.1, which orders issues thematically according to three different yet connected structural dimensions, to propose an integrated agenda to help direct research initiatives on World Heritage Sites. Interesting examples of such an approach used by reviewers elsewhere include Getz's (2008) framework for understanding and creating knowledge about event tourism and Zhang et al.'s (2009) tourism supply chain management framework to identify a research agenda in that field.

More generally, there is a need for a greater use of explicit integrative frameworks. These can provide a general overview of a particular field and serve to put specific studies and problems in context, thereby facilitating a better understanding of existing interrelationships, develop a sense of direction and common purpose and suggest more integrated solutions to problems which may arise (Pearce, 2001). Furthermore, by clearly establishing the shape and structure of research in a particular field, integrative frameworks can also reveal where the gaps lie, suggest questions for future research in a more directed fashion and show how particular studies contribute to our understanding (Pearce, 2001; Zhao and Ritchie, 2007a). In their as yet relatively limited use in tourism research, integrative frameworks have been predominantly employed to synthesize empirical studies, to stress the 'what' dimension of the research being done. However, as has been demonstrated in other fields (Zahra and Pearce, 1989; Hart, 1992), integrative frameworks may also be used to bring together conceptual and methodological dimensions and have the potential to make a very valuable contribution if used in this way in tourism research given some of the trends outlined above.

Frameworks which integrate work on particular themes or in particular parts of the world might then be used as building blocks to draw together more effectively the diverse studies in tourism, thereby bringing greater unity to the field and enabling the more detailed knowledge arising out of more specialized studies to be added more effectively to our body of knowledge. Consolidating the results and lessons of our research in this way may also facilitate knowledge management and the more effective transfer of what we know to others (Chapter 17). Figure 17.1, for example, illustrates the identification of categories of values to form the pillars of education for responsible leadership in tourism. Integration of work within particular language-based literatures may also be a useful precursor to more effective transfers of knowledge among researchers across the globe as it would reduce the linguistic challenges by enabling researchers to focus on the essence of the findings. This would mean going beyond enumerating what is being studied and how (Chapter 12) to a higher level of synthesis and interpretation. Integrative frameworks might also be used to build bridges with other fields of study, for example between tourism and urban studies (Pearce, 2001) or tourism and poverty alleviation (Zhao and Ritchie, 2007a). Of current global issues, the need for integrative studies is perhaps greatest of all with respect to climate change, and in this context, its relationship, both of cause and effect, with tourism, a topic that is deservedly attracting increasing attention as Harrison noted in Chapter 4.

Integrative frameworks are not, of course, a panacea for all of the issues discussed above and in earlier chapters. They are not substitutes for theory, however theories may be defined, and much more effort is needed to strengthen the theoretical foundations of tourism research (Chapters 2 and 3). Just how this might be achieved is not immediately apparent given that this has long been one of the recurrent themes in commentaries on the state of tourism research (Chapter 1). Journal editors have played and will continue to play a key role here by emphasizing that authors need to demonstrate the contribution to theory made by their study (Ryan, 2005; Perdue *et al.*, 2009). Jennings (2007) makes a convincing plea for tourism researchers to consider a suite of theoretical paradigms and usefully outlines seven that might be taken into account when undertaking tourism economics and management research.

Closer engagement with parent disciplines may also strengthen the theoretical basis of tourism studies as well as develop more rigorous methodologies and enhance our research more generally (Chapters 7, 8, 14, 16, and 17). Moscardo (Chapter 16), for instance, shows how tourism researchers have lagged behind others in considering ethical issues while Shaw and Williams (Chapter 7) draw attention to the limited incorporation of work on tourism SMEs into the broader policy arenas. The key point coming through these chapters is that by being less introspective and by engaging more widely with researchers in other areas, tourism researchers can both learn from and contribute to work being done elsewhere. Given the apparent marginalization of tourism in many established disciplines noted earlier, the first steps here may have to come from the tourism specialists rather than their mainstream disciplinary counterparts. Such engagement is not without its challenges, especially given the increasing tendency to measure and rank research outputs (Zhao and Ritchie, 2007b) and the growing role of research assessment exercises that are commonly discipline based. Publishing in the leading tourism journals may establish a stronger profile and enhance the career prospects of those within tourism programmes but it does not necessarily bring one's work to the attention of those working in other related fields. Those researching tourism from within mainstream disciplines face similar issues (Pearce, 1999; Gibson, 2008), the combined effect of which is to discourage interdisciplinary effort.

Broader engagement also behoves us to be a little less precious and more explicit about just what is different about tourism and what characteristics, conceptual and methodological challenges or policy implications this sector shares with other subjects. Are we in fact specialist researchers concentrating on an essentially distinctive phenomenon or are we just rather narrow and inward looking and as a result do we fail to recognize or admit that what we are researching is little more than a specific variation of a broader issue? Most tourism research is likely to have elements of both the specific and the general, a point developed elsewhere (Pearce, 2008) with regard to tourism distribution and illustrated here in Figure 8.2. Likewise, many of the broader ethical issues raised by Moscardo (Chapter 16) are central to much tourism research but we have yet to fully acknowledge and address them. The specificity or generality of tourism also underlies many of the points being made by Aramberri in Chapter 2, whether in discussion of the work of MacCannell and Turner in the search for general theories or attempts to group tourism with other mobilities, an attempt that he argues is a dead end given the distinctiveness of tourists. The avoidance of dead ends or blind alleys was one of a number of open-ended approaches offered by Dann (1999) for advancing research on tourism development at an earlier meeting of the Academy. Others included: reversing conventional wisdom, concept stretching, scope broadening, breaking out of the case, resolving paradoxes and establishing new linkages. Some of these approaches, such as breaking out of the case, would do much to address the fragmented nature of many tourism studies and establish the broader, underlying problems being addressed, while others, such as reversing conventional wisdom or resolving paradoxes, illustrate the scope and opportunity for much needed creativity as a further means of advancing tourism research. In his discussion of the Simmelian perspective Dann (1999: 16) also addresses the generality of many research problems, claiming such a perspective offers an 'ability to abstract out the essences of phenomena, those recurring and immutable forms of reality which, though combined with, stand in sharp contrast to, changing content'.

Tourism researchers also need to become more closely engaged with the industry, policy-makers and other stakeholders and to continue to explore the relationships between stakeholder groups if the results of tourism research are to have practical significance and if tourism as a phenomenon is to be fully understood. Harrison (Chapter 4) goes so far as to speak of academic/practitioner apartheid with regard to tourism and development, a division that needs to be broken down if tourism benefits are to be spread widely. Shaw and Williams (Chapter 7) call for greater engagement to give tourism a louder voice in the policy debate while Cooper and Sheldon (Chapter 17) argue for more work on implementation strategies to improve the sharing of knowledge for the greater public good. Other contributors illustrate how research might improve collaboration among stakeholders. Song, Witt and Zhang (Chapter 9), for example, put forward a practical research-based design for a collaborative approach to tourism supply chain forecasting while Perdue, Tyrell and Uysal illustrate how the concept of tourism value has evolved over time among stakeholder groups (Figure 10.1) and how understanding such measurement is necessary for collaboration and common purpose to be successful. Some of the broader issues raised in the latter study also illustrate that the 'how' question of measuring the value of tourism over time is inherently associated with 'why' the concept has changed as stakeholder attitudes have evolved, suggesting the twofold split in tourism research argued by Aramberri (Chapter 2) is not necessarily a neat one and that the blades of the scissors are not always sharp or far apart.

Conclusions

Tourism research has certainly come a long way in the last two decades, especially in terms of the coverage of topics and the emergence of a separate, identifiable literature. As tourism continues to evolve, considerable scope exists to expand and deepen research efforts in this field. Many of the issues that face the development of tourism at present and in coming years, such as the impact of economic uncertainty, climate change and international security, are dynamic, far-reaching and global in nature. Addressing these issues will call for increasingly robust, sophisticated and focused research. To meet these opportunities and challenges more must be done to consolidate and build on existing studies, to create a 'body' of knowledge which has much more structure, shape, depth and common purpose. Some ways by which this might be accomplished have been outlined in earlier chapters and brought together here. Consolidating what we know and communicating it more clearly are critical steps to provide tourism researchers with the confidence and ability to tackle future problems and issues and contribute to and engage more widely and effectively with other researchers and society at large.

References

Cooper, C. and Wanhill, S. (1997) *Tourism Development: Environmental and Community Issues*, Chichester: Wiley.

Crompton, J.L. (2005) 'Issues related to sustaining a long-term research interest in tourism', *Journal of Tourism Studies*, **16** (2), 34-43.

Dann, G.M.S. (1999) 'Theoretical issues for tourism's future development: identifying the agenda', in D.G. Pearce and R.W. Butler (eds), *Contemporary Issues in Tourism Development*, London: Routledge, pp.13-30.

Dann, G.M.S. (2009) 'How international is the International Academy for the Study of Tourism', *Tourism Analysis*, **14** (1), 3-13.

Getz, D. (2008) 'Event tourism: definition, evolution and research', *Tourism Management*, **29** (3), 403-428.

Gibson, C. (2008) 'Locating geographies of tourism', *Progress in Human Geography*, **32** (3), 407-422.

Hart, S. (1992) 'An integrative framework for strategy-making processes', *Academy of Management Review*, **11** (17), 327-351.

Ioannides, D. (2006) 'The economic geography of the tourist industry: ten years of progress in research and an agenda for the future', *Tourism Geographies*, **8** (1), 76-86.

Jafari, J. (2005) 'Bridging out, nesting afield: powering a new platform', *Journal of Tourism Studies*, **16** (2), 1-5.

Jennings, G. R. (2007) 'Advances in tourism research: theoretical paradigms and accountability', in A. Matias, P. Nijkamp and P. Neto (eds), *Advances in Modern Tourism Research: Economic perspectives*, Heidelberg: Physica Verlag, pp. 9-35.

Kreisel, L. (2004) 'Geography of leisure and tourism research in the German-speaking world: three pillars to progress', *Tourism Geographies*, **6** (2), 163-185.

Lazzarotti, O. (2002) 'French tourism geographies: a review', *Tourism Geographies*, **4** (2), 135-147.

Pearce, D.G. (1999) 'Towards a geography of the geography of tourism', *Tourism Geographies*, **1** (4), 406-424.

Pearce, D.G. (2001) 'An integrative framework for urban tourism research', *Annals of Tourism Research*, **28** (4), 926-946.

Pearce, D.G. (2008), 'A needs–functions model of tourism distribution', *Annals of Tourism Research*, **35** (1), 148-168.

Perdue, R., Meng F. and Courtney, J. (2009) 'Publishing in the *Journal of Travel Research*: an assessment of manuscript acceptance and rejection', *Journal of Travel Research*, **47** (3), 267-274.

Przeclawski, K. (1993) 'Tourism as the subject of interdisciplinary research', in D.G. Pearce and R.W. Butler (eds), *Tourism Research: Critiques and Challenges*, London: Routledge, pp.1-8.

Ryan, C. (2005) 'Authors and editors – getting published: context and policy – an editor's view', *Journal of Tourism Studies*, **16** (2), 6-13.

Zahra, S.A. and Pearce II, J.A. (1989) 'Boards of directors and corporate financial performance: a review and integrative model', *Journal of Management*, **15** (2), 291-334.

Zhang, X., Song, H. and Huang, G.Q. (2009). 'Tourism supply chain management: a new research agenda', *Tourism Management*, **30** (2), 345-358.

Zhao, W. and Ritchie, J.R.B. (2007a) 'Tourism and poverty alleviation: an integrative research framework', *Current Issues in Tourism*, **10** (2/3), 119-143.

Zhao, W. and Ritchie, J.R.B. (2007b) 'An investigation of academic leadership in tourism research: 1985-2004', *Tourism Management*, **28** (2), 476-490.

Index